Tupolev Tu-95/-142 'Bear'

Russia's Intercontinental-Range Heavy Bomber

Yefim Gordon and Vladimir Rigmant
Edited by Jay Miller

AeroFax

Tupolev Tu-95/-142 'Bear'
© 1997 Yefim Gordon

ISBN 1 85780 046 X

Published by Midland Publishing Limited
24 The Hollow, Earl Shilton
Leicester, LE9 7NA, England
Tel: 01455 847 815 Fax: 01455 841 805
E-mail: midlandbooks@compuserve.com

United States trade distribution by
Specialty Press Publishers & Wholesalers Inc.
11481 Kost Dam Road, North Branch, MN 55056
Tel: 612 583 3239 Fax: 612 583 2023
Toll free telephone: 800 895 4585

All rights reserved. No part of this publication may be reproduced, stored in a retrieval system, transmitted in any form or by any means, electronic, mechanical or photo-copied, recorded or otherwise, without the written permission of the publishers.

Design concept and layout © 1997
Midland Publishing Limited and Jay Miller

Edited by Jay Miller

Printed in England by
Clearpoint Colourprint Limited
Daybrook, Nottingham, NG5 6HD

Aerofax is an imprint of
Midland Publishing Limited

The publishers wish to thank the following for their contributions to this book:
Sergei Agavelyna; Tom Copeland; Reuben Johnson; Tony Landis; Pavel Mikhailov; Susan Miller; Margarita K. Obertysheva; Chris Pocock; and Alexander 'Sasha' Velovich

Select photographs from the Jay Miller Collection appear courtesy of the Aerospace Education Center in Little Rock, Arkansas.

Contents

Introduction	3
Acronyms and Abbreviations	4
Chapters	
1 Genesis	5
- 'Bear' Colour Photo Portfolio	17
2 The 'Bear' Flies	25
3 'Bear' Versions	31
4 Tu-142s and other Tu-95s	53
5 Tu-95 & Tu-142 in Detail	83
6 Drawings	113
Index	128

Title page: **Tu-95RTs on Atlantic patrol during the mid-1970s.** Jay Miller collection

Below: **An early production Tu-95 escorted by four MiG-15s during the Tushino Airshow of 1956.** Yefim Gordon collection

Opposite page top: **A Tu-95RTs photographed by US Navy interceptors during a routine fleet surveillance mission.** Jay Miller collection

Opposite page bottom: **Tu-95s, such as this Tu-95RTs were routinely photographed during US Cold War fleet exercises.** Jay Miller collection

Introduction

From my earliest days as an aviation enthusiast and writer to the present, I can think of no other aircraft that has left on me a more striking impression of invincibility than Tupolev's awesome turboshaft-powered Tu-95 bomber.

I first remember seeing crudely-drawn images of this fantastic aircraft as early as the mid-1950s; and decidedly soft photographs taken during fly-overs of Tushino and Moscow shortly thereafter.

I was awestruck by its apparent enormity. Coupled with its enigmatic nature, its obviously fearsome capabilities, and the fact that it bore 'red stars' on its wings and vertical tail, the study of its development history, its operational career, and its stunning performance became a long-term personal pursuit that on more than a few occasions I assumed would never come to any state of fruition.

Never in my wildest dreams during the 1950s did I foresee that, forty years later, I would be participating in the production of a definitive written history of this awesome aircraft. Yefim Gordon's research and writing have, at long last, placed this magnificent cold war warrior in its proper perspective... warts and all. Thanks to Yefim's penchant for accuracy and his equally impressive ability to uncover rare and previously unpublished photographs, we now have a truly worthy history of what the west has come to know all too well as the 'Bear' bomber.

Born in a post-Great Patriotic War era that at the time still was heavily under the influence of Russian dictator Joseph Stalin, the 'Bear' was the direct benefactor of Boeing B-29 technology exported to the Soviet Union purely by accident. As a result of wartime exigencies, these wayward bombers had come to rest in a country that was decades behind its western counterparts in its ability to construct, produce, and field a long-range heavy weapons delivery platform. Nothing flying in Russia at the time of the first B-29's inauspicious arrival was even remotely on-par with the big and very capable American combatant.

The opportunity to replicate en-masse the B-29's powerplant, materials, aerodynamics, landing gear, remotely-controlled turrets, and structural design techniques was not lost on the war-torn Russian aviation community.

The Tupolev Design Bureau – and others – were quick to leap-frog an evolutionary learning curve that had taken US engineering teams decades to build. Almost at the drop of a hat, the bureaux were able to skip thousands upon thousands of engineering trial-and-error man hours. And it's impossible to estimate what Russia was saved in the way of flight test arena blood, sweat, and tears.

What follows, then, is the history of one of the world's most amazing aircraft. Its genesis and operational career, from the early 1940s to the present, is a captivating story... and one the west has aspired to know for over four decades. Thanks to Yefim Gordon, we now have that opportunity.

Jay Miller
Editor

Acronyms and Abbreviations

AD	aviation engine	HF	high frequency	SL	sea level
ADD	Long-range bomber force of VVS	HSI	horizontal situation indicator	SST	supersonic transport
ADF	Automatic Direction Finder	HUD	head-up display	TB	heavy bomber
AFA	large reconnaissance cameras	IAS	indicated airspeed	TBO	time between overhauls
AoA	Angle of Attack	IFF	identification friend or foe	TE	trailing edge
APD	accessory gearbox	ILS	instrument landing system	TK	turbo-supercharger
APU	Auxiliary Power Unit	INS	inertial navigation system	TRD	turbojet engine
Argon	turret control radar	IR	infrared	TRDD	twin-spool/two-shaft turbojet
ASCC	Air Standards Co-ordinating Committee, allocated reporting names to WarPac types, eg 'Bear', 'Blinder'.	KB	constructor/design bureau	Tu	Tupolev Design Bureau
		l/d	lift/drag ratio	TV	turboshaft engine
		LE	leading edge	TVD	turboshaft/turboprop engine
ASO	chaff/flare dispensers	LII	Flight Research Institute	TvRDD	turbofan engine
ASW	Anti-Submarine Warfare	LL	flying laboratory	UHF	ultra-high frequency
BAP	Bomber regiment	LP	low pressure	VFSh	variable-pitch propeller
CAHI	Central Aerodynamics and Hydrodynamics Institute (often referred to as TsAGI in the west)	MAC	mean aerodynamic chord	VHF	very high frequency
		MAI	Moscow Aviation Institute	ViSh	constant-speed propeller
		MAP	Ministry of Aviation Industry	VLF	very low frequency
CCB	Central Construction Bureau (often referred to as the TsKB in the west)	MLG	main landing gear	VOR	VHF omni-directional range
		MR	Maritime Reconnaissance	VPSh	fixed pitch propeller
cg	center of gravity	MTO	maximum takeoff weight		
CIAM	Central Institute of Aviation Motors (often referred to as the TsIAM in the west)	Mya	Myasischev Design Bureau		
		NII	general term for Scientific Test Institute		
		NKAP	State commissariat for aviation industry		
COMINT	Communications Intelligence	NKVD	Russia's secret police		
cp	center of pressure	NPO	*Nauchno-Proizvodstvennoye Obyedinyenye* (Scientific-Production Union)		
csd	constant speed drive				
D	engine				
DA	long-range bomber aviation/became the ADD	OKB	Experimental Design Bureau		
		PD	piston engine		
DB	long-range bomber	PD	pulse Doppler		
DC	direct current	pr	pressure ratio		
ECCM	electronic counter-countermeasures	PRF	pulse recurrence frequency		
ECM	electronic countermeasures	PVO	Protective Air Defense (ended 1983)		
ELINT	electronic intelligence	R	Reconnaissance		
EO	electro-optical	R	jet engine		
EW	Electronic Warfare	RD	turbojet engine		
FLIR	forward-looking infrared	RWR	radar warning receiver		
FR	flight refueling	SAR	search and rescue		
GAZ	a state aviation factory	shp	shaft horsepower		

RUSSIAN LANGUAGE AND TRANSLITERATION
Russian is a version of the Slavonic family of languages, more exactly part of the so-called 'Eastern' Slavonic grouping, including Russian, White Russian and Ukrainian. As such it uses the Cyrillic alphabet, which is in turn largely based upon that of the Greeks.

The language is phonetic – pronounced as written, or 'as seen'. Translating into or from English gives rise to many problems and the vast majority of these arise because English is not a straightforward language, offering many pitfalls of pronunciation! Accordingly, Russian words must be translated through into a *phonetic* form of English and this can lead to different ways of helping the reader pronounce what he or she sees. Every effort has been made to standardize this, but inevitably variations will creep in. While reading from source to source this might seem confusing and/or inaccurate but it is the name as *pronounced* that is the constancy, if not the *spelling* of that pronunciation!

The 20th letter of the Russian (Cyrillic) alphabet looks very much like a 'Y' but in English is pronounced as a 'U' as in the word 'rule'. (See the illustration of the Ye-155U two-seater prototype on page 34.) This is a good example of the sort of problem that some Western sources have suffered from in the past (and occasionally get regurgitated even today) when they make the mental leap about what they see approximating to an English letter.

TUPOLEV BUREAU NO & ASCC KEY

ASCC	Bureau No
'Bear-A'	Tu-95, Tu-95M, Tu-95A, Tu-95MA, Tu-95U
'Bear-B'	Tu-95K, Tu-95KU, Tu-95KD
'Bear-C'	Tu-95KM
'Bear-D'	Tu-95RTs
'Bear-E'	Tu-95MR
'Bear-F'	Tu-142, Tu-142M, Tu-142MK, Tu-142MK-E, Tu-142M-Z
'Bear-G'	Tu-95K-22
'Bear-H'	Tu-95MS
'Bear-I'	Reporting name not allocated
'Bear-J'	Tu-142MR

Left: NATO's Air Standards Co-ordinating Committee (ASCC) gave the reporting name 'Bear' to the Tu-95/-142 family. **Tu-95KM 'Bear-C' illustrated.** Yefim Gordon

Chapter One

Genesis

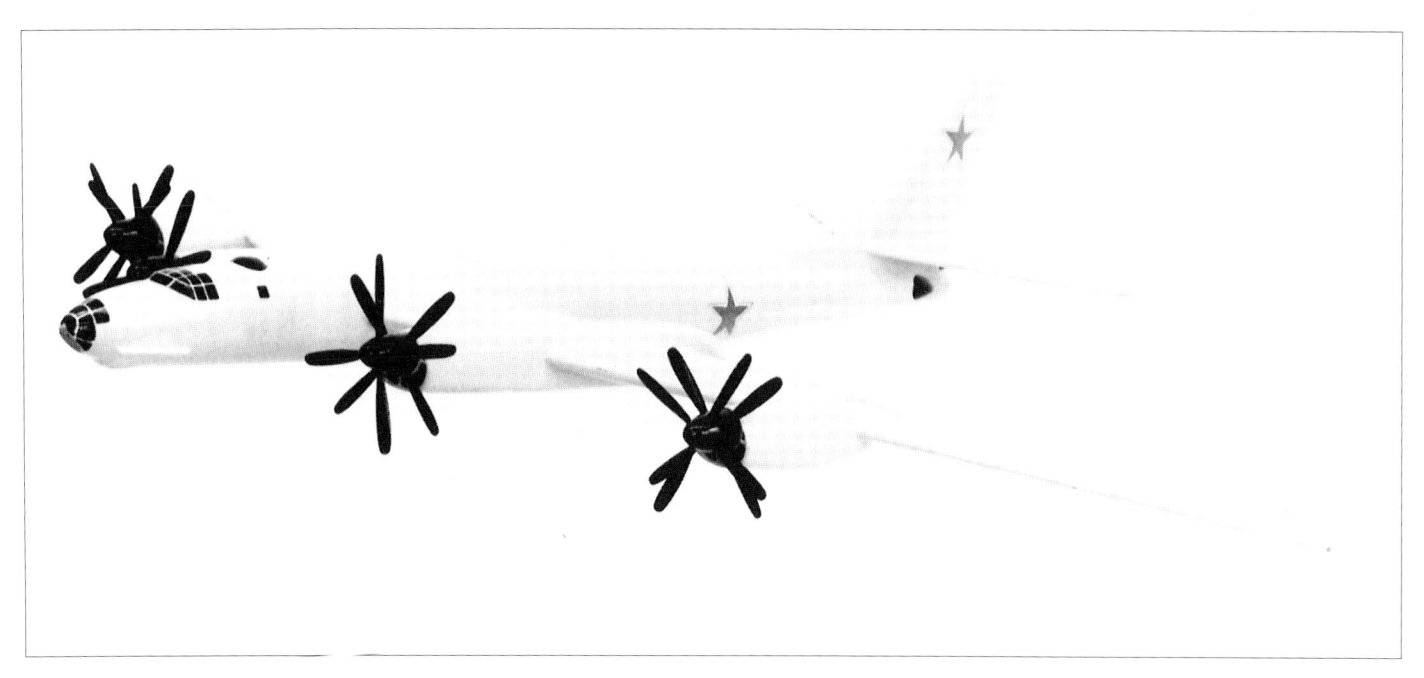

Above: **There are no known photographs of the prototype Tu-95 ('95-1') with its original engine installation. This image depicts a model of the prototype aircraft.** Tupolev

Below: **The great aircraft designer and design bureau chief, Andrei Tupolev.** Tupolev

During 1943, as a result of information acquired through Russian espionage agent Klaus Fuchs – who had successfully penetrated the secrecy surrounding the American nuclear weapons program – the Soviet Government elected to begin work on a nuclear weapon program of their own. General scientific supervision of the effort was entrusted to I Kurchatov. Concurrently, NKVD Chief L P Beriya was asked to serve as director of all Soviet atomic programs. Consequent to this, the Russian armament industry complex, a massive collection of facilities that had resulted from 'The Great Patriotic War' (as the Russians usually refer to the Second World War), was brought into the development consortium. Unlimited capital was provided for research and production.

The nuclear weapon program thrust was defined thus: to create and test the first Soviet atomic bomb in a short period of time with the objective of countering what already was being perceived as a major postwar threat from the west.

Though development of the nuclear weapon was of primary concern, how to deliver that weapon to a target – once it was successfully tested and manufactured – quickly surfaced as a major secondary concern.

Long Range Aviation in Russia, which effectively came into existence during 1942, had not been created initially to address the issue of weapon delivery over intercontinental ranges. At the time, mission objectives were considerably more conservative, particularly in light of the fact that Nazi Germany – less than a few hundred miles distant – was the primary target.

Following the war, a reassessment of long range military aircraft requirements led to the decision to place more emphasis on bomber development. At the time, the long range branch of the Soviet air arm consisted of 1,839 aircraft. The most potent of these were thirty-two Petlyakov Pe-8 four-engine bombers ... marginally referred to as 'heavies'.

There also were a similar number of refurbished American-built Boeing B-17s and Consolidated B-24s. These had landed in Russia as a result of navigation errors, powerplant failures, enemy action, and other similar difficulties and had been absorbed with little equivocation by the Russian Air Force.

Making up the rest of the Soviet bomber fleet were outdated Ilyushin Il-4s modified to serve in the night bomber role and a motley collection of Lisunov Li-2s (license-built Douglas DC-3s) and North American B-25s that had been acquired during the course of the American Lend-Lease program of the Second World War.

Not one of these aircraft could effectively serve as a long-range bomber when pitted against contemporary fighter forces. None had the range to serve as an intercontinental weapon delivery platform.

The range requirement, as it turned out, was perhaps the most critical issue. Russia was one of the world's largest countries in terms of land area, and the ability to fly from home bases to targets that under some circumstances were thousands of miles distant, was paramount, to say the least.

Soviet military commanders did not have difficulty envisioning a scenario wherein US intercontinental range bombers – already extant in the form of the Boeing B-29 in the mid-1940s – could hold Russia hostage. It became apparent that the only way to counter this threat was to develop an indigenous long-range heavy bomber force with similar capability. A radius of action of 3,000 to 4,000km (1,863 to 2,484 miles) was required to pose any kind of threat to the Americas.

Secondary to range, the bomber also would have to be reasonably fast to complicate fighter intercepts, have an exceptional weight-lifting ability in consideration of the first-generation nature of a crude nuclear weapon, and be adequately armed for self-protection.

The Beginning

During 1944 two Soviet aeronautical design bureaus (one under A N Tupolev's supervision and the other under the supervision of V M Myasischev) were tasked with preliminary configuration studies that would eventually lead to the design and development of a full-scale intercontinental range heavy bomber. The two bureaux were instructed to observe the successes enjoyed by Boeing's devastatingly effective B-29 Superfortress which already had begun to wreak havoc on the Japanese mainland and had succeeded in operating routinely in the Pacific Theater of Operation while flying safely over thousands of miles of wide-open ocean.

V M Myasischev's design bureau prepared two project studies. The resulting designs, referred to as the '202' and the '302' were both four-engine bombers. Though differing primarily in the form of propulsion utilized they were also somewhat similar in that the B-29 served as their basic design model.

Concurrently, during 1944, Design Bureau No. 156, supervised by A N Tupolev also had begun work on their '64' bomber project. Though similar in size to the Petlyakov Pe-8, the new aircraft weighed almost twice as much. The '64' thus was a very heavy four-engine bomber combat load was in the vicinity of 4,537kg (10,000lb), and range while carrying this load was estimated to be between 3,000 and 4,000km (1,863 and 2,484 miles). Emulating the B-29, the project '64' aircraft was given a very heavy defensive armament that incorporated the same tactical and technical specifications of Boeing's Superfortress. In some instances, this armament superseded that of the B-29 in coverage and capability.

Above: **The first prototype Tupolev Tu-4. This aircraft eventually was given the NATO codename of 'Bull'.** Yefim Gordon collection

Below: **The second production Tu-4 probably photographed at Zhukovsky.** Yefim Gordon collection

Opposite page top: **The standard production Tu-4 was decidedly difficult to differentiate from its US progenitor.** Tupolev OKB

Opposite page bottom: **The first production Tu-4, No. 0101, following an emergency landing during the course of initial flight trials.** Tupolev OKB

Though design of the '202', '302', and '64' progressed rapidly and with little difficulty, the exigencies of the on-going war prevented initiation of construction. The difficulties lay not so much with technology, but rather with the scarcity of strategic materials.

Not surprisingly, Stalin managed to keep himself apprised of events and advances in both Russian and foreign aviation. Though not a specialist in the field, he was nevertheless sufficiently knowledgeable to ask prying and revealing questions of his subordinates and to make accurate assessments of hardware and strategies.

When it became apparent the Myasischev and Tupolev teams were encountering development difficulties with their new bomber designs, Stalin, along with the leaders of the National Aviation industry and the Commander-in-Chief of the Soviet Air Force, made a decision to reverse-engineer and produce the Boeing B-29. This aircraft, which already had acquired considerable respect among Russian aeronautical engineers and the Russian military, was considered an ideal long range bombing platform. Most importantly, it was determined that with the proper insights, it might be possible to produce the aircraft in Russia using available facilities and personnel.

Fortuitously, three B-29s had made emergency landings in the Soviet Far East during 1944 and were immediately interred by the Soviet Air Force. Within weeks of their arrival, they had been moved to Moscow for detailed examination and possible disassembly.

The American heavy bomber was copied in a miraculously short period of time and was Immediately Introduced into mass production. The priority was so high, no experimental prototype was built for flight testing.

Production of the Tupolev Tu-4 (NATO code-named 'Bull') continued until 1953, by which time no less than 4,100 aircraft had been completed. As a result of a successful nuclear weapon development program, several Tu-4s – as Tu-4As – eventually were modified to carry the Soviet Union's first air-deliverable atomic bomb. These same aircraft also served to accommodate much of the atmospheric testing of Soviet nuclear weapons during the 1950s. One Tu-4A dropped an atomic bomb at the Tozky proving ground during a military training exercise during September of 1964. At the time there was a huge number of infantry troops and equipment on site.

During the early to mid-1950s the Tu-4As were the only nuclear-capable aircraft in the Soviet air force arsenal capable of reaching the US-equipped military bases found at various points along the Soviet borders separating Russia from its European and Middle Eastern neighbors.

As it was, the Tu-4 proved to be a turning point for the Soviet aviation industry. Accessing the Boeing B-29 proved a major technological windfall and allowed the various bomber design bureaux, most notably Tupolev, to shorten a normally lengthy learning curve into a matter of months, rather than years. This rather giant leap forward would prove the foundation of all future Russian heavy bomber development and its fall-out would impact the history of the western world.

The first Soviet atomic weapon was exploded during 1949 ...with extraordinary political and military repercussions across the globe. Production weapons were delivered to operational units within a few years of this event, and as a result, extraordinary emphasis was placed on developing a means for getting the new bomb to a target. The target of greatest concern was, of course, the United States... some 6,400 km (4,000 miles) distant. This was well beyond the range of the Tu-4A – particularly when It was carrying an overweight payload such as an atomic bomb. Only targets in Europe, North Africa, the Middle East, Japan and the Far East were accessible.

Attempts to extend the Tu-4's range via inflight refueling were modestly successful but little emphasis was placed on developing the technology. Only six Tu-4s eventually were modified to incorporate this capability: three were equipped as tankers and three as receivers. It was not until the advent of the Tupolev Tu-16, some years later that inflight refueling became relatively commonplace in Russia.

Other studies tackling the range-to-the-US requirement included the option of one-way missions. In the event of war, Tu-4s that were to attack the US would be flown to their target, a bomb would be dropped, and the crew would then parachute from the aircraft once the aircraft initiated its abbreviated return leg over the Atlantic. A waiting submarine would then retrieve them for the return to Russia.

Concurrent with the one-way flight studies were similar studies exploring the attributes of using the Tu-4 in the stand-off carrier role. Remotely piloted vehicles launched from the Tu-4 would serve to deliver warheads to targets. Like inflight refueling, the initial RPV work of the early 1950s was only a preliminary step and full-fledged Interest in the option was not Initially sufficient to merit a more intense effort.

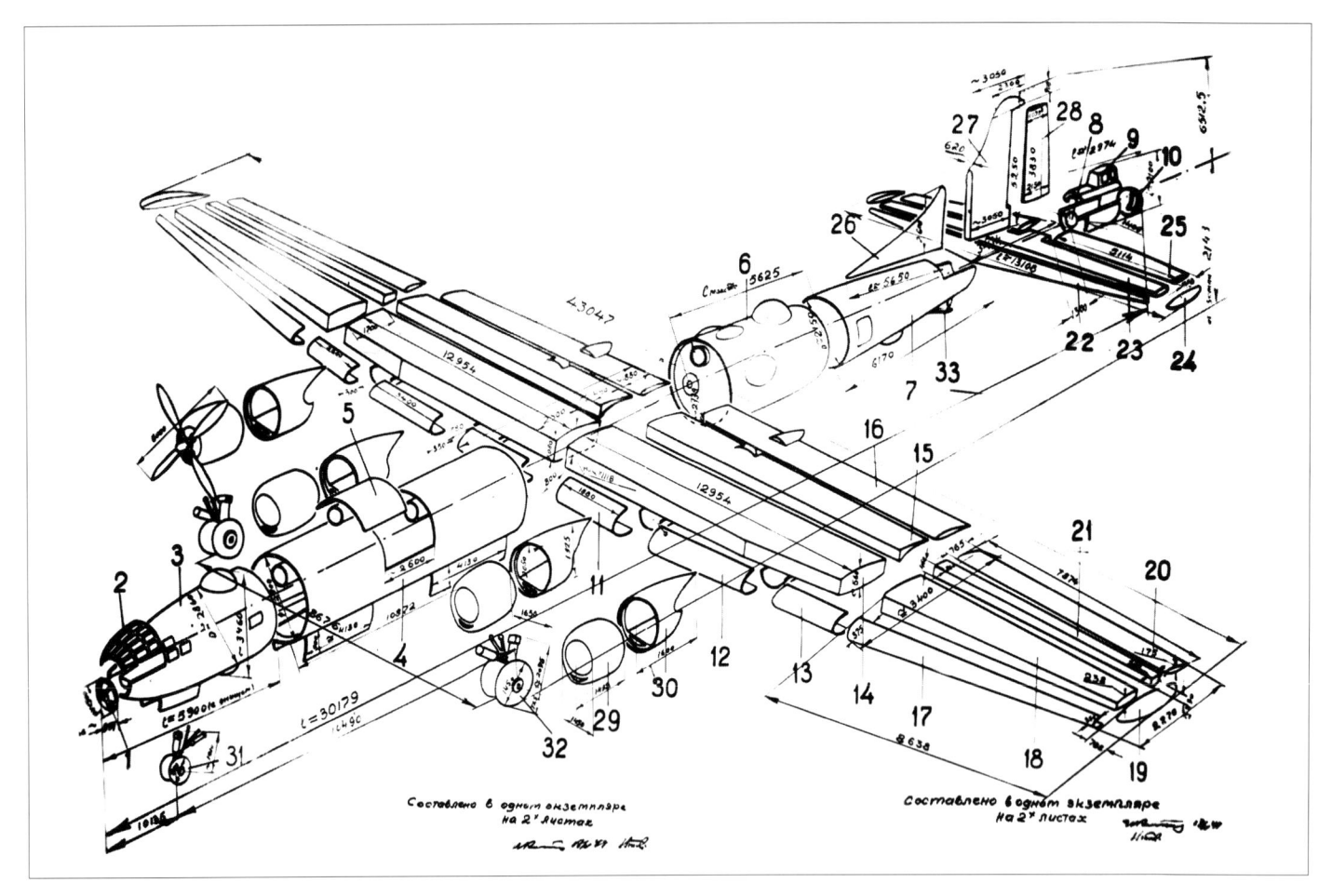

Most of the on-going emphasis solving the range problem pursued the more conventional path of advanced bomber development. The objective was to develop a weapon transport that could span, with payload, the distance between Russia and the US and return …preferably without having to be refueled.

Once the Tu-4 had successfully entered production, Tupolev began looking at developed versions to fill the role of stand-off missile carrier with intercontinental range. These studies resulted In projects 471, 473, 474, and 485 (with the first two numbers indicating the year of origin and the latter indicating the specific project). All were developments of the original Tu-4, differing primarily in having more engines of greater horsepower, larger fuselages, greater wingspans, and increased operating weights.

For example, intercontinental bomber Projects 471 and 485 had six ASh-473 TK turboprop engines, wingspan increased to 56m (183.7ft), and the normal operating weight increased to 86,207kg (190,000lb). Interestingly, information about these two projects

Above: **Exploded view of the Tupolev Tu-4. The component breakdown is remarkably similar to the US Boeing B-29.** Tupolev OKB

Below: **Production Tu-4, No.2805710, after an arctic landing.** Gennadii Petrov collection

Photographs on the opposite page:

Top: **A modified Tu-4 carrying two prototype KS-1 cruise missiles. The latter appear to be manned versions as first used to verify project viability.** Tupolev OKB

Right and below: **The Tupolev Tu-4 was one of the first Russian aircraft to have inflight refueling capability. Only a select few Tu-4s were so modified.** Tupolev OKB

somehow penetrated through the infamous 'iron curtain' and appeared in western aviation journals of the day. The mysterious Russian bomber was referred to as the 'Tu-200' and stated to be analogous to the Convair B-36.

Work on the new bomber project was divided Into two stages. The first explored the various non-Tu-4 options that would permit non-stop intercontinental range flight over distances of 20,000 km (12,420 miles) or more. The second explored taking the basic Tu-4 and enlarging it into a design that would accommodate the range and payload specification. Comparison charts utilizing a variety of engine and airframe combinations were drawn to explore the various options.

The resulting studies showed that the proposed 20,000 km (12,420 miles) range specified for the new bomber was not obtainable. Ranges of from 15,000 to 16,000 km (9,315 to 9,936 miles) were, however, within the realm of possibility. In order to meet this specification, the wing area for the aircraft would have to be from 300 to 340 m² (3,229 to 3,659 ft²) and the takeoff roll at gross weight would have to be from 2,500 to 4,160 m (8,200 to 13,645 ft).

Second-generation studies included exploring options other than multiple engine aircraft of immense size and weight. Instead designs concentrated on four-engine aircraft capable of performing the long-range heavy bomber function. These, in turn, served as a basis for future super-long-range designs that could be developed based on the original aircraft without major modification.

These diverse studies of different configurations utilizing a variety of engine options led to the design bureaux' conclusions that the new aircraft should use the manufacturing and design experience that had evolved from the manufacture of the Tu-4. It was proposed therefore, that the new long-range bomber should be based on the Tu-4 fuselage but mated to a new wing of increased area (200 m²/2,153 ft²) utilizing a low-drag airfoil. Additionally, new and more powerful engines would replace the originals. The aircraft would benefit from an increased fuel capacity, an increased bomb load, and improved aerodynamics.

The first aircraft to incorporate the proposed improvements to the Tu-4 was the Tupolev bomber '80', or Tu-80. This was a severely redesigned Tu-4 with increased takeoff weight and significantly improved range. It represented an indigenous evolutionary development of the Tu-4 along the lines of Boeing's B-50 and the B-29, but emphasized specific Russian Air Force and environmental requirements. The new aircraft eliminated many of the Tu-4's more overt failings while at the same time improving aerodynamics and increasing defensive armament options.

Fuel capacity of the Tu-80 was increased by 15% over that of the Tu-4. This was accomplished by increasing the span of the wing center section and improving the size and location of the integral wing fuel tanks.

Left: **Several MiG-15s were modified by the MiG design bureau to incorporate a probe system for inflight refueling via Tu-4 tanker.**
Tupolev OKB

Below left: **The prototype Tupolev Tu-80, probably during flight testing at Zhukovsky.**
Tupolev OKB

Bottom and next page bottom: **The prototype Tupolev Tu-85, probably during flight testing at Zhukovsky.** Tupolev OKB

New engines were installed as well, these being mounted with higher thrust lines, low-drag circular cowlings, and separate ventral oil cooling ducts.

The Tu-80, which was 3 m (9 ft 10 in) longer than its predecessor, revised the Tu-4's cockpit layout, as well, and positioned the majority of the crew in the forward section of the aircraft. The radio operator, for instance, was moved from the center crew position to the forward. Both the navigator and bombardier were moved to the nose of the aircraft where they could have an excellent forward field of view. A new, conventional stepped windscreen arrangement solved the Tu-4's problem of internal reflections and associated visual distortion. A pressurized communication tunnel was installed to permit crew access to the aft fuselage through the bomb bay.

A new vertical tail, necessitated by the more powerful engines and increased wingspan, replaced the original Tu-4 design. Armament included modified Tu-4-style gun turrets (i.e., remotely controlled) positioned low at their mounting points to reduce drag, and a Cobalt radar system – mounted under the nose inside a dielectric fairing – to assist the bombardier in locating targets.

Aerodynamically, the Tu-80 was somewhat cleaner than the Tu-4. The former, with a drag coefficient of 18, compared quite favorably to the former with a drag coefficient of 17.

Engine performance also was improved. The 18-cylinder ASh-73TKFN radial utilized was capable of 2,026 kW (2,720 hp) at sea level and 1,758 kW (2,360 hp) at altitude (the ASh-73TKFN with fuel injection was more economical to operate than the earlier ASh-73TK). New, more efficient propellers also were developed to more efficiently utilize the ASh-73TKFN's power.

These structural, mechanical, and aerodynamic improvements resulted in the Tu-80 having a range of 5,092 miles (8,200 km). This was an increase of 30% to 35% over that of the Tu-4.

These performance improvements, unfortunately, were not enough to merit Tu-80 production. While its development had been on-going at Tupolev, additional performance had been deemed possible and more advanced designs thus had begun to come to fruition. The Tu-80 successfully completed its flight trials – initiated upon its first flight on 1st December 1949 – but was quickly relegated to flight test work on behalf of forthcoming bombers of considerably more capability.

In fact, work on the Tu-80's successor, the '85' bomber by Tupolev, had advanced rapidly even in light of the successes enjoyed by the earlier design. When completed, the Tu-85 proved to be an even more capable weapon delivery platform. Utilizing the technological advances generated under the Tu-80 umbrella, it became the true forerunner to the ultimate development of the series, the Tu-95.

Construction of the first Tu-85 was completed during September of 1950 and the aircraft made its first flight on 9th January 1951. Flight tests quickly verified Tupolev's performance predictions. The 24-cylinder Dobrynin VD-4K engines, generating some 2,980 kW (4,300 hp) each, proved more than sufficient to give the aircraft the speed and range required for its bombing mission. During one test flight, the bomber flew a 12,018 km (7,463 miles) mission and reached a maximum speed of 638 km/h at 10,000 m (396 mph at 32,800 ft).

The Tu-85's normal bomb load was 5,000 kg (11,020 lb). Maximum bomb load over short ranges was 18,000 kg (39,672 lb). Two separate bomb bays were provided with one positioned ahead of the wing center section and one aft. The largest single bomb that could be carried weighed 9,000 kg (19,836 lb).

The successes enjoyed by the Tu-85 during the course of its flight test program gave the Tupolev bureau and other concerned entities the impression that their long range bomber aspirations had been achieved. The aircraft met its range and payload requirements without difficulty. It was predicted it could, if necessary, reach and bomb the US mainland with only modest effort. Production plans were initiated and a production facility was picked to accommodate manufacture.

Just as production plans were reaching fruition, intelligence studies of US anti-aircraft

defenses and fighter-interceptor developments indicated that a bomber powered by reciprocating engines would have a difficult time surviving. Reduced to the lowest common denominator, it was apparent the Tu-85 was too slow for the strategic bombing mission in the post-Second World War environment. It would be a sitting duck for advanced, radar-equipped, supersonic interceptors such as those then under development in the US.

Underscoring this conclusion was the relative vulnerability of US bombers to North Korean MiG-15s. The limited successes of the former during the course of the Korean War, which by 1952 was serving as a testing ground for the latest in US and Russian aviation technology, had not gone unnoticed by the major participating combatants. Though the US already had curtailed the development of bombers powered by reciprocating engines, the Korean War served to justify expeditious development of their jet-powered successors. Even the enormous Convair B-36, the last major US intercontinental bomber to be primarily powered by reciprocating engines, was adversely impacted. Production was limited to fewer than 400 aircraft.

Assessing the development of bombers in the west, the Soviet military quickly concluded that aircraft such as the Tu-85 were outmoded and not suitable candidates for a full-scale production program and operational deployment. The Tu-85, like its Tu-80 predecessor, was cancelled and work on more advanced heavy bombers powered either by turboprop or turbojet engines were given highest priority.

Of central importance was that these advanced, high-subsonic-speed-capable aircraft be able to carry the Soviet Union's rapidly growing stockpile of first-generation atomic bombs.

During 1950, bureau chief V M Myasischev approached the Soviet military forces with an offer to create a strategic bomber with a maximum speed of up to 950km/h (590mph) and a range of more than 13,000km (8,073 miles).

Providing initiative for this aircraft – proposed with four turbojet engines – had been engine design bureau chief A A Mikulin. Shortly afterwards the proposal was given manufacturing approval by the government. Myasishchev was directed to proceed as rapidly as possible.

The new bomber would have to be capable of carrying a 4,537 kg (10,000 lb) atomic bomb non-stop to the continental US and return. A heavy defensive armament would offset any deficiencies in performance.

The highly classified Myasischev bomber, eventually to become known as the M-4 project, utilized the best aerospace technology and engineers in the Soviet Union's vast aerospace industry. Practically unlimited financial resources were provided in the hope that an unlimited amount of money would expedite development.

A N Tupolev knew about the initial studies referring to the M-4. Not surprisingly, he was ready to compete with Myasischev (a former pupil) for the right to create a strategic high-speed bomber for the Russian Air Force. During the spring of 1948, research on designs to meet the new specification were initiated by the Tupolev engineering staff under the direction of N S Kondorsky.

By this time Design Bureau 156 had received a copy of a TsAGI report entitled 'Researching Flight Characteristics of a Heavy Jet Bomber With Swept Wing'. In the report captured German research into large, swept wing aircraft weighing from 72,595 to 145,191 kg (160,000 to 320,000 lb) and with wing sweep angles of from 25° to 35° at quarter chord, was examined in considerable detail. Some 46 designs utilizing up to eight RD45 or AMTKRD 01 turbojet engines providing from 107 to 215kN (10,889 to 48,000 lbst) of thrust were reviewed in the calculations.

Using the German data as a baseline, additional work by Tupolev expanded upon the available information and then was extrapolated into actual hardware through development of the Tupolev Tu-16.

The earlier Tu-85 also served as an expansion point for the Tupolev experience base. Both aircraft led to the realization that a takeoff weight of at least 136,116kg (300,000lb) and a sweepback angle at quarter-chord of 35° (with an aspect ratio of 9) would be required in order for a large bomber to fly the requisite range and achieve the desired speed-at-altitude... all while carrying a reasonable bomb load.

The swept-wing had been thoroughly studied by the engineers at TsAGI and declared the best option for the new Tupolev bomber. As the aircraft began to emerge in its final form, it became apparent the '85's' fuselage would be suitable when coupled with the proposed new wing configuration. The various powerplant options were quickly narrowed by N S Kondorsky and his team to either turbojet or turboprop propulsion, though which of the two (or a combination thereof) remained undecided at this early stage. It was known that an engine in the 7,460 to 8,952 kW (10,000 to 12,000 shp) range consuming about 0.25 kg (0.6 lb) of fuel per horsepower per hour would be necessary for the performance specifications to be achieved.

Actual work on the design aspects of the new bomber began with upgrade studies of the basic Tu-4 and Tu-85 in response to new tactical and technical issues. Various engine studies led to examination of the TV-2 on the Tu-4 in place of the ASh-73TK (maximum speed was increased to 676km/h (420mph) and range to 6,900km (4,285 miles) as a result). This project (aircraft '94') became the basis for an attempt by Tupolev to undertake a major fleet-wide upgrade of the Tu-4.

The second step in the proposed modernization program was via introduction of an upgraded Tu-85 using either TV-2F or TV-10 engines. In this case calculated flight range was between 16,000 and 17,200km (9,936 to 10,681 miles) and maximum speed was between 700 and 740km/h (435 to 460 mph). Unfortunately, these figures did not give rise to a lot of enthusiasm and a decision was made therefore to continue the study process.

Above: **Aft-view of the Tu-85 illustrates the enormity of its wingspan.** Tupolev OKB

The next step involved investigating the bomber configured with a swept wing and a variety of engine combinations as follows:
- with four AM-3 turbojet engines
- with a combination of four TV-10 turboprop and AM-3 engines
- with four TV-10 engines and two TR-3A turbojet engines
- with four TV-4 engines and two AM-3 engines
- with four TV-10 engines

Additionally, as these studies continued, the anticipated wing area was increased from 274 m² to 400 m² (2,949 ft² to 4,305 ft²) and the quarter chord sweep angles were varied between 0° and 45°. Aspect ratio was explored from 6.8 to 11.75.

Eventually, the studies led to two basic versions of the preliminary design being chosen for extended study. One was equipped with four turbojet engines and the other with four turboprops. The comparison indicated the version using the four TVD's generating anywhere from 8,952 to 30,959 kW (12,000 to 41,500 shp) shaft horsepower was the most suitable option for reaching the range requirement of over 13,000 km (8,073 miles). In the necessary configuration to meet this range specification, the aircraft's calculated takeoff weight reached 181,488 kg (400,000 lb). The calculated maximum speed at 10,000 m (32,800 ft) was about 800 km/h (497 mph). The takeoff roll was estimated to be 1,500 m (4,920 ft).

In comparison, the study calling for the propulsion provided by four TRD turbojet engines each of 900 kg (4,083 lb) thrust, offered a range of only 10,000 km (6,210 miles) and a maximum speed of 900 km/h (559 mph). Takeoff roll was calculated to be over 2,000 m (6,560 ft).

A final review of the various options and performance charts finally led Tupolev to pick the turboprop engine (TVD) configuration over the pure turbojet (TRD). The driving force behind this decision was the high priority placed on range. The first-generation Russian turbojet engines simply did not provide the fuel economy needed for the proposed heavy bomber.

Not surprisingly, the Russian Air Force and its aviation industry advisors, well aware of the progress being made by Myasischev with their M-4 all-jet bomber, did not agree with Tupolev's decision. Discussions eventually led to Stalin requesting that Tupolev meet with him in the Kremlin.

Upon hearing Tupolev's arguments in favor of the turboprop, Stalin elected to continue work on the Myasischev bomber and at the same time, approve initial development funding for the Tupolev strategic bomber, henceforth to be referred to as bomber '95'.

By the date of Stalin's approval, work on the TVD engine, now referred to as the TV-2, developed under the supervision of Chief Designer N D Kuznetsov of Design Bureau 276 (N D Kuznetsov) had progressed to the point where prototype engines were developing in excess of 3,730 kW (5,000 shp) on the test stand. Evolved from the Junkers Jumo 022, the technology for the TV-2 had been captured by the Russians at the end of World War II and quickly developed into full-scale hardware utilizing the assistance of interned German propulsion system engineers.

A prototype engine (initially designated TV-22) successfully passed government static tests during October of 1950. An improved version, tested not long afterwards, delivered 3,446 kW (4,620 shp). The TV-10 and TV-12 engines followed, these producing 7,460 kW (10,000 shp) and 8,952 kW (12,000 shp), respectively. At the time, these were by far the most powerful turboshaft (turboprop) engines in the world. Unfortunately, problems arose that were not easily rectified. It would be nearly two years before these were overcome.

Because of the powerplant delays and their associated impact on the new '95' bomber project, Tupolev flew to Kuibyshev in order to consult with Kuznetsov and review the immense turboprop engine's status. During the course of the meeting it was decided that, in order to meet flight test scheduling requirements, it would be best to temporarily utilize the older, smaller TV-2F in a paired configuration and couple the two engines to one common gearbox. The resulting powerplant was designated 2TV-2F and its maximum power rating was determined to be 8,952 kW (12,000 shp).

Interestingly, development of the 2TV-2F's gearbox proved a major undertaking. At the time, no aircraft-grade gearbox of comparable size, weight, and power capacity had ever been built.

Concurrent with the engine's on-going development cycle, design of a propeller capable of efficiently utilizing the power output also was undertaken. It was soon determined that a propeller with a diameter of 7 m (23 ft) would be required. This was unacceptable for a number of reasons, not the least of which was the simple difficulty in building and producing such an enormous propeller and in manufacturing landing gear tall enough to accommodate it!

In short order, it was decided that a contra-rotating propeller configuration would be best suited for the new engine. Though mechanically complicated and aerodynamically challenging, a design utilizing the contra-rotating option could be conveniently accommodated by the propeller manufacturers and the airframe landing gear could be readily design to meet the more sensible height-above-the-ramp requirement.

Design Bureau 120, supervised by K I Zhdanov, tackled the design of the advanced propeller and its contra-rotating transmission assembly. One challenging aspect of the eight-blade design was that – in combination with the new Kuznetsov engine – it had to provide an efficiency rating of 0.78 to 0.82 in order for the aircraft to meet its performance specification. No previous propeller/engine combination had ever achieved such high numbers.

Following the meeting with Kuznetsov, Tupolev made another trip to the Kremlin. There he convinced Stalin that the new '95' bomber project was worthy of continued support. On 11th July 1951, the USSR Council of Ministers and Ministry of Aviation Industry released a resolution and written order in accordance with which Design Bureau 156 (Tupolev) was 'entrusted to design and build a long-range high-speed bomber in two versions:
- with four interconnected TVDs of 2TV-2F type; and
- with four TV-12 engines.'

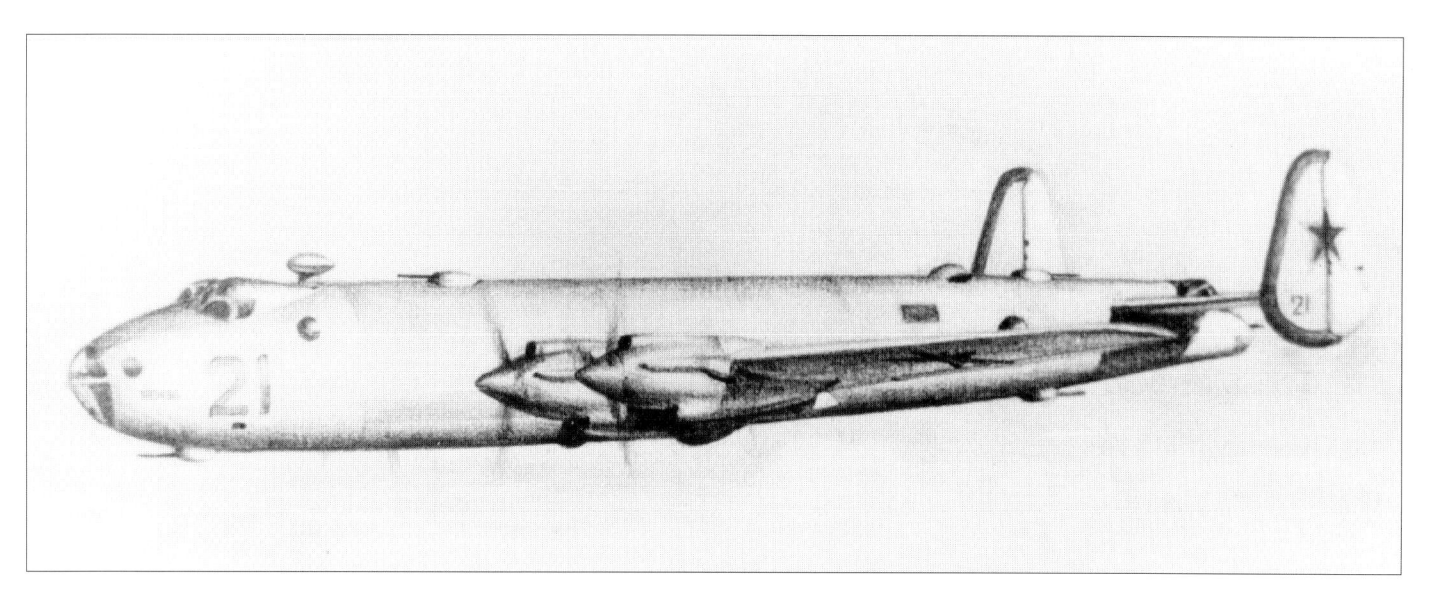

The first configuration had to be ready for flight test by September of 1952; the second had to be ready for flight test by September 1953.

The question of mass production was resolved in four days. On 15th November 1951, the Kuibyshev factory and Design Bureau 18 were ordered to prepare for the production of the '95' aircraft. This would be initiated during January of 1952. Necessary preparations for full-rate production would be completed by 1st September.

Concurrent to this, the Myasischev Design Bureau and Moscow Factory No.23 were preparing to initiate production of the 'M-4' aircraft. It was now well known that the Myasischev and Tupolev aircraft would be competing with each other to see which would be best able to accommodate the Russian Air Force's intercontinental range heavy bomber requirement for the coming several decades. The Soviet Government, and in particular, Stalin, believed that the priority placed on the development of these two aircraft, and the associated outlay of roubles, was justifiable. The perceived threat of nuclear war with the US provided the incentive necessary to expedite development.

While work began to accelerate on the '95's' airframe development and construction, Kuznetsov moved ahead with the 2TV-2F engine. A Tu-4 was bailed to Tupolev for use as a testbed and by the middle of 1952, as the Tu-4LL (175II order), it was ready for flight test with a prototype 2TV-2F engine mounted on the starboard inboard engine position (replacing the standard ASh-73TK radial engine); at a later date, this same Tu-4 would be utilized as an inflight testbed for the definitive TV-2.

Final engineering design of the '95' prototype had been started on 15th July 1951. Under the supervision of S M Eger, this work proceeded rapidly...alongside the actual aircraft which was being built as engineering and manufacturing drawings were released.

At the same time, the Russian Air Force, during August of 1951, began to define the tactical and technical objectives that would be required to efficiently utilize the capabilities of the new bomber. In accordance with those requirements and a resolution of the Council of Ministers, the aircraft was expected to have an operating range of up to 15,000 km (9,315 miles) with payload and an absolute maximum range from 17,000 to 18,000 km (10,557 to 11,178 miles). Cruise speed was expected to be from 750 to 820 km/h (466 to 509 mph) and maximum speed was expected to be from 920 to 950 km/h (571 to 590 mph). Service ceiling was expected to be approximately 14,000 m (45,920 ft). Takeoff roll was estimated to be from 1500 to 1,800 m (4,920 to 5,904 ft).

By December of 1951, engineering design and initial construction of the new Tupolev '95' bomber was moving along rapidly. Final (revised) performance estimates included a cruising speed of from 750 to 800 km/h (466 to 497 mph) at an altitude of from 10,000 to 14,000 m (32,800 to 45,920 ft). Maximum range now was estimated to be from 14,500 to

Top: **Resembling the British Handley Page Halifax, one of numerous '64' heavy bomber studies undertaken by Tupolev.**
Yefim Gordon collection

Bottom: **Another of the many '64' heavy bomber design studies that eventually led to the Tu-95.**
Yefim Gordon collection

17,500km (9,005 to 10,868 miles). Targets were established as being items of a strategic nature including military bases, seaports, military manufacturing factories, political and administrative centers, and other similar entities positioned deep within an enemy's borders that were otherwise inaccessible to other military aircraft or equipment. Additionally, the '95' was optimized to deploy mines and handle other maritime bombing and surveillance requirements.

Tupolev's engineers also had established that the '95's' relatively high speed at altitude, when combined with its exceptional defensive armament, would make it a difficult target for enemy fighters to attack and destroy. Additionally, modern navigation and communication capabilities gave the new bomber a high chance of success, even in adverse weather conditions and/or at night.

An analysis of the 2TV-2F engined version versus the TV-12 engined version indicated that with an 8,167kg (18,000lb) bomb load, the former would have a radius of action of 6,000km (3,726 miles) and the latter would have a range of 7,500km (4,658 miles). This finalized the decision to proceed with the TV-2 aircraft and to make the more powerful engine the standard propulsion system for the production bomber.

Integral with the new bomber's design was the ability to be inflight refueled. This was a first for Russian bombers and a technology and skill that had been little exposed within the Russian Air Force. Regardless, the ability to fly missions in excess of 32,000km (19,872 miles) made the additional effort seemingly worthwhile. With inflight refueling, the '95' would be able to attack any point on the globe and return to base without difficulty.

The '95's' bomb bay was designed to accommodate a bomb load of up to 13,612kg (30,000lb) with a normal bomb load of 4,537kg (10,000lb). Conventional loads, torpedos, mines, and other weapons were optional, with a thermonuclear device being standard for the strategic bombing mission. The bomb bay was environmentally controlled in consideration of the sensitivity of nuclear weapons and their associated systems.

Though it had now been determined that the prototype '95' would fly with the 2TV-2F engine, it was decided that the second prototype would be powered by the definitive TV-2. This engine now was expected to deliver a maximum of 9,325kW (12,500shp), a continuous rating of 8,952kW (12,000shp) and a cruise power of 7,609kW (10,200shp), all at sea level.

Crew accommodations were optimized for eight crew members. There were no ejection seats as the aircraft did not operate in a flight regime where such emergency egress systems were deemed necessary. Additionally, there were serious weight and comfort issues which would have been difficult to address if ejection seats had been included.

In consideration of other economies, it had been stipulated that maximum usage of available hardware from other design bureaux should be used wherever appropriate. This not only saved money, it significantly speeded development time…and thus allowed the aircraft to enter production at the earliest possible date.

Final design studies and engineering documents were transferred to the Air Technical Committee in the presence of the Commander-in-Chief of the Russian Air Force. On 31st October 1951, he approved it.

Initial working drawings for actual construction were nearing completion by September of 1951 and the last of these was delivered approximately one year later. A full-scale '95' mock-up was initiated during August and had been completed by November. During construction, the mock-up was inspected three times by the Air Force Commission. Considerable criticism surfaced as a result, and many changes and improvements were incorporated. During November, the completed mock-up was examined in detail by the Commission and the following month the Russian Air Force Commander-in-Chief approved it for construction.

In the meantime, construction of the prototype had been initiated during October. Factory 156 had been assigned the task of building the first bomber, now referred to as aircraft prototype '95-1' (order number 180-1). Concurrent to this, a second airframe for static testing was begun as well.

The static test article was deemed one of the most important of the many test specimens to be examined. Structural integrity was considered a critical aspect of the immense bomber's development. Tupolev's chief structures engineer was A M Cheryomukhin who headed that department within the bureau's bureaucracy. His department was responsible for most of the more critical aspects of airframe integrity, including the engine location and mounting dynamics.

At yet another factory, No.18, tooling design and requirements as well as the logistical aspects of production were being accommodated. This was complicated by on-going changes resulting from stability and structural studies. These, in turn, had to be integrated into the production line…with a ripple effect from there.

During the design of the '95' bomber it proved necessary to incorporate changes that adversely impacted the production methods and standards that were extant then. Older engineering methods had led to exceptionally large safety margins to accommodate project-

---

Top: **The Tupolev Tu-4LL engine testbed equipped with a single AI-20 engine as configured for the Ilyushin Il-18.**
Yefim Gordon collection

Bottom: **The Tupolev Tu-4LL engine testbed equipped with a single NK-12 engine as configured for the prototype Tu-95.**
Yefim Gordon collection

ed loads. These proved inefficient and wasteful and led to significant increases in airframe weight. In turn, this led to a serious performance degradation. The combined efforts of the TsAGI, Design Bureau 156, and Design Bureau 23 led to new insights into the structures and materials required for large swept wings. This technology was applied to the '95's' wing and as a result, enormous weight savings were realized without jeopardizing the safe operation of the aircraft.

Advanced avionics and electrical systems also were developed specifically for use on the '95' bomber. Aluminum wiring, much lighter than its copper-alloy counterpart, was developed and used for the first time in Russia on the new aircraft; and a lightweight electrical de-icing system was incorporated. Additionally, a lightweight self-contained starter system was developed for the TVD engines.

Control system technology also proved to be not only technologically challenging, but politically sensitive. The TsAGI had become enamored with irreversible hydraulic actuators and insisted they be used on the '95' bomber. Tupolev, taking a more conservative approach, argued that the actuators had a poor reliability record and that the old but dependable mechanical systems then in use were sufficient. This argument continued for a considerable period of time before the TsAGI capitulated to the Tupolev argument. The resulting unboosted mechanical system, though requiring considerable strength on the part of its pilots, eventually proved highly dependable and trouble-free.

Bureau chief A N Tupolev's belief in mechanical control systems versus those powered by hydraulic actuators became somewhat legendary. One of his most famous quotes was, 'The best actuator on earth is the one that stands on his own two feet'.

Not surprisingly, in continuing what it foresaw as the future of bomber design, V M Myasischev's Design Bureau 23 elected to utilize the irreversible hydraulic actuators on their M-4 bomber.

Though this proved a gamble mandated by the all-jet bomber's performance, it would prove a headache that would be many years in being resolved.

Coordinating the '95' bomber effort at Bureau 126, A N Tupolev entrusted his closest assistant, N I Bazenkov with over-all project responsibility. Bazenkov later would become chief of Tu-95 design and also would have similar responsibility for the civil-optimized Tu-114. During 1970, following his death, N V Kirsanov took over as Tu-95 program chief. And by the end of the 1980s, this title had been passed on yet again to D A Antonov.

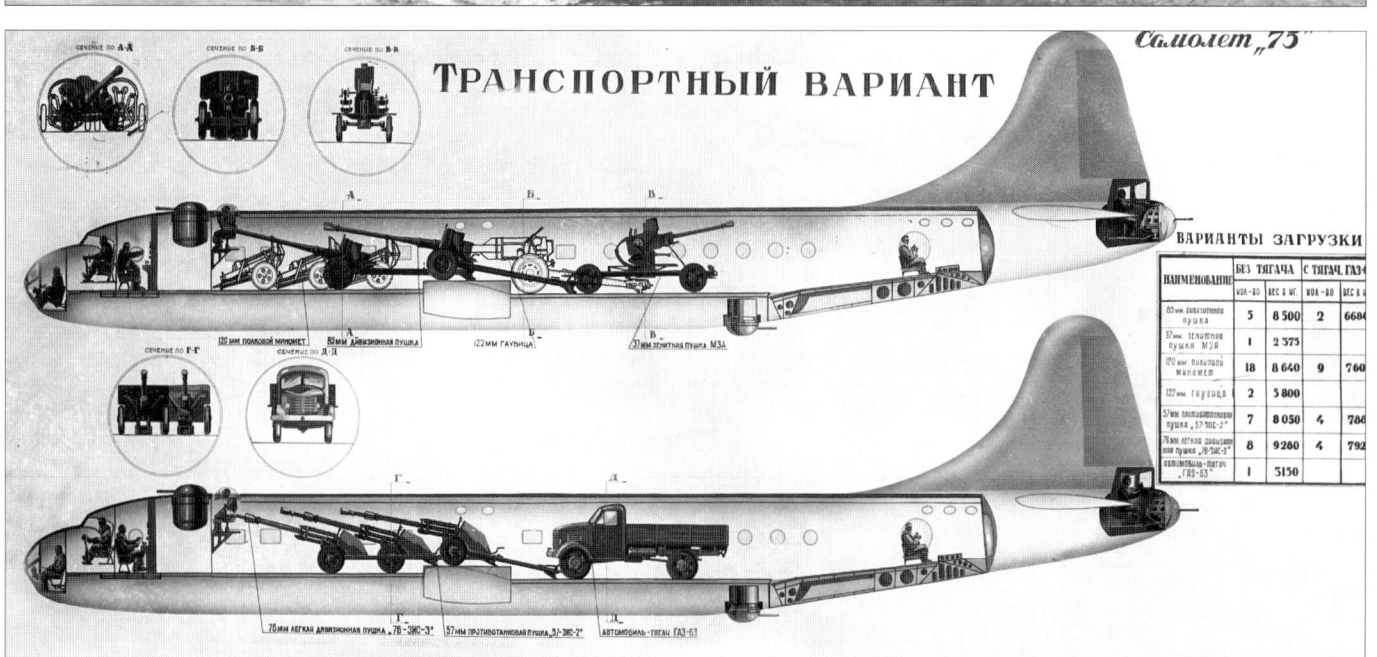

Below: **The Tupolev bureau elected to build a passenger carrying variant of the Tu-4. Referred to initially as the '70', it later became officially the Tu-70.** Yefim Gordon collection

Bottom: **The Tupolev Tu-70 met with some initial success as a transport and accordingly, Tupolev began to explore other uses for the design. Among them was the '75', or Tu-75, which was capable of carrying a great variety of payloads.** Yefim Gordon collection

15

Left and below: **The Tupolev Tu-70 ('70') transport prototype (developed directly from the Tu-4) in flight and under construction at Tupolev's OKB. Several different Tu-70 configurations were envisioned including some with turreted armament systems.** Tupolev

Bottom: **Two drawings depicting turboprop powered versions of the Tu-4. The one on the left illustrates the Tu-4 with four TV-4s and the one on the right depicts the Tu-4 with four TV-02s.** Tupolev

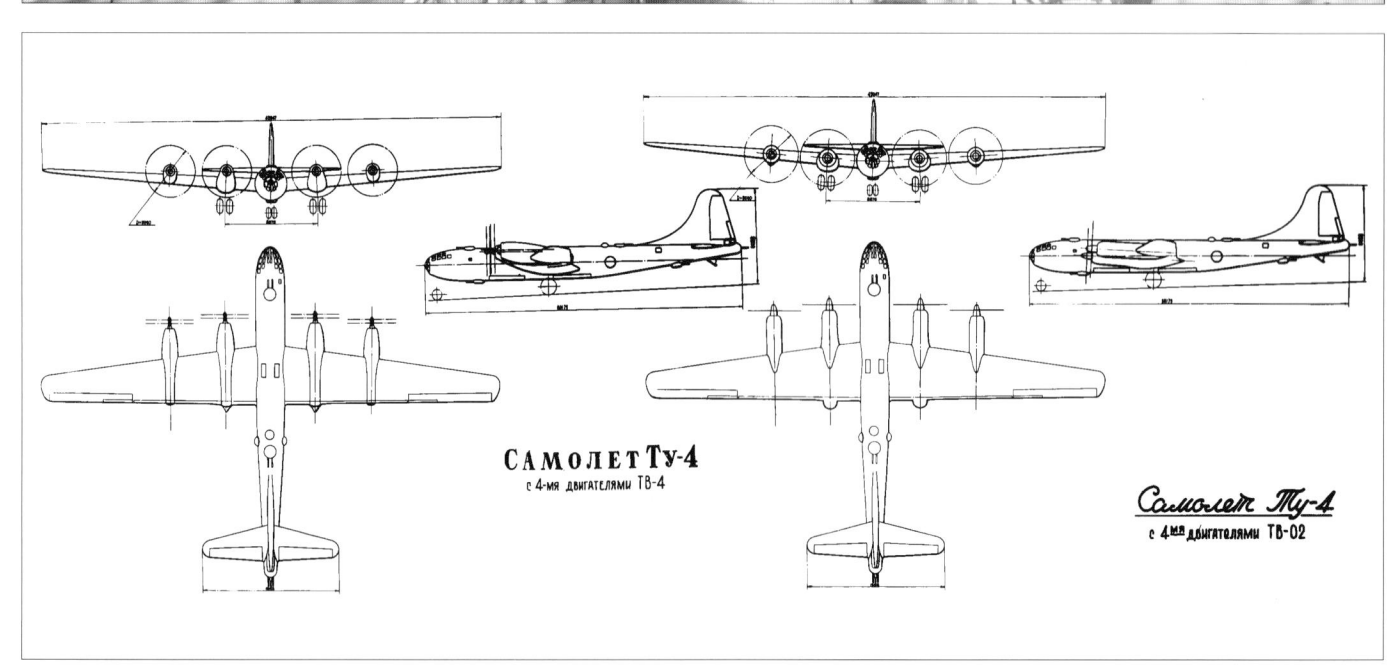

Самолет Ту-4
с 4-мя двигателями ТВ-4

Самолет Ту-4
с 4-мя двигателями ТВ-02

Photo Portfolio

'Bear' Colour

Right: **Tu-142M '93' during low-altitude fly-over.** Yefim Gordon

Middle: **Tu-142M '93' again, on final approach to landing.** Yefim Gordon

Bottom: **Tu-142M '90' sits static at 'Ostrov' Naval Aviation Center.** Yefim Gordon

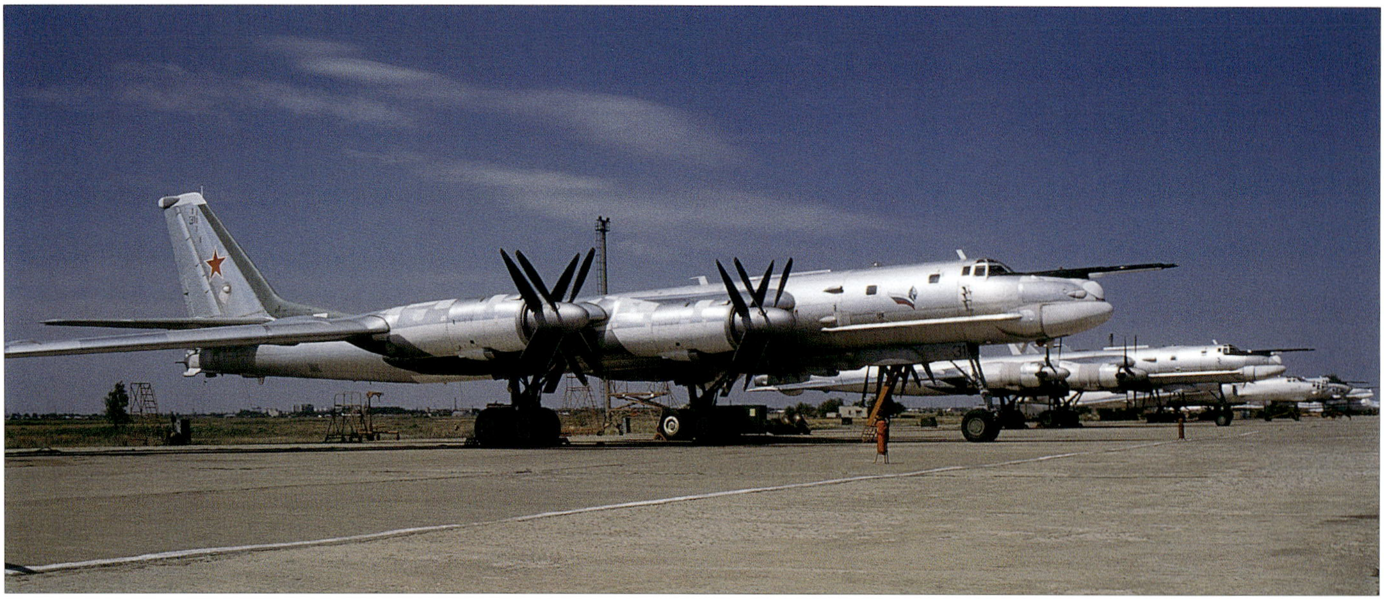

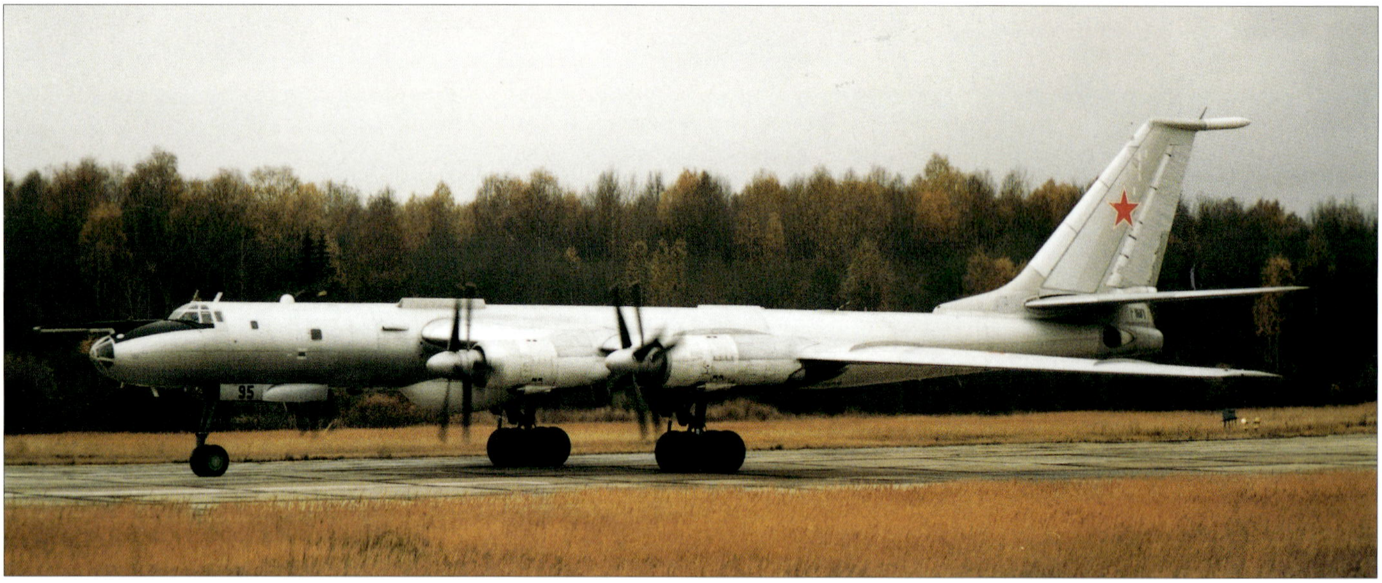
95

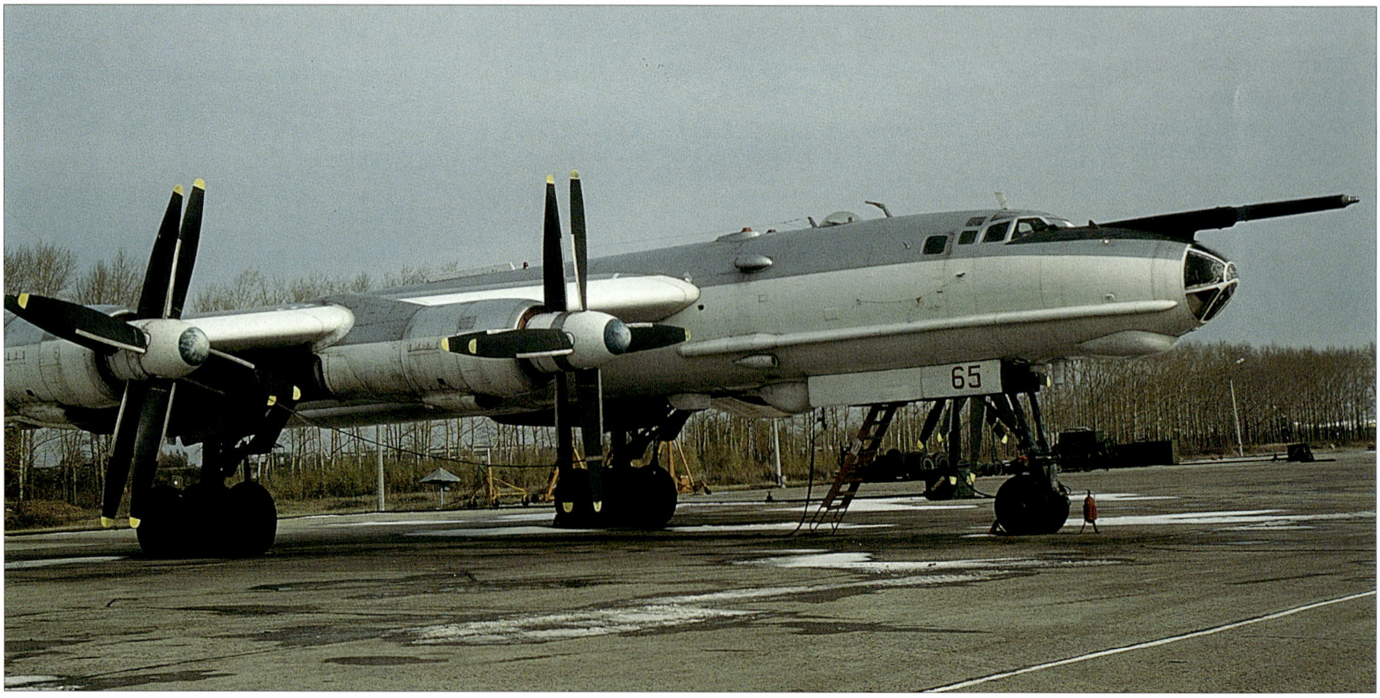
65

Photographs on the opposite page:

Top: **Tu-95MS 'Blue 31' heads a varied line-up.** Yefim Gordon

Middle: **Tu-142M '15' taxies out at the start of a mission from Kipelovo Air Base.** Yefim Gordon

Bottom: **Soon-to-be-scrapped Tu-95MR 'Red 65', with its standard white undersurface markings, at Ryazan Air Base.** Yefim Gordon

Photographs on this page:

Above: **Tu-142MR '15' landing at Kipelovo Air Base.** Yefim Gordon

Right: **Tu-95K 'Red 33' used for training (red band on fuselage) at Ryazan.** Yefim Gordon

Below: **Nose of Tu-95MR 'Red 65' at Ryazan Air Base. Note extended entry ladder in nose gear bay.** Yefim Gordon

Above: **Tu-95MS '33' in operational service.**
Yefim Gordon

Left: **Tu-95MS 23mm tail gun with articulated turret assembly. Readily visible are podded aft-facing radar warning receivers.**
Tom Copeland

Below: **Tu-142M2. Noteworthy is aft facing stinger on vertical fin tip.** Yefim Gordon

Above: **Tu-95MR 'Red 69', a trainer used at Ryazan Air Base for technical improvement trials.** Yefim Gordon

Right: **In response to SALT agreements and the collapse of the Soviet Union, many Tu-95s are being scrapped. A tail gun assembly is shown being disassembled to accommodate this requirement.** Yefim Gordon

Below: **Tu-95M 'Red 71' used for ground training at Ryazan Air Base. Removal of contra-rotating propeller assemblies is a result of SALT accords.** Yefim Gordon

Above: **Tu-142M '93' landing at RAF Fairford during 1994: the first time a Tu-142 had visited Great Britain.** Chris Pocock

Left: **A 'stock' Tu-95RTs on patrol over the Pacific.** Jay Miller collection

Below: **Tu-95MS '36' seen during an exchange visit to Barksdale AFB in Louisiana, USA, during 1992.** Tom Copeland

Above: **Tu-95MR outboard engine contra-rotating propeller assembly.** Yefim Gordon

Right: **Tu-95MS second navigator station which also serves to accommodate defensive electronic countermeasures equipment requirements.** Yefim Gordon

Below: **Tu-95MS first navigation station main panels.** Tom Copeland

Left: **Tu-95MS pilot's instrument panel (left half). Pitch trim wheel is visible on left console along with main control yoke and primary instruments.**
Tom Copeland

Left: **Tu-95MS co-pilot's instrument panel (right half). Pitch trim wheel is visible on right console along with main control yoke and co-pilot's back-up instruments.** Tom Copeland

Left and right below: **Tu-95MS pilot's (left) and co-pilot's console panels. These accommodate communications equipment, some circuit breaker panels and the throttle quadrants.**
Tom Copeland

Chapter Two

The 'Bear' Flies

Construction of the first '95' prototype – powered by four 2TV-2F turboprop engines – had been completed by the autumn of 1952. Following miscellaneous static tests, it was moved in pieces by road to the Zhukovsky flight test and development airfield southeast of Moscow. There, at the Tupolev facility, it was reassembled and on 20th September 1952, approved for initiation of the flight test program.

A hand-picked Tupolev flight test crew consisting of aircraft commander/test pilot A D Perelyot; second pilot V P Morunov; navigator/pilot S S Kirichenko; flight wireless operator N F Mayiorov; flight electronics engineer I E Komissarov; and flight mechanic L I Borzenkov began exploring the characteristics of the new bomber by initiating the first static engine runs and initial low- and high-speed taxi tests.

While the Tupolev flight test crew was preparing for the first flight, a KGB team initiated an above-average black-out to preserve the

Top: **The second prototype Tu-95 ('95-2') with revised engine nacelle configuration.**
Viktor Kudryavtsev collection

Center: **Tupolev Tu-95 bomber cutaway.**
Tupolev Design Bureau

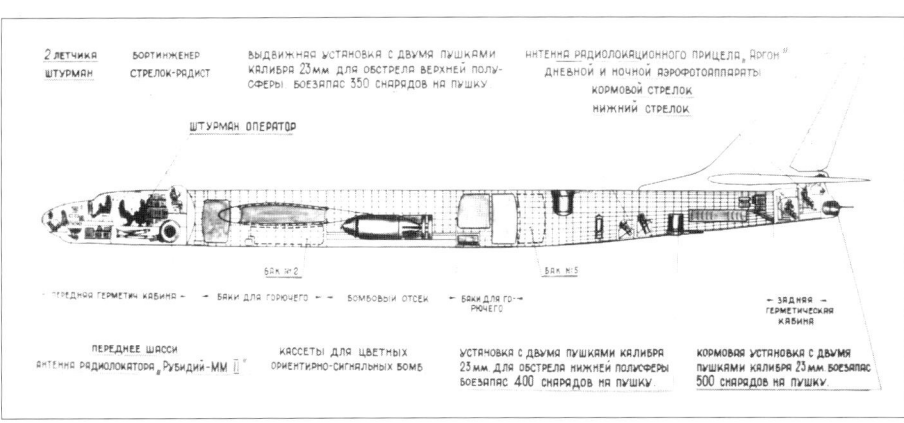

Below: **An early production Tu-95 following take-off.** Yefim Gordon collection

secrecy surrounding the project. They developed and controlled several operations that restricted the outflow of information between the design bureau and the production factory. In addition, they introduced severe control of the residential and farming area on the west bank of the Moscow River where it was easy to observe the runway and some parts of the aircraft parking ramp. Additionally, all work on the prototype was undertaken before truck transports and trains of the Kazanskaya railroad started to pass over near-by roads and railroads.

On 12th November 1952, the prototype '95' bomber, with Perelyot's crew onboard, became airborne for the first time. The flight reached an altitude of just over 1,150 m (3,700 ft) and lasted about 50 minutes.

Two more flights were completed by the end of the year. The next flight took place on 13th January 1953, and by mid-April, a total of sixteen flights had been logged. Then, on 17th April, a massive gearbox failure on one engine led to loss of blade pitch control and near-loss of the aircraft. Perelyot's superb piloting saved the day, however, and the prototype Tu-95 landed at Zhukovsky without further trauma. The aircraft was grounded for five months while the cause of the gearbox failure was uncovered and a solution developed.

TsAGI, in conjunction with Tupolev, eventually traced the difficulty to a material flaw. Finding a solution, the bureau initiated corrective measures that would allow the prototype Tu-95 to fly again.

The Soviet government and the Russian Air Force Command monitored the flight test program with intense scrutiny. Test results were reported to the Government by the Ministry of Aviation Industry and the KGB. Additionally, the Air Force plant representative (at Factory 156), Lt. Col. S D Agavelyan sent reports with considerable rapidity to the Air Force Commander-in-Chief, Col. Gen. P F Gigarev.

Top: **An operational Tu-95M at the moment of touchdown.** Yefim Gordon collection

Above and below: **Second production Tu-95 sits on Zhukovsky ramp.** Tupolev

All the various entities involved in the Tu-95's flight test program were soon extremely overworked and suffering from morale and physical shortcomings. Sleep deprivation eventually proved a serious problem; most members of the engineering and flight test teams were literally working around-the-clock. By the beginning of May the prototype aircraft had completed only 16 flights while accumulating some 21 hours in the air.

Unfortunately, the 17th flight ended in disaster. On 11th May, the prototype crashed. Andrei Tupolev, by chance, was at Zhukovsky on the day of the accident and had monitored the flight and talked with the crew shortly after their departure.

Initially, the flight had proceeded without difficulty. Suddenly, however, Perelyot had radioed, 'I am at the Noginsk area. The third engine is on fire. Free the landing strip. I will be landing directly from route.' Two to three minutes later he radioed, 'We cannot put the fire out. It is spreading. The landing gear and engine nacelles are burning too. We need to fly 440 km more to reach you.' Another message was heard several minutes later: 'The engine has fallen off. The wing and engine nacelle are on fire. I have just commanded the crew to abandon the plane. Watch out'. Nothing else was ever again heard from the crew.

Not long afterwards, a message was received from the Noginsky KGB stating that an aircraft had fallen on the north-eastern part of the town and was burning. A N Tupolev and military representative S D Agavelyan rushed to Noginsky and immediately headed to the accident site. Design bureau and flight test personnel followed shortly afterwards. While Tupolev rode a horse, the rest of those converging on the accident were forced to trek through the marshland on foot. When they finally reached the crash site, all that remained of the aircraft was an enormous crater and an intensely burning fire.

On the crater floor were the Tu-95-1's eight main gear tires. Like everything else, these were on fire and filling the air with acrid smoke and the smell of burning rubber. As the enormity of the accident began to soak in, local peasants voluntarily undertook the unpleasant task of looking for survivors or remains. They soon located what was left of Perelyot. Not long afterwards, the navigator, wrapped in his own parachute, was found dead near by. Reports from peasants in other villages indicated there had been at least a few who had made it to the ground safely by parachute.

Top right: **Test pilot A D Perelyot piloted the prototype Tu-95 on its first flight and flew it to his death when an engine gearbox failed.**
Yefim Gordon collection

Right: **An early production Tu-95, most likely a Tu-95M.** Yefim Gordon collection

A total of four crew members were dead (aircraft commander A D Perelyot; navigator S.S. Kirichenko; flight engineer A F Chernov; and a technician from the Research Scientific Institute of Aircraft Equipment, A M Bolshakov), but seven crew members had survived (co-pilot V P Morunov; flight wireless operator N F Mayiorov; lead engineer N V Lashkevich; assistant lead engineer A M Ter-Akopyan; flight electrician I E Komissarov; flight mechanic L I Borzenkov; and Flight Test Institute engineer K I Vaiman).

A special Government Committee, headed by Minister of Aviation Industry M V Khrunichev, was assembled to investigate the cause of the accident. Various KGB subdivisions, the Air Force, General Headquarters, the Communist Party Central Committee, the Council of Ministers, and many other organizations participated in the investigation as well.

Flight wireless operator N F Mayiorov, who had miraculously survived the ill-fated flight, noted the following in his post-accident report, 'having taken-off in the morning we measured fuel consumption. During a final test of maximum engine thrust at the height of 7,300 m (23,944 ft) the third engine caught fire and burned up. I had been watching the engine through the upper blister. Hearing a strong pop I saw a hole form in the front part of third engine cowling and then noted an intense fire burning there. I reported to the Commander. The engine was shut down immediately and the propellers were feathered. The fire-extinguishing system was activated. The fire continued to burn and as it did, parts of the aircraft began to fall off. We then realized that we could not land the aircraft conventionally. Leveling at an altitude of 5,000 m (16,400 ft) Perelyot flew the burning aircraft away from a densely populated area and over a forest and immediately commanded all of us except flight engineer Chernov to abandon the airplane. I was waiting. I remember looking in the cockpit and observing Perelyot who was very calm. I realized that he intended to attempt an emergency landing. At the height of 3,000 m (9,840 ft) I jumped out.

'While I was descending under my parachute, I was able to see the intense fire and column of smoke on the ground.'

Lead engineer N V Lashkevich during his parachute descent later said he saw the burning third engine fall off the airplane. The propellers on the fourth engine appeared to be fully feathered as well. Eventually, the Tu-95-1 rolled over and entered a nearly vertical descent to the ground.

Perelyot and Chernov were killed when the aircraft exploded. It was apparent they had tried very hard to save the prototype. Later, during 1955, A D Perelyot was posthumously awarded the title Hero of the Soviet Union. During 1957 he was posthumously awarded the prestigious Lenin Prize. Navigator Kirichenko had successfully egressed the airplane but when it hit the ground and exploded, he was caught in the resulting blast and heat. Bolshakov had also successfully egressed the aircraft but apparently had forgotten to firmly attach the seat-pack-type parachute to his body (it later was reported he was not familiar with this type of parachute and did not know how to use it).

As might be expected, the first reaction of the Air Force was a decision by the Commander-in-Chief to blame the Air Force senior military representative at Factory 156, Engineer and Lt. Col. S D Agavelyan. He was formally accused of the accident in a military tribunal court as

perpetrator of the disaster. The submission was prepared by a KGB officer in the main committee of the Soviet Air Force.

The manufacturing division of the Main Air Force Committee and Design Bureau 276 developed and supported their first version of the disaster. This seemed to explain everything in a very simple way: The engine mount on the number three engine had failed and after that the engine had fallen off. Loss of the engine had severed the fuel lines and this had led to the catastrophic fire. Thus the cause of the disaster could be traced to poor manufacturing and engineering technique by personnel of Factory 156. The latter was under the direction of S D Agavelyan and he was accused accordingly. Additionally, TsAGI senior military representative, Engineer-Colonel A I Solovyov, who was responsible for checking the results of the engine mount static test program, also was charged.

The conclusion that an engine mount failure caused the accident was quickly accepted throughout the Russian aerospace community.

It was officially declared as the accident cause by the engine development department under the Administration of Aviation Technical prototypes of the Soviet Air Force. The chief of this department, General Zaikin, later officially filed the order for the Commander-in-Chief of the Air Force that would lead to the conviction of both senior military representatives, Agavelyan and Solovyov.

The Air Force Commander-in-Chief, P F Zhygarev, having read the order in draft form, realized the matter would not simply disappear, even if the two about-to-be-accused men were executed. In his position, he was required to make daily reports to Stalin concerning the status of the '95' aircraft. Everyone in the Russian government was, in fact, following the big bomber's development, including the KGB and Stalin's assistant, Beria. Zhygarev predicted that a lot of generals - himself included - could eventually be playing defendants' roles. Assessing his options, he called Agavelyan and Solovyov into his office and carefully listened to their versions of how the engine mounts had been designed, developed, and tested. Convinced of their innocence, he cancelled the order and thus saved their lives.

Meanwhile, a specially created commission investigated the disaster under the auspices of the Ministry of Aviation Industry. Many commission members, including several engine design bureaus, pointed the finger of blame at Tupolev. Wisely, Tupolev kept silent. His deputies, N I Bazenkov, S M Yeger, K V Minker and others answered the commission's questions on his behalf.

Interestingly, one of the soldiers who had dug out parts of the third engine mount had simultaneously discovered a big chunk of a reduction gear from the 2TV-2F engine's gear box. This was delivered to the TsIAM for detailed study. A material strengths expert, R S Kinasoshvili, was asked to examine the piece. He quickly determined the gear had failed because of metal fatigue and improper material choice.

Not surprisingly, members of the commission refused to accept Kinasoshvili's conclusion that the gear had failed after only ten hours of operational service. The engine bureaux insisted on sticking to their argument that the gear broke after the aircraft hit the ground; and that the cause of the accident was faulty engine mount design.

Top left: **A Tu-95M begins its preflight warm-up prior to an operational mission.** Yefim Gordon collection

Middle: **An early production Tu-95M, probably during a fly-over of Tushino during the late 1950s.** Yefim Gordon collection

Bottom: **Another view of the Tu-95M seen at the top of the page. Noteworthy is white-painted lower fuselage.** Yefim Gordon collection

A commission meeting specifically to address engine manufacturers was called shortly thereafter. At this meeting, it was announced that information from technical documents had surfaced pertaining to Design Bureau 276's testing of the 2TV-2F turboprop engine. In these documents, it was stated that reduction gear failures had occurred during the 40th and 50th hours of static testing. Fires had broken out on both occasions. N D Kuznetsov, head of the bureau, suddenly became pale and fainted.

Tupolev, noting the difficulties surrounding the engine situation, elected not to force the issue with Kuznetsov. Rather than see him given a death sentence, he asked that Kuznetsov be severely penalized. Tupolev felt his engine genius should not be wasted because of a single mistake. Concurrently, Tupolev asked the various engine design bureaus to assist in the refinement of the massive 2TV-2F turboprop engine. This task was considered critical to the development of the '95' bomber… which in turn was considered critical to accomplishing a strategic balance between the Soviet Union and the US.

Further investigation of the 2TV-2F engine indicated that the reduction gear in question had failed as a result of poor manufacturing technique. This anomaly was corrected. Today, the failed gear is part of a 2TV-2F exhibit at the factory where the huge Kuznetsov turboprop engines were manufactured.

As a result of the prototype bomber's accident, the Soviet government took a more sensible approach to the problem and elected to assist Design Bureau 276 in overcoming the failure. Aviation strength standards were calculated for parts such as the failed gear assembly. The development of the new standards took considerable time and it was therefore decided that parts of the engine would be prioritized and analyzed in the order of their importance.

On 15th October 1953, the Ministry of Aviation Industry released a final summary of the prototype '95' bomber's accident: the 2TV-2F engine reducer's intermediate gear failed as a result of insufficient strength and low tolerance to fatigue. Secondary to this was the poor design of the fire extinguishing system in the engine nacelle. The major designers: Tupolev, Myasischev, Kuznetsov, and Mikulin were ordered to provide qualitative accident-free flight testing of the '95' and M-4 aircraft. Tupolev, Kuznetsov and Makarevsky (director of TsAGI) declared that the TV-12 engine scheduled for the second prototype would have to be thoroughly tested on the ground before being mounted on the actual aircraft. Additionally, the complete aircraft would have to go through a new set of static and vibration tests.

Kuznetsov was also to be required to run the new TV-12 engine through a battery of static tests and then a series of actual flight tests with the engine mounted on the TU-LL. testbed. Finally, all design bureaus involved with the new Russian bomber programs would have to test their emergency fire extinguishing systems and prove they worked efficiently. Specific attention would be paid to the '95' and M-4 bombers.

While flight testing of the prototype '95' had been on-going, Factory 156 had proceeded with the construction of the second aircraft (180-2), equipped with four TV-12 turboprops. Engineering for the second '95' aircraft, or as it was sometimes called, the 'understudy,' was started during January of 1952 and was finished a month later. The only difference lay in the design of the engine nacelles and engine mounts, which had been relatively minimal. Construction got underway during February of 1952.

Interestingly, the prototype '95' had weighed 15% more than originally anticipated by Tupolev. The second aircraft, benefitting from the learning curve of the first, came in at only 3% over estimates. This was the result of better detail design and the use of refined, lighter-weight construction materials.

Airframe construction was completed during November of 1952. However, nearly eighteen months would pass before it was determined to be flightworthy. Though static tests consumed a large percentage of this time, Kuznetsov's extremely conservative approach to the engine and engine mount design forced the airplane to sit for some six months while the first flightworthy engines were cleared for delivery. This time the Kuznetsov Design Bureau's engineers wanted to make absolutely certain there would be no repeat of the May 1953 tragedy.

Looking over Kuznetsov's shoulder was the Ministry of Aviation Industry. Their supervision assured that the TV-12's improvements and statics tests were properly accommodated. During December of 1953 the Ministry confirmed that the TV-12's performance was meeting specifications. In fact, take-off and maximum power of the TV-12 exceeded the predetermined values by 2-3% and at the same time specific fuel consumption was only 2-3% higher. Certain engine parameters remained indeterminable without actual flight testing, but the bureau felt confident the TV-12 would perform as promised.

Various engine improvements and miscellaneous engine-related delays eventually impacted the first flight date of the second 'understudy' '95' prototype. Consequently, the Kuibyshev factory moved ahead with production of the type.

Some 15 bombers were built during 1954 and 1955 and moved to factory No.24 (which was also situated in Kuibyshev). These aircraft were engineless as a result of slow TV-12 production (the TV-12 was, by now, being referred to under its official NK-12 designation).

Top and right: **A standard production Tu-95M (c/n 46) in conventional bomber configuration.** Tupolev

P A Solovyov, who headed engine Design Bureau 19, now was given the task of developing a new engine for the '95' bomber. To be referred to as the TVD D-19, it would develop some 11,190 kW (15,000 shp) for takeoff and offer a cruise power of 9,175 kW (12,300 shp). Specific fuel consumption would not exceed 0.16 kg/shp per hour (0.35 lb/shp per hour).

During December of 1954 the first TV-12 engines finally were installed on the '95-2' prototype. At the beginning of January 1955, the 'understudy' was moved to the test airfield at Zhukovsky. On 21st January, this aircraft was cleared for initiation of bureau-sponsored flight tests.

On 16th February 1955, the second prototype '95' bomber, piloted by M A Nyukhtikov and co-piloted by I M Sukhomlin, took to the air for the first time. The flight went according to plan and was completed without incident. Further testing consisted of some 68 flights and a total of 168 flying hours. The last stage of factory sponsored testing took place the following 8th January 1956. All flights but one were completed without major incident.

The single flight that caused concern took place during the summer of 1955. While the aircraft was on approach to landing, flight engineer A M Ter-Akopyan reported by radio to the Zhukovsky tower personnel that the crew could not get the landing gear to extend.

Things on the ground got tense in a hurry. It would be virtually impossible to land the big bomber safely without the gear extended, and it appeared certain the aircraft would be totally destroyed if such a landing were attempted. While ground personnel discussed what to do, the bomber was beginning to run out of fuel. When Tupolev, his deputy, L L Kerber, and others from the bureau got word of the problem, they immediately left their offices in Moscow and drove straight to the airfield.

Kerber and his equipment specialists set up shop on the grass area next to the Zhukovsky runway. With electrical system diagrams in place, they began looking for possible reasons for the gear actuation system to fail. Tupolev nervously paced back and forth while Kerber studied his drawings. The aircraft had only four hours' fuel remaining.

It took Kerber two hours to make an assessment. At that point, he began radioing instructions to the crew. He ordered Ter-Akopyan to turn off all electrical power. As a result, for a while, the 'understudy' flew around Zhukovsky without any radio contact. Finally, when the electrical systems were reactivated, a relay switch that had been stuck was tripped and the landing gear immediately began to extend. The ensuing landing took place without incident.

During the summer of 1955, the 'doubler' was introduced to the General Secretary of the Central Committee Party, N S Khrushchev and Ministry of Defense G K Zhukov (Khrushchev actually entered the '95', sat in its cockpit, and discussed the bomber with Tupolev).

Shortly afterwards, the '95' was demonstrated publicly for the first time at the annual Tushino airshow. The big turboprop bomber made a strong impression on western aviation experts. Within a short while of the fly-over, the '95' was given the official NATO designation of 'Bear'. Interestingly, for two years following the Tushino event, it was assumed by the western press that the aircraft origins could be attributed to the Ilyushin design bureau. For a while it was referred to as the Il-38. Even after its Tupolev origins were determined, the correct designation remained a mystery, as it was called the Tu-20.

In the meantime, flight testing of the '95' second prototype continued without let-up. During September of 1955, the maximum performance tests were initiated, these including maximum range and payload missions. The first of these included a route from Zhukovsky to Khabarovsk and then across to Kamchatka and then back to Zhukovsky. Bombs were to be dropped on the Kamchatsky proving ground.

The first test was conducted without serious incident. The flight covered a distance of 13,900 km (8,632 miles). The final figure was 4,110 km (2,552 miles) less than the original specified range, but it was still sufficient to reach the North American continent – which was its specified target.

During the long range flight, the takeoff weight of the '95-2' was 334,400 lb (151,724 kg). Fuel weight was 168,800 lb (76,588 kg). Cruise speed was 466 mph (750 km/h), maximum speed was 546 mph (880 km/h), service ceiling was 39,852 ft (12,150 m) and takeoff roll was 7,544 ft (2,300 m).

Top left: **An early Tu-95 during the course of the 1956 fly-over at Tushino.** Yefim Gordon collection

Bottom: **A Tu-95M in conventional bomber configuration.** Yefim Gordon collection

Chapter Three

'Bear' Versions

Tu-95/Tu-95M ('Bear'-A)
While factory tests of the prototype continued, factory No. 18 was beginning to build the first production examples for use by the Russian bomber forces. By now, the aircraft was being referred to by its official Tu-95 designator (aircraft of the 'V' class). And by mid-1955, two aircraft from the first two blocks (5 aircraft were scheduled for production in each block) were undergoing assembly in their respective jigs. These production-standard aircraft were considerably different from their predecessors, offering extended fuselages (an additional 2m [6.5ft] was added), a 5% increase in empty weight, and complete and functional sub-systems including full instrumentation and associated electronics.

On 31st August 1955, the first two of the initial production aircraft series, No.5800003 - c/n '5', and No.5800101 - c/n '6' - were released for flight testing. Both aircraft passed a factory-specified flight test program that lasted from 1st October 1955 to 28th May 1956.

Government testing was undertaken utilizing the '95-2' and the first two production samples. Government sponsored testing was initiated on 31st May 1956, and ran through the following August. During the ensuing flight test program, the '95-2' reached a maximum speed of 882 km/h (548 mph) and a service ceiling of 11,300m (37,064ft). Maximum range was 15,040 km (9,340 miles). The two production aircraft, because of their increased weight, had less range and a lower ceiling.

The performance figures gleaned from these tests were considerably lower than what had been anticipated during the 1951 Council of Ministers Resolution. Because of this, the Tupolev bureau took No. 5800101 and placed it in a modification program that ran from 20th August 1956 through 21st February 1957.

New NK-12M turboprop engines with improved specific fuel consumption figures and a modest increase in shaft horsepower (15,000) were installed.

Maximum takeoff weight was increased from 156,080 kg (344,000 lb) to 165,154 kg (364,000 lb) and the fuel capacity was increased from 73,258 kg (161,460 lb) to 81,243 kg (179,060 lb).

In this modernized configuration and as the Tu-95M (manufactured article 'VM') this aircraft completed factory testing during September and October of 1957. During these tests it reached a maximum speed of 905 km/h (562 mph) and achieved a service ceiling of 12,150 m (39,852 ft). Maximum range proved to be 16,750 km (10,402 miles) and operational range proved to be 13,000 km (8,073 miles).

Though these new figures were a considerable improvement over those obtained by the first pre-production series aircraft, they still were not up to the performance numbers specified in the original Council of Ministers Resolution. Regardless, it was decided to start mass production of the aircraft immediately and add it to the Russian Air Force inventory as rapidly as possible. This decision was given even greater impetus when it was discovered that the Tu-95's primary competition, the Myasischev M-4, with a range of 9,040 km (5,614 miles), also had failed to meet its promised range specification.

With the production decision in hand, the Soviet Air Force Long Range Aviation branch began to make plans for the arrival of the first of the Tu-95s and M-4s.

The first of the operationally-configured Tu-95Ms entered production during late 1957 at factory No.18. Nineteen production aircraft initially were released for Soviet Air Force use. These became the first Tu-95s to enter the inventory and their arrival heralded a major new

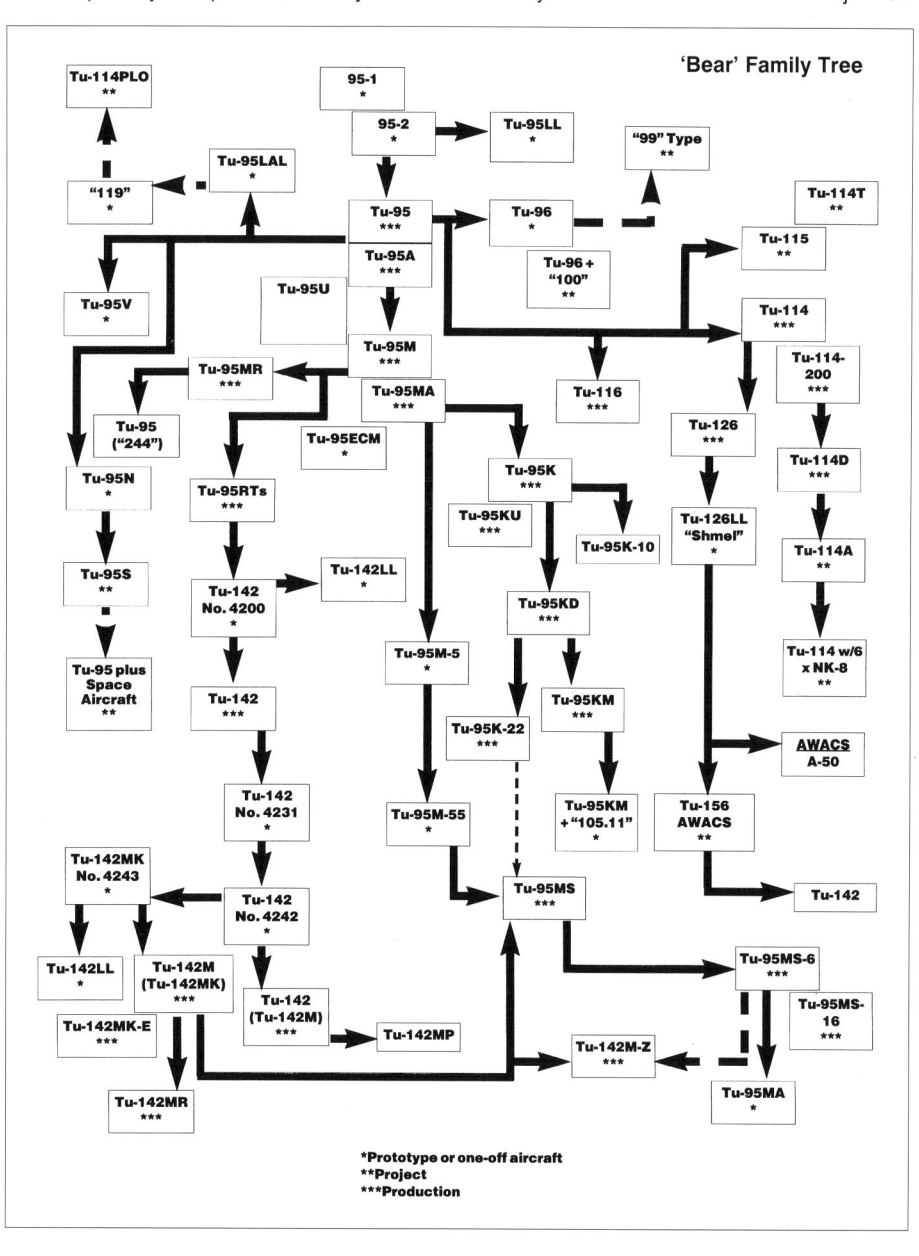

'Bear' Family Tree

*Prototype or one-off aircraft
**Project
***Production

Left: **A Tu-95MR on patrol.** Yefim Gordon collection

Below: **A Tu-95M landing following a training mission.** Yefim Gordon collection

era in the history of Russian Long-Range Aviation.

Total Tu-95/Tu-95M production (excluding the two prototypes) was split by years as follows: 1955 – 4 aircraft
1956 – 23 aircraft
1957 – 8 aircraft
1958 – 14 aircraft

Rigidly controlled test flights of Tu-95M No.410 were conducted during the spring and autumn of 1958. A takeoff weight of 165,154 kg (364,000 lb) was recorded, along with a weapon load of 5,955 kg (13,125 lb) - which was the weight of a Russian megaton-level nuclear bomb. With 4 to 5% of its fuel remaining at the end of a mission, range was 13,200 km (8,197 miles). Maximum speed was 902 km/h (560 mph) and cruise speed was between 720 km/h and 750 km/h (447 mph and 466 mph). These figures became the standard specifications for the Tu-95M and were used as comparison numbers when new aircraft were being flight tested.

In practice, the Tu-95M and the Tu-95 were almost indistinguishable. The standard Tu-95 differed only in having extra air intakes on the top of the engine nacelles. These had been placed there for electrical equipment cooling.

During the 1970s, the Tu-95M and Tu-95 series aircraft began to reach the ends of their respective service lives. All possible and feasible modifications and upgrades had been incorporated within the constraints of the fatigue lives of the airframes, and it was finally decided they should be replaced in the bomber role by newer aircraft. Accordingly, many examples of both types were relegated to the training role where they served out the rest of their operational careers.

The Tu-95 as a bomber went through many modernization programs. These allowed it to stay in Air and Naval Aviation Forces for an extraordinary period of time. Some examples remain operational even as these words are written. With further upgrades, it is presumed examples of these first-generation Tu-95 series will remain in service into the 21st century. Several dozen different first-generation Tu-95s eventually entered the Russian military air services inventories.

Following the initial successes of the first production aircraft, Tupolev's Design Bureau began exploring design options with the basic airframe. Though a few of these studies resulted in one-off prototypes, most remained only paper design studies.

Tu-95A/Tu-95MA ('Bear'-A)

The standard Tu-95, under the designation Tu-95A (manufacturing article 'V', order No. 180) was developed and built specifically for nuclear weapon transport. Differences included a temperature and climate controlled weapon bay, a white fuselage and wing undersurface for protection from the heat generated by nuclear weapon explosions, and a cockpit transparency visor assembly to protect the crew from nuclear heat and light effects.

Utilizing the Tu-95M as a basis, another nuclear-optimized version included the Tu-95MA. This aircraft was similar to the Tu-95 bomber with the exception of the engine nacelle upgrades noted earlier.

Tu-95U ('Bear'-A)

By the late 1980s, virtually all of the Tu-95s and Tu-95Ms remaining in operational service had been converted to trainers. These served primarily to introduce neophyte crews to the Tu-95 aircraft and its unique flight characteristics.

As trainers, the Tu-95s/Tu-95Ms had their weapon systems removed and their bomb bays sealed shut. Most of these training aircraft were based at the Long-Range Aviation training center in Ryazan and at various combat aircraft fields across the country. By the beginning of the 1990s, virtually all Tu-95U trainers that remained were being utilized by these units.

Tu-95Us wear a distinctive red stripe around the aft-fuselage in front of horizontal stabilizer. This has become a distinguishing feature of this version.

Tu-95 with Additional Fuel Tanks

During 1957 and 1958 Tupolev worked to increase the range of the Tu-95 bomber. In conjunction with this thrust, the Kuznetsov Bureau (No.276) also was enlisted to help meet the range performance goal. The engine requirement called for a take-off power of from 13,428 to 14,920 kW (18,000 to 20,000 shp). Concurrently, Tupolev asked that specific fuel consumption be dramatically reduced. It was proposed that with select airframe modifications providing increased fuel capacity and the upgraded engines, it might be possible to achieve ranges of up to 20,000 km (12,420 miles) without refueling.

During the course of the modification and upgrading process, a single production Tu-95 was given additional fuel tanks (under order 244). Tanks 6A and 6B were installed over the

Right: **A Tu-95RTs on patrol over the North Atlantic.** Jay Miller via Tony Landis collection

Below: **A Tu-95RTs warming up prior to a mission.** Yefim Gordon collection

wing center section. An additional tank 5A also was installed between them. This increased endurance of the aircraft to approximately 24 hours. During 1958, to explore this capability, the modified aircraft, equipped with NK-12M engines, stayed airborne for 23 hours 40 minutes.

The fuel tank modification, though proven via the long distance flight, was not integrated into the production fleet. At a later date, extended range was achieved through the introduction of inflight refueling capability. With the advent of the latter, additional internal tankage as an option became moot.

Tu-95 ECM Aircraft

At the end of the 1960s a single production Tu-95 was modified to serve as an electronic jamming system platform. The electronic jamming equipment and its associated operators were installed in the aircraft's bomb bay. Operating across a broad part of the electromagnetic spectrum, the barrage-type system was capable of effectively jamming most known western air defense radars.

Tu- 95MR ('Bear'-E)

As a result of a pressing need for a long-range reconnaissance bomber in the Soviet military service, the Tupolev bureau was asked to develop a reconnaissance version of the Tu-95.

Accordingly, on 20th May 1960, the USSR Council of Ministers generated a resolution that addressed modifying the Tu-95 bomber into the Tu-95R reconnaissance aircraft. It was requested that this aircraft be available as soon as possible. The bureau responded by having an aircraft available the following year and it was being flight tested by the end of 1961.

While airframe development got underway, a new inflight refueling system that also permitted static refueling while the aircraft was on the ground was moved rapidly into development. This latter opportunity forced the issuance of another Resolution which differed only in the fact that it accommodated the new refueling option.

Tu-95M No. 410 thus became the first aircraft with the new capability and the first to be equipped with the new equipment. As such, it became the first Tu-95MR-2.

The Tu-95MR differed little from the Tu-95M. Tu-95MR was equipped with a reconnaissance systems station (all antennas were positioned inside a dielectric fairing in the empennage section just forward of the horizontal tail surfaces) and an extensive camera complement (this was positioned in the bomb bay...which was modified for the pallet and related environmental control systems). The *Rubidiy*-MM radar station was replaced by the newer RMP (RLS) *Rubin*-1D which was integrated with the photography complement. Even in consideration of these changes, all tactical and performance characteristics of the Tu-95M, with the exception of endurance) remained unaffected.

Modification work on Tu-95M No. 410 was conducted at Factory No.18. During the fall of 1964 the work was completed. On November 12, the aircraft entered its flight test program. It became apparent immediately that the electronic systems and the photo-reconnaissance equipment all worked surprisingly well. Three refueling flights also demonstrated the practicality of the inflight refueling system in conjunction with the Myasischev M-4-2 tankers. One of the latter flights was conducted at night to verify this option. Interestingly, during the night flight, the Tu-95MP took on some 45,372 kg (100,000 lb) of fuel.

Flight testing of the new aircraft was completed on 19th December 1964. At that time, the aircraft was turned over to the Air Force where it was placed on an operational status. It was followed by three more Tu-95Ms (Nos.501, 502, and 506) upgraded to the reconnaissance configuration. Aircraft No.506 was not inflight refueling system equipped.

33

Left and below: **A pair of Tu-95RTses at Kipelovo Airbase. These aircraft were assigned to the 392nd Regiment of Naval Aviation.** Yefim Gordon collection

Opposite page top and bottom: **The Tu-95RTs was utilized with considerable regularity to shadow US Navy operations in the Atlantic and Pacific Oceans.** Yefim Gordon collection

The four Tu-95MRs (manufacturing article 'VR') were used with considerable intensity throughout the late 1960s, the 1970s, and well into the late 1980s. Once their service lives were determined over, however, they were converted into trainers and thus became Tu-95Us. They remained operational in that role into the early 1990s.

Tu-95DT

The resolution of the USSR Council of Ministers released on 12th August 1955, essentially gave approval to the Tupolev Design Bureau to initiate work on a Tu-95 transport configuration that would become known as the Tu-114. Initially referred to as the Tu-95DT, it was to be a transport that would require only minimal modifications to the basic Tu-95 airframe. No dramatic design changes would be incorporated.

Tu-95RTs ('Bear'-D)

The world's first maritime reconnaissance/strike complex (including the Tu-95RTs and ICBM carrying submarines) was to include the P-6 anti-shipping missile designed by V N Chelomey, one of the Soviet Union's most prominent rocket engineers. This weapon was to be launched by Project 675 nuclear-powered submarines and Project 651 diesel-electric submarines (the subs had to suface before they could fire the missiles). Since the submarines could not possibly carry a missile guidance radar the mid-course guidance mission was assigned to a specialized aircraft - the Tu-95RTs (*razvedchik-tseleookazatel'* - reconnaissance & target illuminator [aircraft]).

This new aircraft was optimized to provide both long-range reconnaissance and target designation information to surface forces. The aircraft, referred to as the Tu-95RC (implying reconnaissance target designator) became one of the main *Success* system elements. Its mission capabilities included radar observation, electronic surveillance, and photographic reconnaissance of surface targets. It would provide this information to friendly surface vessels and submarines. Of tertiary importance, but built-in to its capabilities, it could also provide meteorological data to surface combatants.

In accordance with USSR Council of Ministers resolution wishes, work on the Tu-95RC started on 21st July 1959. The Tupolev Design Bureau was given two years to complete work required on the Tu-95RTs. This would include installation of the radar and associated target designation systems required for the Success mission.

During March of 1960, the Ministry of Aviation Industry released a directive calling for completion of the first Tu-95RTs aircraft during the first quarter of the year. It was proposed, therefore, that operational aircraft be upgraded to the new configuration. The first aircraft to be modified was Tu-95M, No.510. This aircraft, following conversion, differed from its original configuration as follows:

- the bomb bay doors were removed and a Success system was installed and faired in place.
- a dielectric fairing covering the surveillance radar was mounted under the bomb bay area
- the flare system in the aft fuselage was removed and replaced by a *Square*-2 antenna package. This later was removed, as it was not effective.
- in place of the standard radar, a *Rubidiy*-MM system was set up to transmit data gathered by the Success unit.
- *Alfa* system antennas were mounted in new tip fairings attached to the horizontal tail surfaces.

During the autumn of 1962, the new Tu-95RC configuration was cleared for flight and on 21st September, government tests of the aircraft were initiated. The first flight was under the command of chief test pilot I K Vedernikov. The first stage of flight testing, consisting of 23 flights and a total of 107 hours and 23 minutes of flight time, was completed on 4th June 1963. Flights were flown from the factory airfield in Kuibyshev, from Zhukovsky, and from the airfields at Belay, Cerkov, and Uzina. Difficulties uncovered during the course of these flight tests included incompatibility of the electromagnetic components of the Success equipment and electrical system surges caused by the power supply system. These problems were not easily resolved and thus forced the need for additional test flights and delays. The second stage of testing was therefore not initiated until May of 1964.

The second and final testing stage took until December of 1964 to complete. Problems continued to surface with the complex electrical systems onboard the aircraft, but these were resolved by the time the end of flight testing had been reached. Twenty-two additional flights were completed under the auspices of this Stage 2 work, and the total time logged on the aircraft was 212 hours 57 minutes.

During these Stage 2 tests, the aircraft flew out to its maximum range and tracked real targets while transmitting data back to Russian Navy ships. The tests indicated that the system worked as required over long ranges and permitted the accurate targeting of surface vessels. By resolution of the USSR Council of Ministers on 30th May 1966, the Tu-95RTs was declared operational with the Soviet Navy Air Force.

The Kuibyshev factory No.18 had initiated production of the type three years earlier during 1963. That year, two aircraft were produced. During 1964, five aircraft were built, and from 1965 through 1968, an average of ten aircraft a year were completed and delivered to the Navy. The last five aircraft in the series were completed during 1969. In all, some 53 Tu-95RTs (manufacturing article 'VC') were built with the first being a modified Tu-95M and the rest being purpose-built. The production aircraft (excluding the Tu-95M modification) had *Vishnya* and *Romb* electronic reconnaissance systems with antennas faired into the aft fuselage similar to what was found on the Tu-95MR. Target designation aircraft, essentially Tu-95MRs, were given the multi-purpose ground/air refueling system.

During August of 1964, the Tu-95RC became operational with the Navy Air Force fleet. The type was used operationally until the end of the 1980s. Later, it served as a basis for the development of the anti-submarine warfare-optimized Tu-142 bomber and its several variations.

The aircraft's search radar relayed target data immediately to the surfaced submarine and had sufficient detection range to allow the P-6 missile to be fired from maximum range. Thus, the Mach 1.3 missile could destroy an enemy ship 300 km (166.6 nm) away. This was the first case of a maritime reconnaissance aircraft passing target data to a submarine in real time. This enabled submarine crews to more accurately assess the tactical situation and choose the best targets for the missile strike.

On receiving missile launch orders the sub would surface to periscope depth in order to establish radio contact with the aircraft. The radar data received from the Tu-95RTs was displayed on the radar officer's screen, whereupon the sub's commander would analyze the situation and pick a target. The target's bearing and range would then be determined and entered into the submarine's missile control computer. The computer would analyze target lock-on and kill probability, and the commander would make the ultimate decision to fire.

The submarines could fire the missiles singly or up to four at a time (in a salvo); each missile was guided (almost manually) by a missile aimer looking at a radar display. At a preset range the missile's homing system would activate and take over for terminal guidance to the target. If a group of enemy ships was attacked each one was targeted by a separate operator.

The arrival of advanced, sea-borne missile-optimized armament systems aboard Russian navy ships heralded the need for an aircraft to command and, if necessary, control the weapon systems so that they might be utilized to their greatest effect. Accordingly, a Tu-95 configuration, under a program codenamed Success, was developed to accommodate the Naval Aviation Force's need.

During August 1963, the newly-opened Kipelovo air base located 40 km (25 mi.) from Vologda (north of Moscow) became home for a number of Tu-95RTs long-range maritime reconnaissance and target illuminator aircraft. After a short familiarization and training period the 392nd ODRAP (*otdel'nyy dal'niy razvedyvatel'niy aviapolk* - independent long-range reconnaissance regiment) was formed and went on active duty with the Northern Fleet Air Arm.

The unit was tasked mainly with monitoring the activities of Western navies in the Arctic, Atlantic, and Indian oceans, with ice reconnaissance for civilian agencies as a secondary role. Some crews were on ready alert for SAR tasks. Finally, the unit's pilots located Soviet military space vehicles which splashed down in the Indian ocean after completing their missions. For missions over the Indian ocean, flight refuelling from Myasischchev 3MS-2 tankers had to be mastered. Occasionally, however, the 'Bears' would make refuelling stops at air bases in 'friendly nations' rather than 'hit the tanker'.

Starting in the late '70s, 392nd ODRAP crews flew hundreds of demanding recce sorties from bases in Cuba, Guinea, and Angola. Crews flying sorties over the West and South Atlantic deserved combat pay (even if there was no such thing in the USSR): these missions were often risky as there was considerable danger of being fired upon. However, the results were worth the effort, for instance during the 1982 Falklands campaign the 392nd ODRAP monitored the Royal Navy deployment closely from the moment the task force started assembling in the Bay of Biscay to its arrival on the scene – all British security measures notwithstanding.

The intensive combat training and high mission rate made for a high professional level among the unit's flight and ground crews.

However, the aircraft were subjected to considerable strain, and the frequent and demanding missions took their toll. In January 1971 a Tu-95RTs piloted by Lt. Col. A G Rastyapin caught fire in mid-air and plunged into the Barents Sea, killing all on board. On 3rd September 1971, another aircraft piloted by Col. I F Gladkov, the unit's second commander, crashed on finals to Kipelovo air base. (The 392nd ODRAP's original commander, Lt. Col. A S Fedotov, was killed in a flying accident in 1966).

On 4th August 1976, an aircraft operating out of Cuba crashed on the way home to the USSR after completing a mission near US shores, killing the crew led by Maj. A I Krasnosel'skiy. During January of 1984, one more Tu-9SRTs piloted by Maj. V K Vymyatin crashed on the Kola peninsula. The aircraft had a full fuel load – almost 90 tons (198,400 lbs), and the resulting explosion produced a tremendous fireball that could be seen for miles.

Throughout its service the 392nd ODRAP lost four aircraft and 61 crewmen. In the early '90s the unit was disbanded and its aircraft moved on to other bases.

Tu-96

Developed versions of the basic Tu-95 bomber continued to be studied by Tupolev throughout the life of the aircraft. One of these, optimized for improved high-altitude performance, offered a ceiling of 16,000 to 17,000 m (52,480 to 55,760 ft). This aircraft had a wing with increased area and improved turboprop engines optimized to operate at extreme altitude.

On 29th March 1952, the USSR Council of Ministers released a resolution that called for Tupolev to design and build an advanced Tu-95 that would provide improved high altitude performance. The new aircraft would be referred to as the '96' bomber and would be powered by the TV-16 turboprop engine…then under development. Two '96s' were ordered. The first of these was required to be finished with factory testing by July of 1954 and available for government testing by December of 1954.

Concurrent to this, the Kuznetsov Design Bureau was required to have the first TV-16 engine through bench testing by January of 1954 and available for flight testing by June of 1954.

The Soviet Air Force now released its official '96' specifications and they were as follows:
- range performance with a 40,835 kg (90,000 lb) payload and a maximum cruising speed of 800 to 850 km/h (497 to 528 mph) was -
- 9,000 to 10,000 km (5,589 to 6,210 miles) at 17000 m (55,760 ft)
- 10,500 to 11,000 km (6,521 to 6,831 miles) at 16,000 m (52,480 ft)
- 15,000 km (9,315 miles) at 15,000 m (49,200 ft)
- 17,000 to 18,000 km (10,557 to 11,178 miles) with additional fuel tanks at 14,000 m (45,920 ft)
- Maximum flight speed at the height of 8,000 to 9,000 m (26,240 to 29,520 ft) was 559 to 590 mph (900 to 950 km/h)
- Takeoff run from a first class airfield was 1,500 to 1,800 m (4,920 to 5,904 ft)
- Normal bomb load of 4,537 kg (10,000 lb) and a maximum bomb load while carrying a reduced fuel load of 10,889 kg (24,000 lb)

Defensive armament of the new bomber was to consist of three gun turrets each equipped with two AM-23 (23 mm) cannon. Respective ammunitions complements were 360 rounds per gun for the dorsal mounted unit, 400 rounds per gun for the ventral mounted unit, and 500 rounds per gun for the tail mounted unit. Additionally, the tail gun installation would be equipped with a *Ksenon* radar aiming unit.

The aircraft also was equipped with the *Rubidiy-MM* bomb aiming radar found on the earlier Tu-95 bomber. There also was a *Meridian* long-range navigation unit and a *Materic* blind landing system onboard. As a final touch, the aircraft was equipped with RPDS and RPS long-range communication stations and *Chrom* (interrogation) and *Nikel* (response) identification-friend-or-foe equipment.

Top: **Another Tu-95RTs of the 392nd Regiment of Naval Aviation at Kipelovo.**
Yefim Gordon collection

Opposite page, bottom: **The single Tu-96 prototype.** Tupolev

The TV-16 high-altitude turboprop engine produced 12,500 shp up to an altitude of 14,000 m (45,920 ft). Maximum cruising speed was stated to be 850 km/h (528 mph) at that altitude with the engine power rating staying steady at approximately 12,000 shp. Specific fuel consumption during takeoff was 0.24 kg/shp (0.53 lb per shp) per hour. Maximum consumption was 0.135 kg/shp (0.3 lb) per hour. Dry engine weight was stated to be 3,100 kg (6,832 lb). Design Bureau 120, under the direction of K I Zhdanov, was responsible for the new contra-rotating propeller specifically developed for the TV-12 engine.

The initial design study draft for the '96' aircraft was finished during March 1953. It had been calculated the bomber would have a takeoff weight of 140,653 kg (310,000 lb) and a cruising speed of up to 800 km/h (497 mph). Maximum range was estimated to be 16,200 km (10,060 miles) with a 7% fuel reserve. Absolute maximum range was estimated to be 11,178 miles (18,000 km). Altitude over target was estimated to be 16,800 m (55,104 ft) at a weight of 149,688 kg (330,000 lb). Maximum estimated speed was 560 mph (902 km/h).

When compared to the standard Tu-95, the Tu-96's wing area was increased from 316.5 m^2 (3,403 ft^2) to 345.5 m^2 (3,718 ft^2). Concurrently, wingspan was increased to 51.4 m (168.6 ft). The wing shape also incorporated a subtle change and wing sweep was slightly increased at the mid-span location.

Less noticeable was a change in the design of the cockpit. This was enlarged to permit greater crew comfort on long missions.

Construction of the first '96' aircraft was initiated at the Kuibyshev Factory No.18 during February of 1953 (order 241). Unfortunately, when the prototype Tu-95 (Tu-95-1) crashed, all work on the aircraft was stopped. Consequently, the original 'doubler' configuration and the TV-12 engine were given extensive review.

The first TV-12 engines now were delayed until December of 1954, which pushed delivery of the Tu-96 back until until July of 1955.

Following delivery of the second prototype Tu-95 (the 'Doubler'), work on the '96' aircraft was resumed. It was finally ready for flight testing during the early summer of 1956.

Work on the experimental TV-16 engine did not progress as rapidly as Kuznetsov and Tupolev had hoped. Numerous problems surfaced during static testing and associated development.

Accordingly, it was not installed in the Tu-96 prototype in time for initial flight test work as had been hoped. Instead, NK-12 engines were installed temporarily. With the NK-12s, the Tu-96 made its first flight during the summer of 1956. Subsequent testing also was undertaken using the NK-12s with the understanding the TV-16 would be installed when it was deemed flightworthy.

During the course of this early stage of the '96's' flight test program, the Soviet Air Force went through a change of heart regarding the development and use of high-altitude strategic bombers. By the mid-1950s, it had become apparent that western fighters and western surface-to-air missile systems were achieving performance levels that would make high-altitude bombers vulnerable targets. Therefore, direct delivery of free-falling iron bombs and nuclear weapons was no longer a practical means of target destruction. It would be far more likely that targets could be destroyed using stand-off techniques such as air-to-surface missiles and rocket-boosted bombs.

The Tu-95 was considered ideally suited for this less demanding mission. Thus, it became apparent there no longer was any need for the more advanced '96' aircraft.

The single prototype that was completed thus became a testbed. It was used as an airborne laboratory, still powered by the NK-12 engines. Later, when compared to the all-jet Tu-16, it was concluded that, even with the slightly more powerful NK-12M engines, performance was not suitable. Service ceiling was only 12,400 m (40,672 ft), maximum range was 15,000 km (9,315 miles), and maximum speed was 880 km/h (546 mph).

A study worthy of note at this point was the proposed use of the Tu-96 as a compound strategic strike system. As such, the Tu-96 would have served as a carrier aircraft for the '100' nuclear weapon transport. The latter, developed by the Tupolev design bureau, would have been an aircraft that could have been flown either as a piloted parasitic bomber or an unmanned/remotely controlled weapon delivery vehicle.

In concert with the designer's concept of the system, a Tu-96 would have served to deliver the '100' aircraft to a point some 3,000 km (1,863 miles) from the target. The '100' aircraft would have been launched to proceed on its mission...returning to its home base on its own. The Tu-96, upon releasing the '100' aircraft, was expected to immediately return to base to reload.

Development of the Tu-96 as a carrier for the '100' aircraft went no further than the drawing board. Work was suspended when Tupolev began studying a more efficient carrier aircraft configuration that would involve the '108' aircraft (a supersonic design optimized to carry the '100') and an advanced version of the '100'.

Aircraft '99'

During 1953, the Tupolev bureau began studying the attributes of several different aerodynamic configuration and propulsion system options. Among these were: wing area changing; changing of take-off weight and wing sweep in flight; characteristics of aircraft with four turbojet engines of VD-5 type; and different quantity of turbojet engines (RVD).

The purpose of this research was to determine the optimum aircraft characteristics utilizing pure jet engines versus turboprops.

The design bureau supervised by A D Shvetsov and the design bureau supervised by N D Kuznetsov had developed the first of the successful indigenous Russian turboprop engines during the early 1950s. The core of the Kuznetsov engine, which was given the designation P-8, originally was created for Tupolev's stillborn supersonic strategic aircraft carrier '108'.

Shvetsov's RVD was designed for the Tu-96 high-altitude high-speed strategic bomber. It was calculated the service ceiling of this aircraft would be 16,000 m (52,480 ft) and its speed at that altitude would be 1,000 km/h (621 mph). The total thrust of one RVD engine was then estimated to be 4,537 kg (10,000 lb). This was split between propeller and exhaust thrust almost equally; the propeller's thrust was 2,359 kg (5,200 lb) with an efficiency of 0.8; the jet thrust was 2,178 kg (4,800 lb).

The turboprop engine was designed for normal cruising parameters that included a speed of 1,000 km/h (621 mph) at an altitude of 16,000 m (52,480 ft). During ascent to cruise, power would remain relatively constant, though efficiency of the propellers would decay. At cruise, the engine was to provide 12,000 continuous shaft horsepower. Above 16,000 m (52,480 ft), horsepower would be lost proportional to the altitude increase and the air pressure. Pure jet thrust, on the other hand, was expected to increase linearly from sea level to 16,000 m (52,480 ft) and then stabilize at 2,178 kg (4,800 lb). Above 16,000 m (52,480 ft), thrust would decay per that seen in the turboprop engine. Thus, the total thrust of the RVD actually increased at the rated altitude.

Additionally, in high-speed flight, specific fuel consumption was 0.8 per lb/kg thrust per lb/kg fuel per hour in high speed cruise (by comparison, the VD-5's specific fuel consumption at the same altitude was 1.0 per lb/kg thrust per lb/kg fuel per hour).

As part of the '99' bomber project, Tupolev also studied versions of the VD-5 and RVD in the Tu-96 airframe. These configuration studies included buried engines and engines that were pylon mounted. Some of the RVD configurations called for from two to six engines. A version with four pylon-mounted engines proved to be the most efficient.

The '99's' wing studies included configurations with areas varying from 300 to 450 m² (3,229 to 4,843 ft²). Sweep angles varied between 45° and 55°. Takeoff weights also varied, with the smaller configurations offering gross takeoff weights of 136,116 kg (300,000 lb) and the greatest reaching weights of 226,860 kg (500,000 lb). Tunnel tests of some of these configurations were conducted at the TsAGI facility just outside of Zhukovsky.

Left top and second from top: **Two images depicting the prototype Tu-95K launching a modified MiG-19. The MiG served as a manned surrogate for the forthcoming Kh-20 air-to-surface missile.** Yefim Gordon collection

Bottom three: **Tu-95Ks equipped with early versions of the Kh-20 air-to-surface missile.** Yefim Gordon collection

Difficulties associated with the design, construction, and static testing of the new jet engine for the '99' bomber led to a decision to install four VD-7s (a developed version of the VD-5) turbojets, instead. These each had a static thrust rating of 11,797 kg (26,000 lb). Using this engine, the estimated range of the new aircraft was to be between 12,000 to 13,000 km (7,452 to 8,073 miles), which was superior to that claimed for the Myasischev M-4. The maximum estimated speed was 950 to 1,000 km/h (590 to 621 mph).

Concurrent with this Tupolev upgrade, the Myasischev design bureau now moved ahead with an improved M-4 equipped with four VD-7s. With these new powerplants, the bureau was able to claim a significant improvement in range for the M-4, this being over 13,000 km (8,073 miles).

The new Myasischev bomber successfully completed its first flight during 1956 and two years later, it entered full-scale production. As a result, the Tupolev '99' bomber project became moot and was abandoned. Nothing further was done with the design.

Tu-95 Missile Carrier

Rapid development of western anti-bomber defense systems during the 1950s forced the development of stand-off weapons and their associated transports. Russian bombers thus were forced to accommodate the new requirement or be shelved. In keeping with this new assignment, Russian long-range bomber units were forced to become less bomb oriented and more stand-off missile oriented. This new capability permitted Russian aircraft, such as the Tu-95, to launch and accurately deliver weapons on targets that otherwise were heavily defended.

Top: **Sans Kh-20, a Tu-95K lifts off on a training mission.** Yefim Gordon collection

Right: **A Tu-95K passes over Domodedovo during the noteworthy 1967 May Day airshow.** Yefim Gordon collection

Lower Right: **A Tu-95K during an Atlantic patrol mission.** Jay Miller via Tony Landis collection

Bottom: **A Tu-95K without Kh-20 missile. Noteworthy is size of nose-mounted missile communications antenna fairing.** Yefim Gordon collection

Tu-95K ('Bear'-B)

Tupolev, even in consideration of the new stand-off missile salient, was well equipped to accommodate the new challenge. Their Tu-95 was ideally configured in terms of range, payload, and other associated attributes to carry a large stand-off weapon.

This proved important when the Tu-95 was compared head-to-head with Myasischev's attractive but less efficient M-4(3M) bomber. Perhaps most importantly, the under-fuselage height of the Tu-95, when compared to the M-4, was indisputably superior. There was little question as to which aircraft could most easily accommodate air-to-surface missiles.

On 11th March 1954, the USSR Council of Ministers released a recommendation that the Tupolev bureau be entrusted with the development of a modified Tu-95M, to be referred to as the Tu-95K, for transporting and launching the Kh-20 air-to-surface missile. Concurrently, the Mikoyan design bureau would be responsible for the Kh-20 prototype's design and development. The guidance system for this missile would be developed by the B M Shabanov design bureau (No.1). The entire system would be referred to as the K-20.

The stand-off missile's '-20' designations were not chosen arbitrarily, as it had been planned for the Tu-95, in operational service, to be given the military designation Tu-20. However, during Tu-95 development, so many documents with the '95' designation were produced by the design bureau and government bureaucratic entities, it was decided it would be easier and less complicated if the '95' designator was left intact. The number '20', in the meantime, had surfaced in relation to the missile system and its hardware, and as a result, it was decided to utilize it in relation to the stand-off weapon. When information concerning the new system leaked and appeared in western references, it erroneously referred to the aircraft, and not the weapon system. Russian intelligence thus elected to leave the missile system designation in place in the hope it would disappear - as far as the west was concerned - under the mistaken Tu-20 designator.

Tu-95K design work was initiated during the spring of 1954. Drawings were completed and approved on 26th October. During the following year, the full-scale mock-up was completed and approved by Air Force representatives. Changes from the bomber included the following:

- the search and missile guidance Yad double antenna radar position was removed from the nose section
- a BD-206 beam-type suspension system was installed in the aircraft's bomb bay; this unit permitted the missile to be partially extended into the slipstream for engine ignition prior to launch; at launch it was extended fully into the slipstream and released for flight
- the configuration of the Tu-95's fuselage tanks was changed and one additional tank was added to accommodate the Kh-20's fuel requirement.

The missile suspension system required significant rebuilding of the Tu-95's fuselage. Work specifically had to be undertaken to modify the bomb bay area. Considerable redesign was required to accommodate the missile and its launch systems. Virtually all hydraulic, pneumatic, and electrical lines associated with the empennage had to be redesigned and/or rerouted.

Additional work had to be undertaken to accommodate the redistribution of aerodynamic loads. Models were built to study these changes. The resulting aeroelastic issues lead to the redesign of several major and minor structural components.

Tupolev's engineering studies were quickly passed on to factory No.18 where modification work was undertaken on Tu-95s No.001 and No.404. These two aircraft were to serve as the K-20 carrier-configured testbeds for the type.

Modification work to aircraft No.001 took from 1st March through 31st October 1955. Two months later, on 1st January 1956, it made its first flight. The second aircraft, No.404, followed during the summer of 1956.

Before flights with the Kh-20 in place were undertaken, a series of simulated system and hardware tests were devised to prove the safety and viability of the K-20 equipment. Simulators in the form of MiG-19s equipped with the K-20 guidance system were developed and flight tested. Two versions of the MiG-19 modification were flown, one being an unmanned aircraft referred to as the SM-20, and the other being a piloted version referred to as the SM-20P.

Launches with follow-on remote control from the Tu-95K prototypes were successfully undertaken during late 1956.

The SM-20P proved particularly useful during the flight test program and on numerous occasions it was launched and accurately guided to a remote target. Though pilots were on board, they participated in controlling the aircraft only after the target had been successfully located and electronically destroyed. Many famous test pilots flew the SM-20P, including noted MiG test pilot Sultan Amet-Khan.

Factory Tu-95K tests of the K-20/Kh-20 system were divided into three stages. The first

Top: **A pair of Tu-95KUs wearing protective covers are flanked on the right by a single Tu-22.** Yefim Gordon

Left: **A Tu-95KU immediately after takeoff.** Yefim Gordon

Below: **A Tu-95KD. Readily visible is the extended tailwheel for over-rotation protection.** Yefim Gordon collection

Top: **Tu-95KD can be distinguished from the standard Tu-95K by its nose-mounted inflight refueling boom.** Tupolev

Bottom: **A Tu-95KD equipped with two externally mounted ventral containers for conventional bomb carriage.** Yefim Gordon collection

began on 4th August and ended on 15th October 1956. Aircraft No.001 flew thirteen missions in response to the test program requirements. When problems were encountered, they were addressed and corrected on the spot. The second stage of testing, involving nine flights, was accommodated by Tu-95K No.404 from 15th August through 13th October 1956. The third and last stage of the flight test program spanned from mid-October through 24th January 1957. During this latter program, the SM-20 and SM-20P were utilized to perfect the missile remote control and guidance systems.

All tests after the third stage testing involved actual launch and flight trials of the Kh-20 missile. These began on 6th June 1957 and ran through 29th July 1958. During the year provided for this work, the K-20 system was perfected and significant confidence was gained. Accordingly, by the end of the flight test work during mid-1958, it was proposed that the Tu-95K and the K-20/Kh-20 stand-off missile system and missile be placed in production.

Joint government testing of the K-20 system was undertaken from 15th October 1958 through 1st November 1959. The first production Tu-95Ks, (which had entered the manufacturing process at factory No.18 during March of 1958) were utilized for these tests.

Tests conducted with the initial production Tu-95Ks included utilization of the Kh-20 missile under actual operational conditions. Included in this assessment was operation of the K-20 system and flight of the Kh-20 missile in a heavy electronic countermeasures environment. The system received favorable marks for dependability and ease of maintenance, support, and operation. Later, the system was tested against moving surface vessels in the Barenzevo Sea. It was found the Kh-20 could be effective against large ships as well as conventional fixed surface targets.

A resolution of the USSR Council of Ministers dated 9th September 1960 acknowledged integration of the K-20 system and Kh-20 missile into the operational inventory of the Soviet Air Force.

Production of Tu-95K aircraft (manufacturing article 'VK') continued until 1962. Besides the two prototypes, there were 47 production aircraft (3 built during 1958; 17 built during 1959; 17 built during 1960, and 10 built during 1961). Later 28 Tu-95Ks (27 production aircraft and one prototype - No.404) were modified to the Tu-95KD standard. The remaining 20 carrier-configured aircraft were utilized operationally until the early 1980s. At the end of their service careers, some of these aircraft were modified for the training role and served as such into the early 1990s.

Tu-95KU ('Bear'-B)

Introduction into service of the Tu-95K eventually led to the need for a missile carrier trainer. Accordingly, the Tu-95KU (manufacturing article 'VKU') was developed. In addition, several of the combat aircraft were set aside for the training role during the late 1980s.

Tu-95K-10

On 2nd July 1958, the USSR Council of Ministers passed a resolution requesting the Tupolev design bureau to explore the possibility of a Tu-95K modification that would permit the transport of four K-10 air-to-surface missiles under the Tu-95's wings. The K-10, designed primarily for Tu-16 transport, was smaller than the Kh-20 and thus would allow the Tu-95 also to carry a free-falling nuclear weapon in its bomb bay. Work on this project proved that the proposed installation would not be practical as the impact on performance would be catastrophic. Accordingly, the project was cancelled before hardware could be manufactured.

Tu-95KD ('Bear'-B)

Installation of the K-20 system and Kh-20 missile in the Tu-95 had an adverse impact on the aircraft's range. The range penalty, in fact, was

4,200 km (2,608 miles). To remedy this shortfall, inflight refueling was given serious consideration as an operational system for the first time.

On 2nd July 1958, the USSR Council of Ministers released another resolution calling for Tupolev to perfect inflight refueling for the Tu-95. Work on this system had, in fact, been undertaken during initial development of the Tu-95, but it was not until the advent of the missile carrier configuration that an actual need had finally arisen. Inflight refueling capability had not been provided on the original Tu-95s and Tu-95Ms because their range using internal fuel proved sufficient for their assigned mission.

On 28th April 1958, the Military Manufacturing Commission attached to the USSR Council of Ministers released a document suggesting that the Air Force and Tupolev equip production Tu-95Ks with a wing-tip-to-wing-tip inflight refuelling system (similar to the system then being used on the Tu-16). This recommendation was shortly afterwards approved and accepted.

Later, however, when actual engineering of the Tu-95 system was undertaken, the extraordinary span and flexibility of the big bomber's wing quickly revealed the fact that the wingtip refueling system utilized on the Tu-16 could not be used on the bigger aircraft. It therefore was decided to utilize a conventional probe and drogue system that had, by then, been flight tested on the Myasischev 3M bombers.

On 20th May 1960, the USSR Council of Ministers released their resolution concerning equipping all Tu-95K aircraft with the *Konus* inflight refueling system. Flight testing was to be undertaken during 1961. Tupolev quickly tackled the various design issues and during May of 1961, Tu-95K, No.2103, was set aside at factory No.18 for modification with the *Konus* system. This aircraft was to become the first of the Tu-95KD series (manufacturing article 'VKD'). Up to 4,537 kg (10,000 lb) of fuel per minute could be transferred.

Changes resulting in the Tu-95KD were as follows:
- a refueling boom was mounted on top of the nose section, just ahead of the cockpit
- an externally mounted fuel probe and faired fuel line were visible, with the latter prominent on the starboard side of the fuselage; this ran back to a tank at mid-fuselage
- a fuel scavenging system was provided
- a compressed air system was provided to operate the refueling probe mechanicals
- *Pritok* radio equipment was provided which permitted communication between the tanker and the receiver aircraft

In addition to the inflight refueling system, a conventional ground refueling system also was available on the Tu-95KD.

Top: **A Tu-95KM shortly after takeoff. The Tu-95KM was simply an upgraded Tu-95KD.** Yefim Gordon collection

Bottom: **Tu-95KM upgrades included avionics, defensive armament, and navigation systems.** Yefim Gordon collection

Joint testing of the Tu-95KD under the auspices of the Air Force and Tupolev took place from 5th July through 8th September 1961. Eighteen flights were conducted with an average flight duration of 38 hours. A second series of tests followed between 17th October 1961 and 30th January 1962. Some sixteen flights were undertaken with an average duration of 43 hours. During all these flights, the tanker aircraft was a Myasischev M-4-2 with drogue refueling equipment. The tests were deemed successful and production was initiated.

The first of the production series aircraft was Tu-95KD No.2502. It was completed at factory No.18 during 1962. In all, some 23 aircraft in the series were built (10 in 1962; 8 in 1963; 4 in 1964; and 1 in 1965).

Additionally, some 28 Tu-95Ks (including the prototype, No.404) were upgraded to the Tu-95KD standard. Thus, in total, some 51 aircraft were equipped with the refuelling system. The total number of Tu-95K/Tu-95KD missile carriers completed was 71 (including the second Tu-95K prototype).

Above: **A Tu-95KM with an advanced version of the Kh-20 air-to-surface missile suspended from its bomb bay pylon.** Yefim Gordon collection

Below: **Tu-95KM surrounded by fuel trucks and other miscellaneous support vehicles.** Yefim Gordon collection

Tu-95KM ('Bear'-C)

At the end of the 1960s all Tu-95KDs, including purpose-built and upgraded aircraft were run through a modernization program. Once modernized, they became Tu-95KMs. These aircraft differed from the earlier Tu-95KD as follows:

- the PRS-1 radar gun sight was replaced by the PRS-4 sight
- the *Romb-4* passive electronic reconnaissance system was installed on some aircraft
- the SPO-2 radar warning system was replaced by the SPS-3
- the KS-6D navigation system, Doppler sensor drift unit, DISS-1 velocity meter, and radar electronic equipment for the RSBN-2S short-range navigation system were installed
- the RV-UM radar altimeter replaced the RV-2
- the ARK-11 automatic radio compass replaced the ARK-5
- an RSB-70A radio was installed
- an RSIU-5 radio replaced the RSIU-4

Significantly, the Mikoyan-developed Kh-20 air-to-surface missile also was modernized and received a new designation, Kh-20M.

In modernized format, the old Tu-95K, with its new Kh-20M, the K-20 system, and other upgrades became the Tu-95K-20. Maximum radius of action varied between 6,340 and 8,250 km (3,937 and 5,123 miles) and launch-point-to-target-range of the Kh-20M was 450 to 600 km (270 to 373 miles). It should be noted, however, that the carrier aircraft had to be within 260 and 380 km (161 and 236 miles) of its target. These figures were deemed palatable by the Air Force during the 1960s decade.

Unfortunately, the system had one essential defect: the controller in the carrier aircraft had to maintain guidance contact with the Kh-20 until just before target contact.

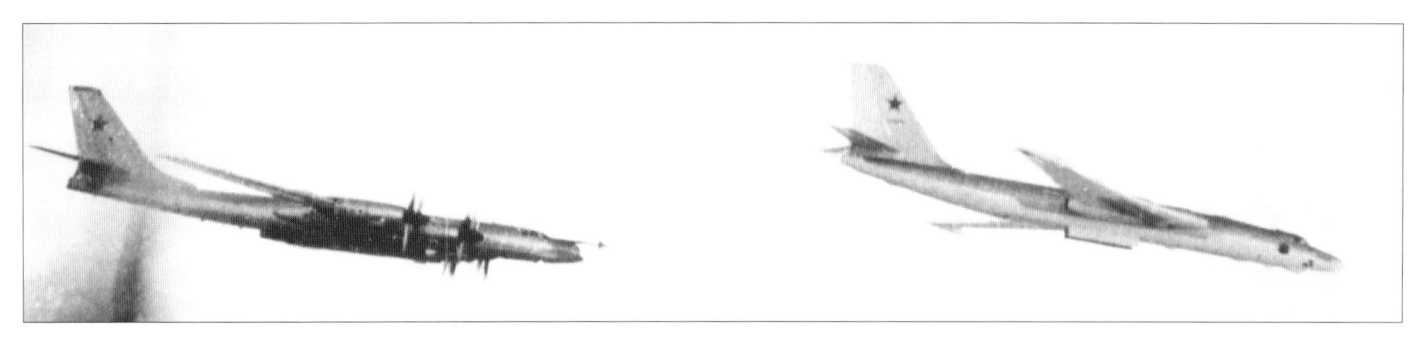

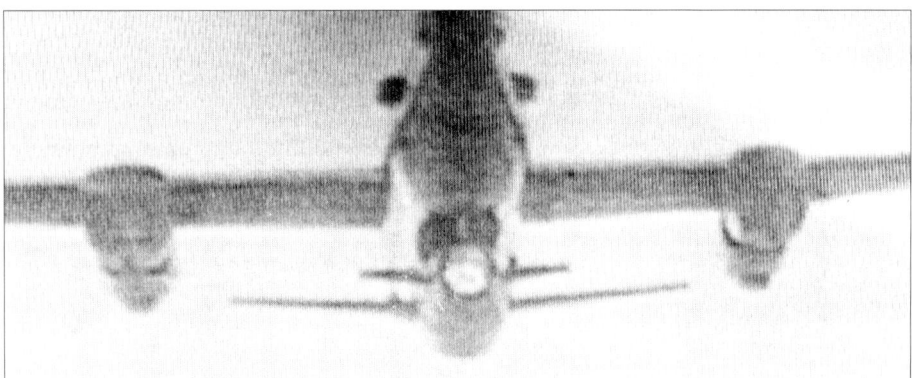

Top: **A Tu-95KM receives fuel from a Myasischev M-4 tanker using a probe and drogue system.** Yefim Gordon collection

Left: **Tu-95KM with its Kh-22 missile. Engine of the latter is running in full burner moments before launch.** Yefim Gordon collection

Lower left: **Distinctive tailcone of the Tu-95K-22 is readily discernible.** Yefim Gordon collection

Bottom two: **Tu-95K-22 in flight and while taxiing out for a training sortie.** Yefim Gordon collection

This shortcoming decreased the system's combat efficiency and increased the carrier's vulnerability to enemy action. Additionally, the time required to guide the Kh-20 to its target also increased the opportunity for electronic countermeasures and jamming.

At the end of the 1960s several Tu-95KM's were modified to accommodate two underwing filter pods which were utilized for aerial sampling requirements.

This system was developed specifically to explore the results of above-ground nuclear testing, primarily in China.

Tu-95K-22 ('Bear'-G)

Improved enemy defenses during the late 1960s and early 1970s markedly decreased the chances of success of the Tu-95KM in delivering its Kh-20 missile to a target. The advent of the new K-22 system and Kh-22 missile quickly led to discussions calling for an upgrade of the Tu-95KM to accommodate this new weapon system.

Top and bottom: **Tu-95K-22s. The miscellaneous systems upgrades, led to external modifications in the form of fairings and antenna pods.**
Yefim Gordon collection

Initial K-22/Kh-22 studies – based on preliminary design information – had, in fact, been undertaken by Tupolev during 1963. Ten years later, during February of 1973, the USSR Council of Ministers made the decision to reconfigure the outdated Tu-95KM missile carriers with the K-22 and Kh-22 system. As such, the new aircraft became Tu-95K-22s and the weapon system was given the designation K-95-22.

On 31st January 1973, the first production Tu-95KM, No.2608, was delivered to the Kuibyshev aviation factory (formerly referred to as factory No.18) where it was to be modified to the Tu-95K-22 standard. Unfortunately, the required drawings and technical data permitting the upgrade did not become available until May of 1974. Work on the modification thus did not get underway until some five months after it was originally intended.

Reconfiguration of the aircraft included the following changes:
- the tail gun was removed and replaced with an electronic countermeasures system
- a *Yad* radar unit was installed
- missile pre-launch and launch equipment was installed
- the BD-206 suspension unit for an Kh-22 missile was installed in the bomb bay
- two BD-45K mounts from a Tu-22M were attached under each wing inboard of the inboard engine nacelles to accommodate one Kh-22 under each wing root

The re-equipped aircraft could carry one missile under the fuselage and two missiles under the wings (one on each side).

The first flight of the modified aircraft was completed on 30th October 1975. The first Kh-22 launch took place during 1981. During the interim five year period, production of the Tu-95K-22 and upgrading of select Tu-95KMs was completed. Following introduction of the type into the operational inventory during 1987, it became a mainstay weapon system in the Soviet Air Force. It remains operational with the Russian Air Force as of this writing.

Noteworthy is the fact that some Tu-95K-22 aircraft were modified to accommodate filtering pods for nuclear sampling.

At the end of the 1960s decade, the Tupolev bureau began studying other missile options for the Tu-95 beyond the Kh-22. One of these was the KSR-5. During February of 1973, a decision was made to equip 33 Tu-95/Tu-95M bombers with the KSR-5 missile (known under the system designator of K-95-26) and its associated *Volga* launch system. The new configuration consisted of the Tu-95M-5 carrier aircraft, two KSR-5 missiles, and the *Volga* system. It was similar in many respects to the K-26 system found on the Tu-16K-26 carrier (also capable of carrying two KSR-5 air-to-surface missiles).

During October of 1976 the Kuibyshev factory (No.18) completed modifications of a Tu-95M to the new configuration. As the Tu-95M-5, the new aircraft had launch pylons under each wing for a single KSR-5 missile, the *Volga* system, a new *Rubin* 1KV radar unit, and an electronic countermeasures compartment and associated antenna in the aft fuselage in place of the rear gunner's compartment.

First flight of the new aircraft was completed during the autumn of 1976. Work continued through May of 1977, and then was terminated. It was determined the Tu-95/Tu-95M offered no significant advantages over other aircraft types equipped with the new missile system. The aircraft to be modified later became the prototype Tu-95MS.

Tu-95 SPECIAL MISSION AIRCRAFT
Tu-95V

During 1953 the Soviet Union exploded its first thermonuclear device. Within two years, an operational weapon rated at three megatons had entered the inventory. At the same time, western nuclear weapon efforts increased substantially, with numerous devices being tested in the Pacific and elsewhere. In effect, a race for increased destructive power had begun...with the limiting factor being only the size of the delivery aircraft's weapon bay.

During the Autumn of 1954, the Soviet Union began work on an aircraft-deliverable weapon rated at 100 megatons. It quickly became apparent the Tu-95 was the only viable delivery option for this proposed behemoth.

Initial bomb studies called for a gross weapon weight of no less than 36,298 kg

Top and bottom: **The Tu-95V was a one-off test variant designed specifically to accommodate the world's largest aircraft-borne nuclear weapon. The device is reported to have been rated at 50 megatons.** Yefim Gordon collection

(80,000 lb). This was about 20% of the maximum gross takeoff weight of the aircraft... and a figure that Tupolev and his engineers found unpalatable. In fact, it was determined that a Tu-95 carrying a 36,298 kg (80,000 lb) weapon would not be able to fly to the Russian nuclear weapon testing ground, much less to a target many thousands of miles distant.

Accordingly, a reduced-size super-weapon was initiated, this one having a gross weight of 18,149 kg (40,000 lb) and yielding a no-less formidable 50 megatons. At 12% to 15% of the gross takeoff weight of the aircraft, this was a considerably more feasible figure for the Tupolev engineering team to digest.

From the very beginning, nuclear weapon designers I V Kurchatov and U V Khariton had proposed to use the Tu-16 and Tu-95 as the delivery aircraft. However, the various modifications that were proposed to accommodate the new bomb were extensive, and the load dynamics demanded extensive redesign of the aircraft's structure.

Following previous practice in the Soviet Union, the new nuclear weapon was referred to by an official name, *Vanya* or *Ivan* (the first Soviet nuclear bomb had been referred to as *Tanya* or *Tat'yana*). Consequently, the Tu-95 version assigned to carry it became the Tu-95V. A total of 242 were built.

On 17th March 1956, the USSR Council of Ministers tasked the Tupolev design bureau with the development of the Tu-95 upgrade that would permit it to carry the forthcoming super nuclear weapon. Initial studies had begun long before the Council of Ministers order had been released. They had, in fact, taken place during 1954, immediately following the first discussions between I V Kurchatov and A N Tupolev. Tupolev's deputy for armament systems, A V Nadashkevich, became the project supervisor.

During the first quarter of 1955, technical specifications for the *Ivan* weapon were provided to Tupolev so that work could begin on the redesign of the Tu-95's bomb bay. As it was assumed the bomb's weight would amount to 15% of the aircraft's gross takeoff weight, the critical issues then became dimensional limits, rather than structural. It was decided that the BD-206 bomb shackle unit (similar to that used to suspend the Kh-20 missile in the Tu-95K) would be used. Additionally, BD7-95-242 (DB-242) suspension devices were integrated into the unit to permit each of the Der 5-6 released units to support as much as 8,167 kg (18,000 lb) each.

A problem surfaced concerning synchronization of the electro-mechanical bomb release units. This was eventually solved when a refined system that accommodated the security issues surrounding a nuclear weapon drop were successfully developed.

Design of the BD-242 support system went rapidly and without too much difficulty. It was positioned at the end of the bomb bay and perpendicular to the longitudinal axis of the fuselage in consideration of the load bearing structure of the frame.

The BD-242 was attached directly to load bearing beams. These were mounted on the sides of the bomb bay. At the front and rear of the bomb bay were bulkheads. Total bomb bay opening dimensions included a width of 1.78 m (5.84 ft) and a length of 7.15 m (23.45 ft). Notably, the Tu-95V's fuselage fuel tanks had to be modified to accommodate the bulk of the bomb.

The bomb shackle system passed its bench test series without difficulty and the synchronized release mechanism was found to work satisfactorily.

Tu-95 No.302 was modified by Tupolev to accommodate the bomb bay modifications. This aircraft then was tested at Zhukovsky where it was declared acceptable by the Air Force during September of 1959. The tests were conducted under the supervision of Air Force Colonel S M Kulikov. They were completed without further effort.

The aircraft now was cleared to drop the world's most powerful nuclear weapon. As it turned out, actual tests of the modified Tu-95V dropping a live nuclear weapon were halted for political reasons. Russian Premier N S Khrushchev was scheduled to visit the US and it was deemed undiplomatic for a massive weapon to be tested while the Premier was on US soil.

As a result, the single completed Tu-95V was delivered to the military airfield in Uzin and there used as a training aircraft. It would stay that way for over two years.

During 1961, as the cold war began to heat up again, the Tu-95V was refurbished back to its original nuclear-capable configuration. By this time, the first of the super bombs was again ready for testing. Unfortunately, between initial mock-up studies and the final configuration of the actual weapon, it had grown by some 3,630 kg (8,000 lb) and a 800 kg (1,763 lb) retarding parachute system had been added as well. The extra weight resulted in a weapon that was bigger in diameter than originally estimated and as a result, the Tu-95V's bomb bay doors had to be removed.

In its new and revised configuration, the Tu-95V was delivered to the North airfield in Vaeng. Shortly afterwards, it was painted white underneath for thermal protection.

Right: **The Tu-95N was modified from airframe '101'.** Jay Miller

Bottom: **The Tu-95N was modified to carry the 'RS' reconnaissance aircraft. When the latter was cancelled, the Tu-95N was relegated to display in the Russian Air Force Museum at Monino.** Yefim Gordon

Most importantly, a functional nuclear bomb was mounted in its bomb bay.

On 30th October 1961, the Tu-95V, piloted by Durncov departed Vaeng and flew non-stop to Novaya Zemlya (New Land). At a test site there, Durncov and his crew released their enormous 18,149 kg (40,000 lb) doomsday bomb at an altitude of 4,500 m (14,760 ft) and then headed home. The resulting blast, estimated in power to be anywhere from 75 to 120 megatons (Khrushchev claimed 100 megatons while reading speeches after the fact), proved monumental.

After the test, the Tu-95V sat derelict at the Vaeng airbase. It was not flown again until the advent of the Tupolev Tu-144 supersonic transport…at which time it was put back into service as a transport. Carrying Tu-144 subassemblies, it flew from Moscow to Novosibirsk (Siberia), delivering pieces to the factory for assembly. Eventually, the Tu-95V ended its days at Semipalatinski airfield where it was used as a static training device until the mid-1980s.

Tu-95N

During 1955, Design Bureau 256, supervised by Chief designer P V Tsibin, initiated work on a project under the auspices of the supersonic strategic strike system, or 'RS'. This system was to consist of a Tu-95N carrier aircraft with an 'RS' supersonic reconnaissance aircraft suspended in its bomb bay.

The 'RS' was designed to be a very high-speed vehicle capable of cruising speeds in excess of 3,000 km/h (1,863 mph). It was to be powered by two ramjet engines. Maximum range was to be from 12,500 to 13,500 km (7,763 to 8,384 miles).

On 30th July, 1955 the USSR Council of Ministers ordered initial development of the 'RS' aircraft. Tupolev was tasked with development of the transport. The Tu-95 was immediately picked as the only possible option. The new configuration would be referred to as the Tu-95N. During the second half of 1956, a joint effort with the Tsibin design bureau generated the initial design studies that would lead to hardware development.

Tupolev chief designer I F Nezval' was picked to head the Tu-95 modification effort. Initial work was carried out at the bureau's Zhukovsky facility and then later transferred to the bureau's branch facility at Tomilino.

Suspending the the 'RS' inside the Tu-95's bomb bay was no simple chore. A number of items required serious modification, not the least of which was the bomb bay itself and the bomb bay doors. The 'RS' and its various support system were predicted to have a pre-launch weight of from 27,223 to 36,298 kg (60,000 to 80,000 lb). The disposition of the aircraft and its miscellaneous equipment became complicated by limited space and dimensional restrictions. As a result, much of what was done to facilitate the modification was explored via a full-scale mock-up.

By the end of the summer of 1957, working drawings were being released to factory No.18. There, Tu-95, No.101, became the first aircraft to be modified to the Tu-95N configuration.

During 1958, the modification program had been completed on the first Tu-95N and the aircraft was flown from the factory to Zhukovsky airfield where the flight test program was to be conducted. Not long afterwards, however, the USSR Council of Ministers made the decision to stop all work on the 'RS' system. The Tu-95N remained at Tupolev's flight test facility until the mid-1960s, at which time it was flown to the Air Force Museum at Monino. It remains on display there to this very day.

Tu-95 Hypersonic Aircraft Carrier

During the 1950s and 1960s, the Tupolev bureau explored a large number of design configurations optimized for flight research in the hypersonic speed regime. Part of this proposed

study included the modification of a Tu-95 to the carrier aircraft configuration. In particular this aircraft was to have been modified to accommodate the launch requirements of the experimental '130' aerospace aircraft.

Work on the '130' was expected to lead to the rocket-propelled 'Star' aircraft which was to be launched into orbital flight by the UR-200 carrier.

The launch system to have been adopted by the Tu-95 was to have been similar in many respects to that utilized in the Boeing B-52A that served as the carrier aircraft for the North American X-15.

The Tupolev and 'Star' programs were terminated following the success of S P Korolyov's R-7 rocket and the *Vostok* and *Voskhod* manned space vehicles. During the late 1960s, however, the Mikoyan bureau's *Spiral* testbed led to the modification and use of a Tu-95 as carrier.

Tu-95 *Vostok* Location Aircraft

On 22 September 1960 the Government Aviation-Technical Committee of the USSR Council of Ministers ordered the Tupolev design bureau and factory No.18 to modify several older Tu-95 bombers for search and rescue missions as part of the *Vostok* manned spaceflight program. These aircraft were to be equipped with the *Pritok* system which was specially created to facilitate finding the big Russian space capsules. The Tu-95 modification program was completed during November of 1960 and the aircraft entered service shortly thereafter.

Tu-95KM '105.11' Carrier Aircraft

During the late 1960s and early 1970s, under the supervision of G E Lozino-Lozinsky the A I Mikoyan design bureau investigated an aerospace plane design referred to as *Spiral*. A scaled-down testbed, the '105.11', was built to explore the subsonic flight characteristics of the design. During flight testing, it was suspended from the bomb bay of a modified Tu-95, No.2607, and dropped following ascent to altitude.

Among the many modifications to the *Spiral*-carrying Tu-95 was a special access door in the pressure bulkhead aft of the cockpit that permitted the '105.11' pilot to enter the research aircraft while at high-altitude.

Flight testing of the '105.11' was completed by the end of the 1970s and the type was turned over the Air Force Museum at Monino. The Tu-95KM remained in operational service, however, and it eventually was reconfigured for other flight test program needs.

Tu-95LL

During the mid-1950s it became apparent that there was a need for a laboratory to accommodate in-flight testing of new and improved turbojet engines. One of the few aircraft that was large enough to accommodate the test instrumentation, test engineers, and mechanical systems associated with inflight propulsion research was the Tu-95.

On 29th July 1957, the Ministry of Aviation Industry ordered the Tupolev design bureau to modify the second Tu-95 ('95-2') prototype into a flying laboratory for testing a turbofan engine equipped with an NK-6 afterburner. This combination would generate from 34,316 to 37,300 kW (46,000 to 50,000 lb st) thrust. This engine later was expected to serve as the propulsion system for the '105A' (Tu-22) supersonic bomber.

Modification of the famous 'Understudy' prototype was undertaken at factory No.18. As the Tu-95LL, it was ready to fly during 1958.

The NK-6 afterburner became the first propulsion item to be tested using this aircraft. Later, it was used for testing and refining five turbofan engines including the NK-144A for the Tu-144, the NK-144-22 for the Tu-22M, and the NK-22 for the Tu-22M1 and the Tu-22M2.

Engines being tested utilizing the Tu-95LL were mounted in a special nacelle that was suspended from a trapeze mechanism positioned in the bomb bay. In the advent of an inflight emergency the engine could be jettisoned. All connectors would be automatically guillotined to facilitate severing of the engine package from the carrier.

An automated fuel system was provided. Fuel for engine operation in flight came from the

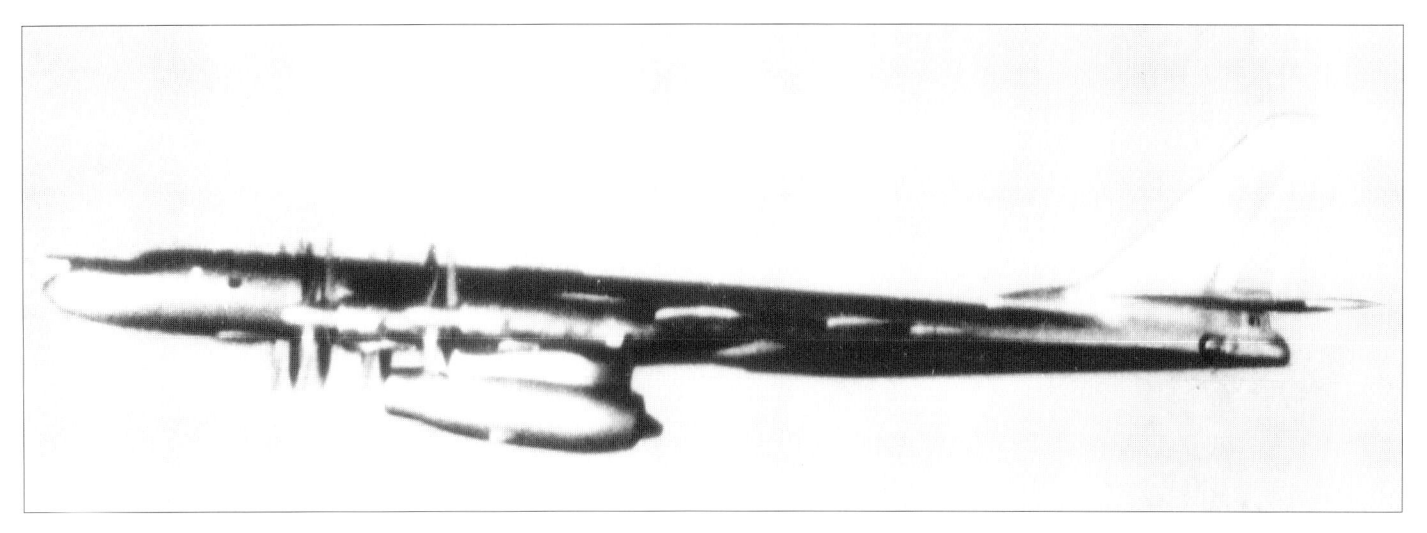

Opposite page top: **The Tu-95N as currently displayed outdoors at the Russian Air Force Museum at Monino.** Jay Miller

Opposite page bottom: **Close-up of the 'RS' reconnaissance aircraft ingress/egress hatch at the forward end of the Tu-95N bomb bay.** Jay Miller

Top: **Inflight of the Tu-95LL during the course of an engine test. Identity of this particular engine is unrecorded.** Yefim Gordon collection

Bottom: **Interior details of the Tu-95LAL nuclear powerplant testbed.** Yefim Gordon collection

Tu-95LL's internal fuel tanks. Dual engine controls capable of being operated either by the pilot or the test engineer, were provided. The former's control was positioned on the center console, and the latter's control was mounted on a special test panel. Test instrumentation measured 172 parameters at 371 control points.

The successful design ideas found on the Tu-95LL later were utilized in the design of the Tu-142 and Tu-142M flying laboratories. The Tu-95LL remained in operational service for some fifteen years until it was lost in a major accident. At that time, its mission was filled by the first Tu-142 prototype which also was modified to accommodate engine test work.

Tu-95LAL

With the initial successes realized by surface vessels utilizing nuclear powerplants, it was only natural that such propulsion systems be considered for aircraft. Under the supervision of I V Kurchatov, work was initiated on studies calling for the development of nuclear powerplants for aircraft. Heading the aircraft powerplant studies was A P Alexandrov.

On 12th August 1955, the USSR Council of Ministers approved development of special facilities optimized for prototyping and developing nuclear power for aircraft.

Studies resulting from the research at these facilities explored nuclear ramjets, nuclear turbojets, and nuclear turbofan engines. Reactors with air and intermediate metal cooling were designed. Thermal and fast nuclear reactors were studied in great detail. Importantly, the problems associated with biological exposure to radiation were paid particular attention.

The Tupolev bureau, upon reviewing available data on aircraft powered by nuclear engines proposed a twenty year program of study and prototyping that would lead to the development of a nuclear powered military aircraft. Both subsonic and supersonic designs were proposed.

It also was proposed that an underground test facility be developed. Once airworthy hardware was available, it would be flight tested aboard a modified Tu-95.

On 28th May 1956, the USSR Council of Ministers ordered the Tupolev design bureau to initiate design studies calling for a nuclear flying laboratory based on the Tu-95 bomber. This laboratory would be utilized to study the effects

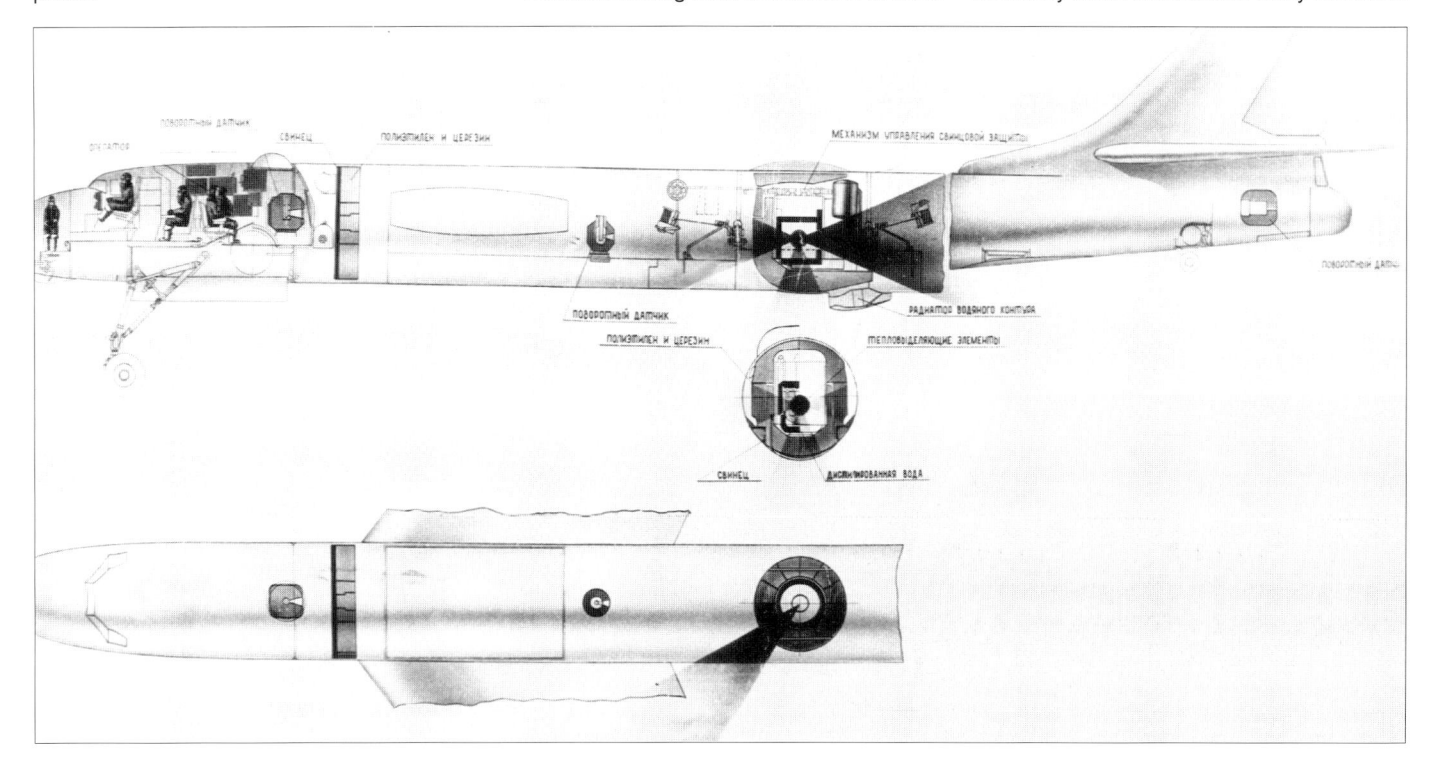

Top: **The Tu-95LAL was perhaps the most exotic of the many Tu-95 variants to fly. External modifications were few but significant and included the reactor fairing on top of the fuselage and the coolant tanks suspended from the outer wing panels.** Victor Kudryavtsev

of radiation on instrumentation and equipment as well as on the aircrew and ground support personnel. It would, in effect, become a radiation effects laboratory.

Work on the modification to the Tu-95 was conducted by the Tupolev bureau at its Tomilino facility (in a Moscow suburb). The Tomilino facility was supervised by an old and experienced Tupolev principal, I F Nezval.

Modifications to the aircraft were extensive. The Tu-95's center fuselage was reconfigured to accommodate the support structure for the reactor. Completely new materials were utilized for the latter including polyethylene in combination with resin and carbon additives. All of this required the mastering of totally new construction techniques. Tupolev's non-metal technology department, supervised by A S Phainshtein and in conjunction with experts in the chemical industry eventually rose to the occasion and created a structure that was both strong and highly resistant to the effects of nuclear radiation. The design of the unit and the materials utilized to build it were checked out by nuclear experts and were accepted for use not only in the aircraft, but also on the underground test stand.

During 1958 the support structure for the Tu-95 nuclear powerplant installation was completed and transported to Semipalatinsk for mating with the reactor. Shortly afterwards, the first airworthy Russian nuclear reactor was completed and declared ready for shipping, also to Semipalatinsk.

Concurrently, the first hot reactor was tested in the underground nuclear facility during late

Below: **The Tu-95LAL's flight test program was abbreviated, but the lessons learned convinced Tupolev and the Russian government that nuclear power for aircraft was not a practical option.** Victor Kudryavtsev

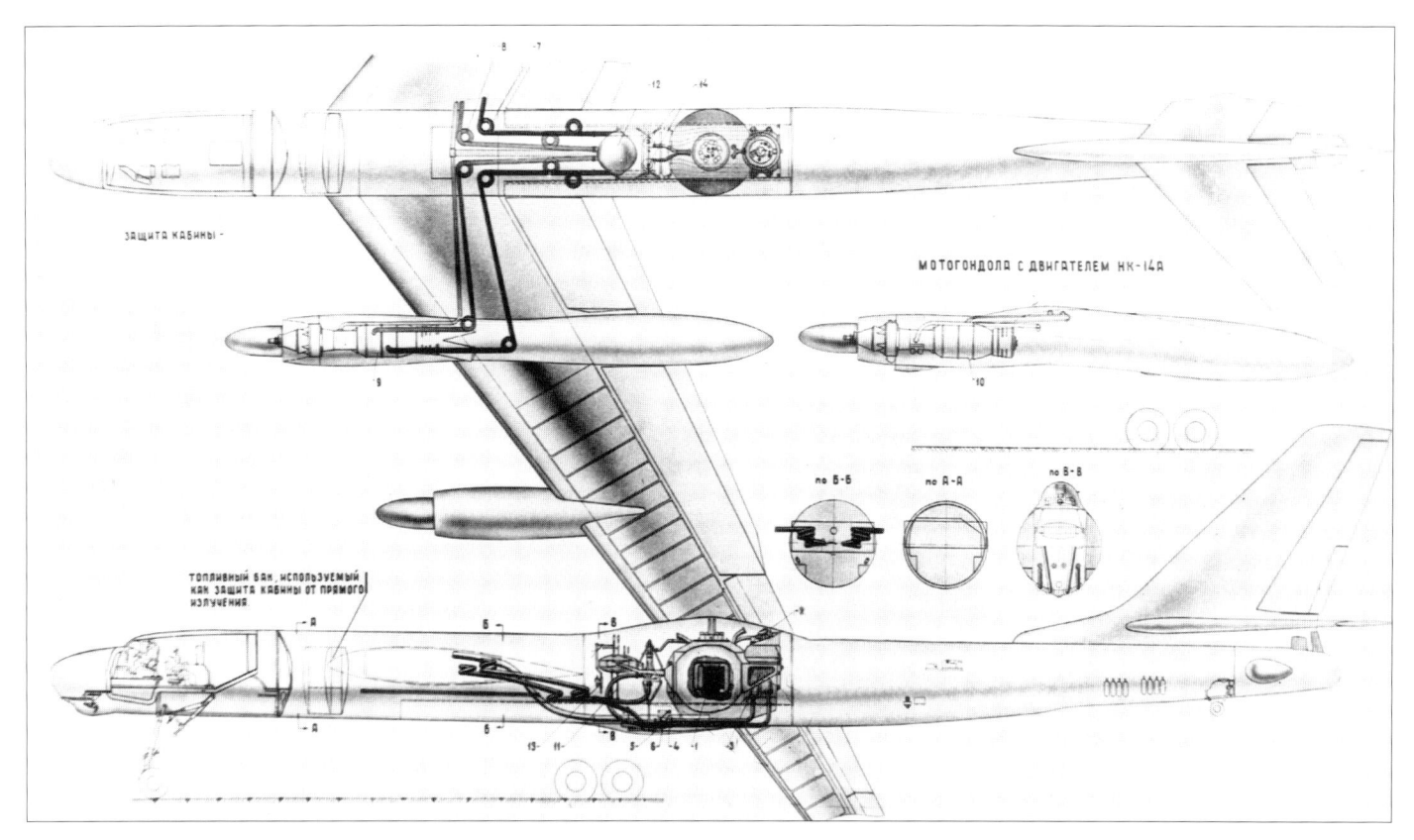

1959. Not long after these tests began, the predicted power level obtainable with the reactor was reached. It was then declared ready for the proposed flight test program.

Production Tu-95M, No.408, following modification during 1961, was set aside as a testbed and eventually became the aircraft chosen to become the Tu-95LAL flying nuclear laboratory.

Following modification and initial flight test work, the Tu-95LAL was equipped with its reactor and from May to August of 1961, flew thirty-four missions related to nuclear propulsion in flight.

Flights with the reactor both 'hot' and 'cold' were flown. Assessing biological reactions to a radioactive environment were the primary mission objectives.

The crew and researchers all sat in the forward section of the fuselage in a pressurized environment. Radiation sensors monitored radiation levels throughout the compartment. A bulkhead made of lead and a matrix of polyethylene and resin served as the radiation barrier between the crew and the reactor. A radiation level sensor was also installed in the bomb bay in close proximity to the reactor. A third sensor was installed in the rear cabin aft of the bomb bay. Two more sensors were mounted in the outer wing panels.

The reactor itself was mounted in the aircraft's bomb bay. It was suspended in a water jacket for cooling purposes and had a radiation attenuating coating of lead and resin to reduce hazardous emissions. The radiator and associated plumbing for the water cooling system were located in a prominent fairing under the fuselage. The reactor's control system was hooked up to a research engineer's panel positioned in a forward compartment just aft of the cockpit area.

The test program quickly proved the efficiency of the radiation barrier system. Exposure rates for the crew members were extremely low. This encouraged the various engineering staffs and gave rise to confidence in the ability of humans being able to work in close proximity to nuclear reactors.

The Tu-95LAL flying laboratory had the following specifications: takeoff weight was 131,579 kg (290,000 lb); landing weight was 99,819 kg (220,000 lb), normal range was 4,700 km (7,568 miles); normal flight duration was 6.4 hours; and cruise speed was 750-800 km/h (466-497 mph).

Though the short flight test program had been both successful and productive, the economics of the nuclear powered aircraft program began to impact its justification. When it was concluded the entire national budget for two years would be consumed by the project, it was elected to terminate the effort and pursue other avenues of bomber development.

Other issues contributing to the nuclear powered aircraft program's demise included the unwieldy nature of the radiation protection systems and associated shielding materials, and the fact the US had effectively terminated its nuclear powered aircraft program (thus eliminating it as a technology threat).

Tu-119

Based on the initial results from the Tu-95LAL and the initial successes of the nuclear powered aircraft program, the Tupolev bureau began design development of the Tu-119 ('119' aircraft). Fabrication of the first aircraft was scheduled for 1965.

The new bomber was to be powered by N D Kuznetsov's NK-14A nuclear turbofan engines.

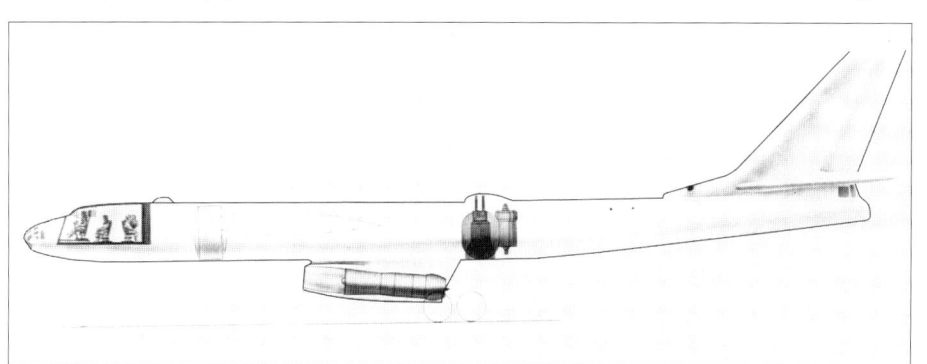

This page: **Two of several design approaches considered for what was proposed to become the Tu-119. In both cases, the nuclear reactor was positioned just aft of the wing center section in what originally was the bomber's aft bomb bay.** Yefim Gordon collection

During 1964, two experimental engines were scheduled to be installed in a modified Tu-95. This aircraft would serve as the '119' testbed.

Placement of the reactor followed the design criteria established with the Tu-95LAL. The bomb bay location of the reactor was the same as that on Tu-95LAL. The lines leading from the reactor to the engines passed through the fuselage, up through the wings, and then out to heat exchangers attached to the two inboard engines. The two outboard engines remained standard NK-12M turboprops. Fuel for the latter was to be carried in conventional tanks mounted in the wing torsion box.

The nuclear reactor was to be encased in lead. Some radiation also was to be absorbed by the conventional fuel tanks.

With the demise of Russia's nuclear-powered bomber program, the Tu-119 was halted during the course of preliminary design. Like its western equivalent, Convair's X-6 (a modified B-36 initially and later, a modified B-60), it never reached the hardware stage.

TYPE:	'95-1'	'95-2'	Tu-95	Tu-95M	Tu-95MR	Tu-96	Tu-95K
Year of First Flight	1952	1955	1955	1957	1964	1956	1956
Powerplant	4 x TV-2F	4xNK-12	4xNK-12	4xNK-12M	4xNK-12MV	4xTV-16/NK-12	4xNK-12M
Power kW (shp)	8,952 (12,000)	8,952 (12,000)	8,952 (12,000)	11,190 (15,000)	11,190 (15,000)	9,325/8,952 (12,500/12,000)	11,190 (15,000)
Number of Crew/Passengers	9 to 11	9	9	9	9	8	9
Wingspan m (ft)	49.8 (163.8)	50.04 (164.17)	50.04 (164.17)	50.04 (164.17)	50.04 (164.17)	51.4 (168.63)	50.04 (164.17)
Wing Area m² (ft²)	(?)	284.9 (3,066)	283.7 (3,053)	283.7 (3,053)	283.7 (3,053)	345.5 (3,719)	283.7 (3,053)
Length m (ft)	44.35 (145.5)	44.35 (145.5)	46.17 (151.4)	46.17 (151.4)	48.5 (159.1)	46.2 (151.5)	46.9 (153.8)
Takeoff Weight kg (lb)	141,561 (312,000)	153,358 (338,000)	156,080 (344,000)	165,154 (364,000)	165,154 (364,000)	312,000 (141,561)	364,000 (165,154)
Fuel Weight kg (lb)	77,441 (170,680)	76,588 (168,800)	73,230 (161,400)	75,980 (167,460) 85,054 (187,460)	75,980 (167,460) 85,054 (187,460)	(?)	72,995 (160,880)
Bombs/Armament kg (lb)	10,889 (24,000)	10,889 (24,000)	10,889 (24,000)	10,889 (24,000)	(?)	(?)	10,708 (23,600)
Empty Weight kg (lb)	71,755 (158,148)	64,265 (141,640)	75,408 (166,200)	76,497 (168,600)	(?)	64,310 (141,740)	78,040 (172,000)
Payload kg (lb)	(?)	(?)	(?)	(?)	(?)	(?)	(?)
Maximum Speed km/h (mph)	945 (587)	880 (546)	890 (553)	905 (562)	910 (562)	880 (546)/902 (560)	860 (534)
Cruising speed km/h (mph)	(?)	750 (466)	750 (466)	720 (447)/750 (466)	750 (466)	(?)	750 (466)
Service Ceiling m (ft)	13,700 (44,936)	12,500 (41,000)	11,800 (38,704)	11,900 (39,032)	11,900 (39,032)	17,000 (55,760)/ 12,400 (40,672)	11,600 (38,048)
Range km (miles)	15,200 (9,439)	13,900 (8,632)	12,100 (7,514)	13,200 (8,197)	13,120 (8,148)	16,200 (10,060)	12,500 (7,763)
Range w/Single Refueling km (miles)	18,400 (11,426)	(n.a.)	(n.a.)	(n.a.)	10,377 (16,700)	(?)	(n.a.)
Combat Radius km (miles)	(?)	(?)	(?)	(?)	(?)	(?)	6,340 (3,937)
Combat Radius w/Single Refueling km (miles)	(n.a.)	(n.a.)	(n.a.)	(n.a.)	(n.a.)	(n.a.)	(n.a.)
Takeoff Run m (ft)	1,580 (5,182)	2,300 (7,544)	2,350 (7,708)	2,730 (8,954)	1,800 (5,904)	2,780 (9,118)	2,380 (7,806)
Takeoff Weight kg (lb)	141,561 (312,000)	151,543 (334,000)	153,358 (338,000)	364,000 (165,154)	165,154 (364,000)	117,967 (260,000)	165,154 (364,000)
Landing Run m (ft)	1,370 (4,494)	(?)	1,500 (4,920)	1,500 (4,920)	1,500 (4,920)	(?)	1,700 (5,576)
Landing Weight kg (lb)	(?)	(?)	108,893 (240,000)	108,893 (240,000)	108,893 (240,000)	84,392 (186,000)	108,893 (240,000)
Defensive Armament	6x23mm (AM-23)	6x23mm (AM-23)	6x23mm (AM-23)	6x23mm (AM-23)	6x23mm (AM-23)	6x23mm (AM-23)	6x23mm (AM-23)/Kh-20M

TYPE:	Tu-95KM	Tu-95MS	Tu-95RTs	Tu-116	Tu-114	Tu-126
Year of First Flight	1961	1979	1962	1957	1957	1962
Powerplant	4xNK-12MV	4xNK-12MP	4xNK-12MV	4xNK-12M	4xNK-12MV	4xNK-12MV
Power kW (shp)	11,190 (15,000)	11,190 (15,000)	11,190 (15,000)	11,190 (15,000)	11,190 (15,000)	11,190 (15,000)
Number of Crew/Passengers	9	7	9	7/20 to 24	5/170 to 200	24
Wingspan m (ft)	50.04 (164.1)	50.04 (164.1)	50.04 (164.1)	50.04 (164.1)	51.1 (167.6)	51.1 (167.6)
Wing Area m² (ft²)	283.7 (3,053.5)	289.9 (3,117)	283.7 (3,053.5)	283.7 (3,053.5)	311.1 (3,348.3)	311.1 (3,348.3)
Length m (ft)	48.7 (160) w/probe	49.13 (161.1) w/pr.	48.5 (159) w/pr.	46.17 (151.4)	54.1 (177.4)	54.1/55.9 (177.4/183.4 w/pro.)
Takeoff Weight kg (lb)	165,154 (364,000)	167,877 (370,000)	165,154 (364,000)	130,309 (287,200)	157,441 (347,000)	155,172 (342,000)
Fuel Weight kg (lb)	71,688 (158,000)	81,670 (180,000)	(?)	75,608 (166,640)	57,623 (127,000) 61,706 (136,000)	(?)
Bombs/Armament kg (lb)	10,708 (23,600)	(?)	(?)	(n.a.)	(n.a.)	(?)
Empty Weight kg (lb)	79,401 (175,000)	(?)	(?)	71,688 (158,000)	84,846 (187,000)	(?)
Payload kg (lb)	(?)	(?)	(?)	2,269 (5,000)	20,417 (45,000)	(?)
Maximum Speed km/h (mph)	860 (534)	830 (515)	885 (550)/910 (562)	870 (540)	870 (540)	790 (491)
Cruising speed km/h (mph)	750 (466)	(?)	680 (422)/770 (478)	(?)	750 (466)	650 (404)/700(435)
Service Ceiling m (ft)	11,600 (38,048)	10,500 (34,440)	10,300 (33,784)	10,000 (32,800)/ 12,000 (39,360)	10,000 (32,800)	10,700 (35,096)
Range km (miles)	(?)	10,500 (6,521)	13,460 (8,359)	8,000 (4,968)	7,000 (4,347)	10.2 hours
Range w/Single Refueling km (miles)	(?)	14,100 (8,756)	16,350 (10,153)	(n.a.)	8,400 (5,216)	18 hours
Combat Radius km (miles)	6,340 (3,937.14)	(?)	(?)	(?)	(?)	(?)
Combat Radius w/Single Refueling km (miles)	8,520 (5,291)	(n.a.)	(n.a.)	(n.a.)	(n.a.)	(n.a.)
Takeoff Run m (ft)	2,780 (9,118)	2,540 (8,331)	(?)	1,700 (5,576)	2,200 (7,216)	2,400 (7,872)
Takeoff Weight kg (lb)	165,154 (364,000)	167,877 (370,000)	(?)	(?)	148,820 (328,000)	150,635 (332,000)
Landing Run m (ft)	1,700 (5,576)	(?)	(?)	1,350 (4,428)	1,750 (5,740)	1,200 (3,936)
Landing Weight kg (lb)	108,893 (240,000)	(?)	(?)	(?)	117,967 (260,000)	(?)
Defensive Armament	6x23mm (AM-23)/ Kh-20M	6xRKV-500A or 16xRKV-500A	6x23mm (AM-23)	(n.a.)	(n.a.)	(n.a.)

Left: **Rare image of a Tu-95MA equipped with wing root section weapon pylons. This particular aircraft is carrying an experimental missile, identified by some sources as being the cancelled AS-X-19, on its right pylon.**
Jay Miller collection

Opposite page: **The prototype Tu-142MR. Aircraft is painted in standard maritime scheme seen on fully operational Tu-142MRs.**
Yefim Gordon collection

Chapter Four

Tu-142s and other Tu-95s

Tu-95 PLO

At the beginning of the 1960s, the Tupolev design bureau initiated design work on an aircraft with a large radius of action while carrying a system for detecting, tracking, and destroying enemy submarines. The proposed new aircraft would not work as an autonomous unit, but rather would be part of a larger, complex hunt and kill system. The aircraft proposed by Tupolev, a highly-modified variant of the Tu-95, became the Tu-95PLO. It was a dedicated ASW platform and it was to be equipped with the following special equipment:
- omnidirectional sonobuoys
- anti-submarine bombs and mines
- anti-submarine homing torpedoes

The new aircraft had to be capable of carrying up to 8,167 kg (18,000 lb) of weapons. While carrying this load, the aircraft was expected to have an on-location endurance of from 3.5 to 10.5 hours, depending on the distance to the patrol station.

System and sensor shortcomings eventually ended the Tu-95PLO program. The lack of a powerful surveillance radar, a magnetometer, and an infrared search and track system effectively terminated interest.

Tu-142

On 28th February 1963 the USSR Soviet Council of Ministers released an order requiring the Tupolev design bureau to design and build a long-range anti-submarine warfare aircraft.

Known as the Tu-142 (and utilizing the Tu-95RTs as its basis) it was equipped with a search and track system and an ASW weapon system.

Integrated into the new aircraft was a sophisticated and accurate navigation system that also was part of the weapons system targeting hardware.

A secondary task included electronic reconnaissance. Accommodating the associated requirements were the *Kvadrat*-2 and *Kub*-3 electronic warfare systems.

Concurrent with the basic mission requirements was a secondary item specified by the Soviet Air Force. The new aircraft would, of necessity, be required to operate from rough and poorly prepared fields. Accordingly, a new main landing gear was designed for the Tu-142, this accommodating no less than six wheels and tires on each bogie. Because of the increased size of this unit, the gear wells had to be increased in size along with the aft inboard engine nacelles.

The Tu-142's wing was refined also. The airfoil section changed and two-section flaps were installed. As a result, wing area was increased to 289.9 m² (3,120 ft²). The flexible rubber fuel tanks of the earlier Tu-95 were replaced by rigid metal tanks that were part of the wing torsion box assembly. Elevator area was increased by some 14% as well. Irreversible hydraulic actuators were installed to reduce the pilot workload.

The Tu-142's defensive armament also underwent a change. The aft cannon was retained, but positioned next to it was a small suite of electronic countermeasures equipment.

It was also suggested that the Tu-142 be equipped with several systems that were deemed appropriate for its performance and mission objectives. One of these was a boundary layer control system. Even in consideration of the landing and takeoff speed reductions that would result, this idea eventually was abandoned due to complexity and cost.

Another suggestion called for an ejection-seat-type crew emergency egress system. Accordingly, the crew would have to egress conventionally in an emergency, if they were to get out at all.

As development of the Tu-142 progressed, it became apparent to Tupolev engineers that the new aircraft would have to have a new cockpit design if it was to physically accommodate the many new systems scheduled for installation. Thus, the Tu-142's cabin was modified by lengthening it approximately 1.5 m (3.42 ft). This upgrade was not incorporated into the first prototype, but the second aircraft was so modified.

The first Tu-142 prototype, aircraft No.4200, was built at the Kuibyshev aviation factory. By the summer of 1968 it was ready for initiation of flight testing. Externally, the new aircraft appeared to be essentially the same as the Tu-95RTs production aircraft. This similarity, in fact, was not superficial, as the airframe changes were subtle. This would facilitate the production transition from the Tu-95RC to the new configuration.

As with the Tu-95RTs, the Tu-142 had a side-looking radar unit mounted ventrally at near mid-fuselage. The weapon bays were positioned aft of that. The ventral and dorsal cannon turrets were removed. In the nose, instead of a large dielectric radome normally allocated to the *Uspeh* system, a smaller fairing was installed covering an infrared search system. Additionally, instead of the *Arfa* system found on the Tu-95RTs, a new antenna system was positioned in fairings on the horizontal stabilizer tips.

The Tu-142, No.4200, prototype became airborne for the first time on 18th July 1968, taking off from the lengthy main runway at Zhukovsky. The pilot was I K Vedernikov. The second prototype, No.4201, took to the air for the first time the following 3rd September. This aircraft was the first to have the 1.7 m (5.6 ft) cabin extension. However, it did not have a full equipment complement. The third Tu-142 became airborne for the first time on 31st October 1968. It also had the extended cabin, but was equipped with the full equipment suite specified by the 1967 decision and mandated by the Ministry of Aviation Industry and the Air Force.

The three prototypes successfully completed the factory flight test program and shortly afterwards, that of the Soviet government. Actual flight characteristics of the Tu-142 aircraft were not a concern as the design did not represent a major change from the Tu-95 configuration. Its ASW search and destroy systems were in fact the items of most importance.

During May of 1970, the first production Tu-142s were introduced for operational test and evaluation by Soviet Navy ASW units. Surveillance of the movement of atomic submarines in the world's oceans proved the items of highest priority during the initial operational trials. When they were completed successfully, the aircraft was cleared for actual operational use. Accordingly, during December of 1972, the USSR Council of Ministers passed a resolution declaring the Tu-142 to be operational with the Soviet Navy.

By the time work on the Tu-142's search and targeting system (STS) got under way full details of the *Berkut* (Golden eagle) search radar and its capabilities were not yet available, but some of its shortcomings were already known. Still, these were not eliminated straightaway and had to be dealt with later during flight tests.

Considering the capabilities of the Tupolev OKB, the general belief was that the Tu-142 would not take long to design and the prototype would commence tests in late 1964. However, these estimates proved a little optimistic and the deadline had to be moved twice - first by two years and then by another year and eight months.

Came January 1968, and the State commission monitoring project status convened for yet another session. Mildly berating the OKB for slow progress, it set a new deadline - the third quarter of 1968. And even that had to be moved to the first quarter of 1969.

The State commission convened once again in January 1969 to check on progress - and found that things were in a rather sorry state: the Tu-142 prototype had made only six test flights from the factory airfield in Kuibyshev.

By then the type's progenitor, the Tu-95, had accumulated quite a lot of operational experience and the designers were aware of its bugs. The cramped flight deck was the main source of annoyance. To solve this problem, several modifications were made to the prototype. A 1.2 m (4 ft) cylindrical plug was inserted into the forward fuselage. A new raised flight deck glazing was incorporated to improve visibility, and the pilot's and first officer's seats were fitted with reclining backs for greater comfort.

The Tu-142 had its share of failures during flight tests – including some rather curious ones like several occasions when the tubeless tires came off the wheels on takeoff or landing. This led to some claims to the petroleum and chemical plants which had produced the substandard tires. Stage I of the flight tests was finally completed in June 1970; trials and debugging of the *Berkut* radar were delayed until August.

The specific operational requirement (SOR) for the Tu-142 contained a highly unorthodox clause: the aircraft had to be capable of operating from dirt strips. This unprecedented clause for a heavy aircraft crammed with sophisticated and sensitive mission electronics was included at the insistence of the AV-MF (Soviet naval aviation) top command. To meet this requirement the designers had to make extensive modifications. The aft portions of the inboard engine nacelles were widened considerably and flattened; these accommodated huge 12-wheel main gear bogies with three rows of four wheels and a complex retraction sequence. Flap area had to be reduced to make room for the new nacelles.

A disconcerted A N Tupolev wrote a letter to the Soviet minister of defence, arguing that operating such an aircraft from dirt strips was pointless. On 6th October 1970, the minister wrote back, stating his agreement. Consequently the Tu-142s were fitted with lighter four-wheel main gear bogies in much slimmer nacelles (identical to those of the Tu-114 airliner), and flap area was increased accordingly. Unfortunately, there is no knowing how much money went down the drain because of all these conversions and reconversions. Concurrently the aircraft were refitted with more efficient airscrews.

The modified Tu-142 was flight tested once again; the SIGINT and ECM packages and some other equipment were removed for the occasion, giving a weight reduction of 3,700 kg (8,157 lbs). The results were not entirely encouraging; curiously, takeoff performance had deteriorated, being 2,150 to 2,300 m (7,053 to 7,545 ft) rather than the 1,800 to 2,000 m (5,905 to 6,561 ft) stated by the SOR. On the other hand, range was improved and was now quite close to the target figure.

In August 1972 two airframes were selected for fitting with the new *Korshun* (Kite) search radar. And finally, on 14th December 1972, a decree was signed by the Central Committee of the Communist Party of the USSR and the Council of Ministers, allowing the Tu-142 equipped with the *Berkut*-95 search radar to enter service – rather belatedly.

Top: **An early production Tu-142 equipped with ventral search radar optimized for ocean surveillance.** Yefim Gordon collection

Bottom: **The first production Tu-142 being prepared for flight at Kipelovo Airbase.** Yefim Gordon collection

Opposite page, top: **A standard production Tu-142 at Kipelovo Air Base.** Yefim Gordon

Opposite page, bottom: **A naval aviation Tu-142M.** Aviatsiya & Kosmonautica

Item 2 of said decree was formulated as follows: 'to award and pay a 1st-degree State Award for the design, testing and entry into production of the Tu-142 aircraft to (whomever) and a 3rd degree State Award for the design, testing and entry into production of the *Berkut-95* system to (whomever) pursuant to the Directive on State Awards approved by Decree of the Council of Ministers No.28-10 (8th January 1966). The document was signed by Leonid Brezhnev and Anatoliy Kosygin (head of the Council of Ministers).

On 22nd June 1969, the Northern Fleet Air Arm started picking personnel for a long-range ASW regiment operating Tu-142s. The first group started conversion training in Nikolayev on the Black Sea on 4th March 1970, and was ready to fly about three months later. However, the second group did not begin training until December 1971, so it was a long time before the unit was finally operational under Lt. Col. V I Dubinskiy.

Attaining initial operational capability was hampered by slow deliveries. The AV-MF was to receive 36 Tu-142s during 1972; however, only 12 were actually delivered. All of them were Batch 1 aircraft fitted with the famous 12-wheel main gear bogies.

The reason for late deliveries were the delays in testing and production. The culprit was the Ministry of aircraft industry (MAP - *Ministerstvo aviatsionnoy promyshlennosti*) which switched Tu-142 production from the Kuibyshev aircraft plant to the Taganrog machinery plant No. 60 named after Georgiy Dimitrov. This was done without consulting the AV-MF – possibly by some arrangement of the top brass to give the Taganrog plant something to build since it was standing idle at the time. Technical documentation also was shipped from Kuibyshev to Taganrog not long afterwards and production under the TMZD umbrella was initiated.

However, Taganrog had no experience building heavy landplanes, nor a runway long enough for the Tu-142. New assembly shops were needed for the programme, new machinery had to be installed (Taganrog had lots of obsolete equipment dating back to the '30s), new jigs and tooling had to be manufactured, the workforce had to be re-trained – to say nothing of the new airfield, which was a must. This was a massive task and required considerable time to execute.

To give credit where credit is due, the engineering staff at Taganrog took this task in stride. Moreover, rather than just turning out Tu-142s as per OKB drawings, they introduced numerous improvements – particularly in the flight deck, thus easing pilot workload considerably.

Tu-142 ('Bear'-F Mod.1)

Initial operational use of the Tu-142 revealed several shortcomings. The Soviet Navy found rough field capability to be limited and flight characteristics in general to be less than satisfactory. An immediate weight reduction program became the item of highest priority, the expectation being an improvement in the aforementioned performance shortfall.

As a result of the shortcoming, a modification plan was instigated with the aircraft's failings being addressed at every opportunity. Beds for crew rest during long duration flights were installed in the cockpit of Tu-142, No.4211. Tu-142, No.4231 had its infrared system dismantled and part of its electronic countermeasures system removed. The larger main landing gear bogies were replaced with a beefed-up four-wheel unit similar to that found on the standard Tu-95. These modifications resulted in an aircraft that was 3,630 kg (8,000 lb) lighter than when it was originally built. Importantly, aircraft No.4231 had significantly better flight characteristics than its unmodified stablemates.

In total, the Kuibyshev facility, with the exception of the first prototype, produced 18 Tu-142s (2 during 1968, 5 during 1969, 5 during 1970, 5 during 1971, and 1 during 1972).

Tu-142M ('Bear'-F Mod.2)

The last aircraft produced during 1972 at the Kuibyshev facility, No. 4242, became the standard configuration for the production aircraft delivered from the Taganrog facility.

This aircraft was equipped with the extended cockpit and the newer two-axle main gear bogie configuration found on all but the first aircraft. Other equipment was similar to that found on Tu-142, No.4231. Concurrently, the modernized and updated aircraft were given the Tu-142 designator at Tupolev.

Throughout most of 1973 the Taganrog factory made preparations to accommodate production of the basic Tu-142 as built by the Kuibyshev factory. Production finally got underway during 1975 and continued over the next two years. In order to distinguish Taganrog aircraft from those produced earlier by the facility in Kuibyshev, the Taganrog Tu-142s were given the internal factory designator Tu-142M (similar to the designator adopted by Tupolev)

Somewhat surprisingly, Naval Aviation did not adopt the new identifier. Accordingly, the aircraft remained designated simply Tu-142, as in the past.

Tu-142M/Tu-142MK ('Bear'-F Mod.3)

Operational experience with SAR aircraft and helicopters worldwide indicated that acoustic-band sonobuoys with trigger devices were becoming increasingly less effective against submarines as these were getting quieter and harder to identify. Submarine designers kept working at making their craft more stealthy, managing to make submarines sound almost like the natural noises of the ocean. Research by ASW experts indicated that sonobuoys with a 2 to 10 Hz noise reception band were needed to hunt down modern subs.

Noises in this range are generated, e.g., when propeller blades pass the submarine's elevators and rudders because of fluctuating cavitation on propeller blades. Protruding structures of the submarine's hull generate vortices which disturb water flow in the propeller disc, causing pulsations of propeller thrust. Such pulsations are common to all submarines, including those with five-, six-, or seven-bladed low-speed propellers; occasionally, flow departure from propeller blades generates vortex noise with frequencies of up to 100 Hz.

Contemporary Soviet sonobuoys, however, could only detect noise in the 3 to 10 kHz band. All this showed clearly that more modern underwater noise detection and processing techniques were required for acoustic detection of submarines. Characteristic pulsating low-frequency and infrasonic noises had to be defined since they travel large distances through water without dissipating.

Western SAR aircraft were equipped with low-frequency sonobuoys since 1960. Several high-performance models were in use; importantly, Western navies used fairly sophisticated data processing methods and equipment. Besides, sonobuoys with explosive sound sources (ESS) were used for detecting submarines in deep waters; the explosive charges varied in power, shape, sound spectrum etc.

In 1961-1962 the Soviet Union conducted R&D in using ESS for locating submarines. The two research programmes were called 'NIR' (*naoochno-issledovatel 'skiye raboty* – research) and *Yel'* (fir tree). In 1965, work began on operational sonobuoy systems with ESS; the defence industry directive to this effect stated that the system was to be integrated with the *Berkut* search radar installed on the Il-38 and Tu-142. Besides the actual design effort – the *Udar* (blow) program – the possibilities of

---

Top: **A standard production Tu-142M during refueling process. Noteworthy is extended tailwheel.** Yefim Gordon collection

Second from top: **A Tu-142M shortly after takeoff. Gear retraction sequence has begun.** Gennady Petrov collection

Second from bottom: **Standard production Tu-142Ms.** Yefim Gordon collection

Bottom: **A Tu-142M flaring for landing.** Gennady Petrov collection

Top: **Tu-142Ms at Ostrov Naval Aviation Center.** Yefim Gordon

Below: **A Tu-142M viewed from under the nose of a Tu-95MR.** Yefim Gordon collection

using ESS in the future were investigated; however, the latter effort was soon abandoned.

As the *Udar* program proceeded it became clear that the Il-38 could not carry the new system without major modifications and upgrades to the STS (search radar). Moreover, the existing TsVM264 computer would have to be replaced with a more capable *Orbita* computer. This and insufficient development of other hardware (the ESS launchers were not ready, nor was the launch technique developed) led to the *Udar* programme being put on hold. However, data obtained during this effort and its sequel *Udar*-75 were put to good use when designing the Tu-142M's STS.

The Tu-142M's equipment suite was developed pursuant to a directive of the USSR Council of Ministers issued on 14th January 1969. The SOR was approved same year in March.

Usually research and development work on Soviet aircraft and their systems, even the most primitive ones, proceeded under tight security wraps. Thus, the meeting held at Kipelovo air base in May 1970 was something of a sensation – as at least 100 people attended the meeting included high-ranking officers, designers, representatives of the AV-MF operational training centre, various defence industry plants, as well as local aircrews and ground crews operating the Tu-142.

Of course, the information revealed at the meeting was scarce - nothing more than a few colourful charts and tables plus a few words about the general concept of the aircraft. Still, this was good enough for the aircrews which were sick and tired of the *Berkut* radar's limitations and believed that something new would come soon to replace it. However, it was another nine years before the new aircraft attained IOC with the Northern Fleet Air Arm, with loads of bugs still to be ironed out.

Development work on the Tu-142M and its systems followed the worst Soviet traditions of procrastination. The full-scale mockup was completed a year late, and flight tests began in 1975 rather than in 1972 as originally scheduled.

Production of the modernized anti-submarine Tu-142 with the old target acquisition system (the Tu-142M) began during 1975 at the Taganrog factory. Two pre-production examples, Nos. 4243 and 4244, became the prototypes for the follow-on production aircraft.

Work on a new target acquisition system, referred to as the *Korshun* unit, progressed satisfactorily, however, and as a result the equipment complement on the production aircraft changed. It was decided, therefore, to install the *Korshun* unit on all succeeding Tu-142s. Accordingly, the first two Tagonrog machines were updated with the equipment and were assigned the Tu-142MK designator.

Aircraft No.4243 successfully completed its first flight on 4th November 1975. It was piloted by I K Vedernikov. Concurrently, a third Tu-142MK, No.4264, was completed with the *Korshun* system in place.

Three prototypes took part in Stage A of the trials program. The first aircraft, or *etalon* ('standard'; the first aircraft built by the production factory, not the OKB's experimental plant), operating out of Feodosiya on the Crimea peninsula was used for search radar evaluation and verifying its ability to handle complex tasks. The second Tu-142M, based at Zhukovsky, served for performance testing, while the third prototype was a testbed for the MAD, ESS launchers and other equipment and operated from various air bases, including Sleezevo on the Kamchatka.

When the preliminary trials were completed the WS (Soviet Air Force) C-in-C, the AV-MF C-inC and the Minister of Aircraft Industry signed a memo giving the go-ahead for full-scale production. This was rather strange, since the Tu-142M's performance fell utterly short of the design requirements. In fact, only seven of the SOR's 31 items were complied with, and those were relatively unimportant ones. Thus, the premature decision to launch full-scale production was bound to cause problems – and promptly did.

Stage B of the trials began in April 1978, terminating in October; the three trials aircraft made a total of 136 test flights during this period. Deliveries to AV-MF units began next year, despite the fact that the aircraft was beset by teething troubles. The new *Korshun* radar, avionics suite and ASW equipment turned out to be a real can of worms, proving extremely

57

unreliable as soon as the Tu-142M entered service. Besides, tests indicated that the STS had little growth potential and was becoming obsolete even before it became operational. Hence in July 1979 - more than a year before the *Korshun*-equipped Tu-142M entered service – the Military/Industrial Commission (a consulting body on general policies of military hardware production; not to be confused with the State commission which deals specifically with tests of individual weapon systems) ruled that its STS needed upgrading.

On 19th November 1980, the Council of Ministers issued a decree clearing the aircraft for service, and on 6th December same year the Minister of Defence signed an order to this effect. The decree said, among other things:

'…The Ministry of Aircraft Industry, the Ministry of Electronics Industry and the Ministry of Defence are authorized to recommend up to 2,000 of their employees and military experts for awarding orders and medals of the USSR for their active contribution to the design, testing and operation of the long-range ASW aircraft.' The decree was signed by Brezhnev and Tikhonov (the then head of the Council of Ministers).

The ASW weapons system included the Tu-142M aircraft, the NPK-142M avionics suite (NPK or *navigatseeonno-peelotazhnyy kompleks*), the updated *Korshun*-K search radar, a bombing computer controlling the release of bombs, torpedoes, sonobuoys and mines, the MMS-106 *Ladoga* MAD,. the *Strela*-142M (Arrow) communications suite, the *Nerchinsk* sonar set, assorted offensive weapons and the *Sayany* defensive weapons system.

The main flight data of the Tu-142M, including field performance, were little different from the basic Tu-142. Fuel load was increased by 3,000 kg (6,613 lbs); however, this did not improve range or endurance because of the increase in all-up weight and the added drag caused by various new fairings. Thus, range was 12,000 km (7,500 miles) at a 185-ton (407,848 lb) MTOW. Aerial refuelling increases range by 2,000 km (1,250 miles).

In order to install various new equipment the forward crew compartment of the Tu-142M had to be changed considerably. Despite the relatively high level of automation the crew was enlarged to eleven: pilot, co-pilot, first navigator, second navigator, combat navigator (sic), two sonar systems operator, communications officer, chief flight engineer, tail gun barbette operator and tail gunner. It was obviously possible to eliminate at least two crewmen and reduce all-up weight by approximately 1,500 kg (3,306 lbs) by deleting the tail gun barbette and associated equipment.

The engineers designing the STS were facing enormous problems - naturally enough, since they were to develop a system capable of detecting modern 'stealthy' submarines. The system looked very well on paper but not all of its features could materialize easily.

Four types of sonobuoys, explosive sound sources, a new MAD, new data processing equipment and much more was developed in an attempt to tackle the problem. The effort was spearheaded by the system's chief designer A M Gromov, a person of modest character but great engineering talent.

In order to use the aircraft's sensors efficiently, interface operators with the on-board data processors and graphic displays inform the crew of friendly and hostile activity in the air, on the surface and under water, the Tu-142M featured tactical situation displays at the crew's stations, including the flight deck.

The *Korshun*-K STS incorporates all of the features described above. It enables the crew to seek and destroy submarines (both surfaced and submerged), trade tactical information with other ASW aircraft and C³ centres, process search data and perform navigational and tactical tasks automatically or semi-automatically. The STS comprises equipment rigidly installed on the airframe, sonobuoys and ground testing equipment.

The main weakness of all prior ASW systems was the lack of tactical situation displays enabling the crew to make better tactical decisions. This was eliminated in the *Korshun*-K STS. It includes a tactical information display subsystem TIDS) which uses a preset range of

Top: **A standard production Tu-142M being towed at Kipelovo Air Base.** Yefim Gordon

Opposite page bottom: **A Tu-142M-2 making a fly-by with its aft weapon bay doors open.** Yefim Gordon

commands stored in a computer's hard drive. The TIDS may operate in a display mode or data processing mode.

The main and auxiliary TIDS displays (incidentally, the one in the flight deck was added at the insistence of this author) display the tactical situation in the form of special symbols with two-digit codes for threat classification, vectors and circles. This includes the aircraft's position and speed vector, sonobuoy drop positions, headings for directional buoys, positions of detected subs and up to six other parameters. The TIDS automatically switches from display mode to data processing mode, operating as a single-address digital computer.

To facilitate working with images and increase data presentation speed the combat navigator is armed with an optical 'pointer' (light pencil) projecting a big cruciform cursor on the display. If this is pointed at any place on the display and certain keys are pressed a 'go-to' function is activated – the aircraft is automatically guided to the cursor position.

A special computer processes inputs from the control panel and data coming in from all components of the *Korshun*-K STS. It continuously keeps track of the aircraft's position, sonobuoy splashdown positions, monitors submarine movements, trades information with other aircraft via data link, provides control inputs to the autopilot in the automatic or semi-automatic flight mode during tactical maneuvers and launches weapons ('shooting to kill').

The *Korshun*-K STS employs four models of sonobuoys (RGB-75, RGB-15, RGB-25 and RGB55A) as the principal source of data about submerged targets. The first two are used for detecting subs and the other two for pinpointing them and monitoring their movements. However, RGB-15 buoys can be used jointly with small high-explosive bombs (explosive sound sources) for pinpointing targets.

The RGB-75 buoy picks up acoustic signals (low-frequency audible and infrasonic bands) generated by submarines, transforms them into electric signals and transmits them to the aircraft for further processing. The buoy is 1,214 mm (3 ft 11¾ in) long and weighs 9.5 kg (20.94 lbs); the Tu-142M carries 24 of them. The buoy operates continuously after hitting the water.

The RGB-15 buoy picks up acoustic signals (low-frequency audible and infrasonic bands) generated by submarines, as well as signals generated by explosive sound sources, transforming them into electric signals and transmitting them to the aircraft. The buoy's receiver has a 2 Hz – 5 kHz waveband. In the active mode (ie, when ESSs are used) distance from buoy to aircraft is determined by the radar's DME channel, using the data link; however, the buoy has no self-contained beacon.

In operating condition, the RGB-15's hydrophone is a cylinder of 80 mm (3.14 in) dia. and 1,400 mm (4.5 ft) long and weighs 9.5 kg (20.28 lb). It incorporates six receivers and can be submerged 20, 150 or 400 m (65, 492 and 1,312 ft); maximum operating time is 2 hours. The Tu-142M carries 16 RGB-15s.

As described earlier, the RGB-15 can be used separately or in conjunction with ESSs. In the former case the noises picked up by the buoy are transmitted to the aircraft where the operator analyzes them, using a KR-P graphic equalizer which displays frequencies of 2-6 Hz; frequencies up to 5 kHz are analyzed through headphones. While the buoy's capabilities in the visual waveband analysis mode are somewhat worse than of the RGB-75, the audio analysis may offer some advantages in noise classification.

If used with ESSs the RGB-15 picks up and transmits both primary signals (when the ESS detonates) and echoes reflected from the target. Detection range may be 10 to 15 km (6.25 to 9.3 miles) or more. Sometimes this combination works as a primary search means in the active mode, especially when searching for low-noise submarines.

Passive directional RGB-25 buoys are used to detect audio-frequency signals emitted by subs and determining their position; the signal is then processed and transmitted to the aircraft. The buoy's antenna is a collapsible three-dimensional framework made up of five separate grids joined by cylindrical hinges; the three inner grids carry 34 acoustic receivers. The antenna weighs 7 kg (15.5 lbs). It is powered by an electric motor and rotates at 6 to 12 rpm, scanning the sea around the buoy.

When a submarine comes into range the RGB-25 picks up the noise, amplifies it and converts it into radio signals before transmitting them to the aircraft. A compass is used to determine the current heading the acoustic system is pointed at. The buoy's position and distance from the aircraft is calculated using the search radar's and DME channel. The RGB-25 is submerged 20 or 150 m (64 or 479 ft) and remains operational for about 40 min; target headings are determined with an error margin of 3°. The Tu-142M carries 10 buoys weighing 45 kg (99.2 lbs) each.

The RGB-55A is likewise a directional sonobuoy; however, it is an active buoy designed to send signals allowing the buoy's position to be determined. It also allows the operator to determine the radial component of the submarine's speed.

The buoy's hydroacoustic transmitter is triggered by a special command from the aircraft, sending an audible signal through the water. The echo reflected from the target is then transmitted to the aircraft. This enables the operator to determine signal return time and the Doppler frequency shift and thus calculate the distance between buoy and target and the speed of the latter. Thus, two or three buoys allow the crew to pinpoint the submarine and determine its speed and heading. If no acoustic signal is transmitted the RGB-55A works as a passive non-directional buoy.

RGB-55As are delivered in sets of 16; the Tu-142M carries up to 15 such buoys with four different acoustic signal frequencies, depending on the mission.

The buoy weighs 55 kg (121.25 lbs) and operates at depths of 20 to 200 m (65 to 656 ft) for up to an hour; minimum detection range 5 km (3 miles). The length of the acoustic signal is variable. All sonobuoys are scuttled automatically when their operation time expires.

The RGB-15 and RGB-55A are powered by one Model 15-9 battery, the RGB-25 and RGB-75 each have two identical batteries. The Model 15-9 is a disposable battery activated by salt water, with a negative electrode made of magnesium alloy sheet and a positive electrode made of silver sulphate. (Later this battery was found to be too expensive and replaced by a cheaper one.) However, this is not enough to power the buoy in the active mode, so the RGB-55A has an additional Model 64NKPL1.5A nickel-cadmium battery with 64 cells in a metal casing.

Three types of explosive sound sources (ESS) are used with the RGB-15 sonobuoy in the active mode. These are the MGAB-OZ, MGAB-LZ and MGAB-SZ free-fall bombs (MGAB = *malogabaritnaya aviabomba* – literally 'compact bomb') with different charges (OZ = *odinochnyy zaryad* – single charge; LZ = *leeneynyy zaryad* – linear charge; and SZ = *speeral'nyy zaryad* – spiral charge).

MGAB-OZ bombs with a 200 or 800 g (7 or 28 oz) are used if the suggested distance from target to buoy is equal to or less than the sea depth. The safety catch of the bomb is removed as it hits the water.

MGAB-LZ bombs are used in shallow areas with an even seabed, since they minimize reverberation interference. The linear charge is shaped like a 2 m (6.5 ft) string and weighs 100 g (3.5 oz). It is extracted from the bomb casing by the water flow after impact and detonates at a preset depth. The aircraft can carry up to 240 MGAB-LZ bombs.

In complicated hydrological conditions and areas with an uneven seabed, parachute-stabilized MGAB-SZ bombs are used. They have a coiled string charge weighing 200 g (7 oz) with up to 40 coils. The *Wast* generates a series of 4 kHz signals; the number of signals depends on the number of coils in the spiral.

All three models of ESSs can be set to detonate at a depth of 25, 150 or 400 m (82, 492 or 1,312 ft).

The *Korshun*-K system is closely connected with the NPK-142M avionics suite which has duplicated control channels. The suite offers automatic and semi-automatic flight control modes with control inputs from the navigation system and the STS. It includes the *Bort*-142 trajectory control system and the AP-15PS autopilot.

The Tu-142M's armament comprises bombs, ASW torpedoes, special stores and defensive armament. The weapons system hardware includes bomb, torpedo and sonobuoy racks, bombsight (NKBP-7) and release controls (ESBR-70 electric bomb release unit, drop sequence module, detonation depth setting module etc.), detonator controls and bomb/torpedo hoists.

All offensive armament is released automatically, triggered by the tactical computer.

Tactical and navigational tasks are solved separately; eg., only the navigation suite is used when the aircraft is en route to the search area, and in the search area the aircraft is controlled by the STS.

Since the *Korshun*-K STS makes use of active sonobuoys and ESSs, knowing the speed of sound in water is important. Therefore, the

Tu-142M is fitted with the *Nerchinsk* system with two buoys which, when dropped, transmit data on the speed of sound at different depths. The data are picked up by a special *Istra* receiver and, after being deciphered, are recorded electrographically on a paper strip.

In an emergency, the pilot or combat navigator may jettison all offensive armament, setting it for detonation or non-detonation.

The defensive armament consists of a DK-12 tail gun barbette with two 23-mm AM-23 cannons, a PS-153K optical sight and a VB-153 aiming computer. The latter may receive inputs from a PRS-4 *Krypton* gun-laying radar.

The increasing importance of communications led to all communications equipment being united into an on-board communications suite. It provides intercomunications between crew members, voice and data link with shore-based C³ centers, surface ships, other aircraft and records all incoming and outgoing voice and data communications.

The MMS-106 MAD 'stinger' acts as a secondary source of information about submerged targets. It comprises a magnetic anomaly sensor, an orientation module, a measurement channel and other supporting systems. The magnetic anomaly sensor (ie., the MAD 'stinger') is located atop the fin, pointing aft – probably the worst possible location since large static charges are accumulated here and is covered by a dielectric fairing. The MAD display is in the forward crew compartment.

A typical ASW sortie looks like this. After reaching the search area the aircraft scans it with the search radar and then drops RGB-75 sonobuoys (the most widely used type). If the buoys detect the presence of a submarine, more precise data about target position may be required before tracking commences. To this end, RGB-I buoys (usually used with the Berkut STS) or RGB-15s may be dropped.

RGB-15s may also be used in conjunction with ESSs, or RGB-55As may be used in the active mode (which is the least advisable and least common technique). These are unstealthy methods, and the chances of detection are reduced. Sub tracking is done by placing straight or curved 'barriers' (series of sonobuoys) along the suggested directions where the submarine may go; RGB-15s and RGB-55As may be used for this.

Depending on the objective received by the crew the aircraft may attack and destroy the sub either immediately after discovering it or after tracking it for some time to see if it is getting too close to friendly ships.

As was already mentioned, the Tu-142M entered service with the AV-MF in 1979, and the early service period was most disappointing since the STS, the avionics suite and sonobuoys turned out to be extremely unreliable. Operational experience showed both weaknesses of the equipment and flaws in the design policy: much time was needed to process data supplied by the sonobuoys, the operator had to manually compare 'equalizer graphs' since there was no provision for this to be done automatically, the directional buoys had huge sidelobes etc.

The MAD represented the most difficult equipment to perfect. Its sensitivity was much lower than required, and this was not helped by its unfortunate location. The flight manual said the crew had to switch off four of the aircraft's eight generators, the hydraulic pump and some electronic equipment items to operate the MAD.

Early operational experience with the Tu-142 did not allow the AV-MF to fully assess its capabilities simply because for almost two years the sonobuoys that were to go with it were not used. The reason is unbelievable – the buoys were so damn classified that operational units never saw a whiff of them! After the buoys were finally declassified, for the next four years no one could tell for sure if the signal received was a real submarine or a false alarm because the data recorders used for debriefing was far from perfect. Finally, in 1985 some aircraft were fitted

Top: **A Tu-142 flares for landing.**
Gennady Petrov collection

Bottom: **The Tu-142M prototype.** Yefim Gordon

Top: **The Tu-142M prototype. Angle of MAD boom at top of vertical fin was varied slightly from that of production aircraft.** Tupolev Design Bureau

Bottom: **A Tu-142M with conventional MAD boom.** Tupolev Design Bureau

with the new *Uzor*-5V magnetic data recorder (pronounced 'oozor'); the situation became more or less clear, and the designers of the previous inefficient equipment faced some serious claims.

Aircrews found conversion to the new STS difficult since the new system was very different in ideology from its predecessors. Though it's not recorded officially, logic told that the combat navigator should be in control in the search area since he has more tactical information than anyone else, while the pilot would be responsible for flight safety and for getting the mission accomplished. To speed up conversion training, representatives of research institutes and test navigators would fly training sorties with regular crews. Ironically, it often turned out that service navigators who had clocked much time on the Tu-142 were more expert than the test navigators who were supposed to be the best of the best.

Production of the Tu-142M (Tu-142MK) superseded that of the Tu-142M at the Taganrog factory during 1978. The Soviet Navy, unlike the production facilities, elected to utilize their own designation system on these new aircraft. Those equipped with the new ASW system became simply Tu-142Ms and the older aircraft, without the newer equipment, retained their simple Tu-142 designator.

Tu-142MK ('Bear'-F Mod.3)

During 1969, while factory testing of the Tu-142 continued, the Tupolev bureau proposed an ASW variant of the aircraft equipped with a new search-and-find system consisting of the following: a side-looking radar; an infrared sensor system; a towed magnetometer; an infrared seeker unit; a gas analyzer; and a modernized flight navigation system integrated with the flight control system. The latter could control the aircraft automatically in flight while searching for submarines.

A variant of the original Tu-142 configuration, with the extended cockpit and the original three-axle main landing gear bogies, was chosen to serve as the basic production model. Initially, the new equipment complement proved difficult to maintain and keep on-line. Therefore the Tu-142 equipped with the old target acquisition system was retained in production.

The new ASW system completed its pre-production test program during 1980 and the first three aircraft equipped with the *Korshun* unit entered the operational Soviet Navy inventory during November. Unlike the earlier Tu-142, the Tu-142MK was equipped with a magnetic anomaly detection unit. This was mounted at the top of the vertical tail to position it as far from other metal parts of the aircraft as possible. Additionally, the aircraft had the NPK-142M navigation system which provided automatic flight control inputs, a new communication system complement, and an improved electronic countermeasures suite.

Tu-142MK-E ('Bear'-F Mod. 3)

During the 1980s, eight Tu-142MKs were delivered to India and given the export designation of Tu-142MK-A. One of these aircraft later crashed while in Indian service.

The Tu-142MK-A differed from the standard Tu-142 in having a slightly less sophisticated equipment complement.

Tu-142M-Z ('Bear'-F Mod. 4)

The Tu-142 was updated several times during the course of its lengthy production run. One of these resulted in the Tu-142M-Z upgrade. This was the product of a more sophisticated ASW system and an improved electronic countermeasures suite. Additionally, the NK-12MV engines were replaced by the more powerful NK-12MP. An auxiliary TA-12 powerplant also was installed. The Tu-142M-Z entered production in the late 1980s.

In order to enhance the Tu-142M's ability to track down modern 'quiet' nuclear-powered submarines the Tupolev OKB began another upgrade program in the mid-1980s. The aircraft was fitted with the latest *Korshun*-KN-N STS, the two N's denoting the *Nashatyr'-Nefrit* (Ammonia/Jade) ASW complex; this included the *Zarechye* (a region of Moscow) sonar system. In addition to production RGB-IA and RGB-2 buoys associated with the *Berkut* STS the aircraft could carry RGB-16 and RGB-26 buoys associated with the *Nashatyr'-Nefrit* complex. The new version was designated Tu-142M-Z, the Z standing for *Zarechye*.

The additional equipment installed on the Tu-142M-Z doubled the aircraft's efficiency while reducing the expenditure of sonobuoys 1.5 times. The aircraft could detect submarines

Top three: **A Tu-142MK-E used by the Indian Navy. Nose close-up provides marking details.** Beriev Design Bureau

Bottom: **The prototype Tu-142MR prototype at Beriev's Taganrog facility.** Beriev Design Bureau

travelling at down to 800 m (2,624 ft) in rough seas of up to 5 points on the Beaufort scale.

The prototype, a converted Tu-142M, entered flight tests in 1985; state acceptance trials began in late 1987. In the course of the trials program the prototype searched for nuclear-powered submarines of the Soviet Navy's Northern and Pacific Fleets and showed excellent results as compared to production-standard aircraft. Soon the new model supplanted the Tu-142M on the Taganrog production line.

Deliveries began shortly afterwards, and the Tu-142M-Z became fully operational with the AV-MP in 1993. Besides an improved STS, the aircraft had a modified ECM suite and some changes to other systems.

The Tu-142M-Z was the last ASW aircraft based on the Tu-142 airframe. The last aircraft left the Taganrog plant in 1994, putting an end to the long production of the 'Bear' family.

Tu-142MZ-C

As part of the *konversiya* policy the Tupolev OKB and the Taganrog aircraft plant proposed using a handful of Tu-142M-Z aircraft operated by both enterprises as cargo aircraft. The aircraft's range enabled it to make non-stop cargo flights to any location in Russia (the CIS). The ASW equipment (sonobuoy racks etc.) would be removed to make room for a 17,004 kg (37,477 lb) payload; the MTOW would be 185,049 kg (407,848 lbs). The proposed cargo version was designated Tu-142MZ-C. (That is how it was spelt in Tupolev advertisements. Really, it should be Tu-142MZ-K for *kommercheskiy* - 'commercial', ie. cargo.)

Cruising speed is 740 km/h (462.5 mph), un-refuelled range is 9,150 km (5,718 miles) with a 7,002 kg (15,432 lb) fuel reserve. Cruising altitude is 7,800 to 10,600 m (25,590 to 36,190 ft), max endurance is 12.6 hrs. Takeoff run with full payload is 2,540 m (8,333 ft).

Tu-142MP

This designation surfaced when a Tu-142M was modified to test a new anti-submarine warfare suite. The modified aircraft became the one-off Tu-142MP.

Top: **The Tu-142MR prototype (left) and a standard production Tu-142 at Kipelovo Air Base.** Yefim Gordon

Second from top: **The Tu-142MR prototype seen at Kipelovo Air Base. Particularly noticeable in this shot is the non-production-standard nose and the different tail boom configuration.** Yefim Gordon

Third from top: **A standard production Tu-142MR showing off its distinctive thimble-type nose radome. It is seen at Kipelovo Air Base.** Yefim Gordon

Fourth from top: **Nose of a standard production Tu-142MR at Kipelovo Air Base.** Yefim Gordon

Bottom: **A production Tu-142MR taking off from Kipelovo Air Base.** Yefim Gordon collection

Tu-142MR ('Bear'-J)

The Taganrog design bureau, under the Beriev name and utilizing the talents of Chief Designer A K Konstantinov, developed a special communication/relay Tu-142 configuration referred to as the Tu-142MR. The ASW Tu-142MK was used as the basis for the new aircraft. Taganrog produced several production examples for use by Soviet Naval Aviation.

These aircraft differed from others in the series in having a trailing wire-type antenna system in place of the side-looking radar system. Additionally, a communication antenna was faired into the vertical fin tip in place of the magnetic anomaly detection unit found on the Tu-142MK.

The Tu-142MR served as a relay aircraft for submarine communication requirements.

The Tu-142MR prototype differed from production aircraft in having a simplified equipment fit in the nose and tail. Still, it served with the 76th Naval Aviation Regiment for quite a long time along with fully-equipped production aircraft, operating from Kipelovo air base.

Top: **The Tu-142LL on final approach. Noteworthy is the early three-axle main gear bogie configuration.** All Yefim Gordon collection

Left: **The Tu-142LL shortly after takeoff. Exhaust nozzle with plug assembly is noteworthy.**

Bottom left: **The Tu-142LL is now rarely used and has fallen into a state of disrepair.**

Bottom: **The Tu-142LL conducted many of its test flights from Zhukovsky.** Yefim Gordon

Tu-142LL

During the early 1970s, the first prototype Tu-142, No. 4200, was reconfigured as a flying laboratory for inflight testing of new turbojet engines. It replaced the older Tu-95LL. For this new assignment, all anti-submarine warfare gear and armament were removed and systems required for the engine test programs were installed following removal from the Tu-95LL.

The following engines were tested using the Tu-142LL: the NK-25 for the Tu-22M3, the RD36-51A for the Tu-144D, and the NK-32 for the Tu-160. The Tu-142LL was used until the mid-1980s at which time airframe fatigue life became an issue of considerable concern.

A second aircraft was modified for the flying laboratory role. This was the first Tu-142MK, No.4243. During 1990 this aircraft set several time-to-climb and altitude-in-horizontal-flight records for class.

Top and bottom: **The Tu-95M-5 prototype, probably at Zhukovsky during the course of its short-lived flight test program. Visible suspended from the bomb bay area is what appears to be a Kh-55 missile.**
Tupolev Design Bureau

Cruise Missile Carriers

The modification of American Boeing B-52s to carry the AGM-86 and the creation of the Rockwell B-1B with its stand-off missile capability encouraged the Soviet military and political leadership, as well as the military industrial complex, to introduce a fundamental change in its strategic bomber program.

As in the US, the Soviet Union elected to explore cruise missile options in a two-pronged effort. One was the decision to develop the Tupolev Tu-160 variable-sweep-wing intercontinental range supersonic bomber; the other was to develop an interim cruise missile carrier in the form of an updated and improved Tu-95.

Tu-142MS

During the 1970s, a cruise missile carrying version of the anti-submarine warfare Tu-142M (Tu-142MK), to be called Tu-142MS, was studied. It would be optimized to carry the Kh-55 long-range missile. The modernized aircraft would be equipped with two rotary-type launchers for carrying up to 12 MDB Raduga RKV-500A cruise missiles.

Difficulties in placing two launchers in a position that would permit acceptable c.g. limits led to a decision to equip the aircraft with a single launcher and 6 RKV-500As.

Tu-95M-55

During July of 1977 the Opyt factory (the number assigned during the mid-1960s was 156) was entrusted with the modification of the cruise missile aircraft at the Taganrog facility where the Tu-142MK were being built. The resulting aircraft would be Tu-95MSs. The flying laboratory to study the various options and systems associated with the RKV-500 program was designated Tu-95M-55. The Tu-95M-5 prototype was utilized for this testbed.

During the initial stage of the program, only a single launch pylon was installed and only one missile was capable of being carried. As work on the engineering side progressed, however, it was decided to create two options, one offering the single pylon, and a second offering a configuration that would permit the carriage and launching of two missiles.

Modification work by the Kuibyshev aviation factory on what became the Tu-95M-55 aircraft was completed during July of 1978. During the course of the reconfiguration, all electronic countermeasures and other miscellaneous gear was removed, and the reconfigured tail surfaces were returned to their original configuration. Equipment to accommodate the new missile launch system was installed as well, this including electro-hydraulic missile ejection system test instrumentation, and a new flight/navigation suite that was integrated with the new weaponry complex. The aircraft thus became a sophisticated multi-purpose laboratory with at least two options available for missile carriage and launch.

The Tu-95M-55 successfully completed its first flight on 31st July 1978. The test program that was initiated shortly thereafter continued for the following four years. During that time, many different Kh-55s were tested in both dummy and actual hardware form. The results of these tests proved instrumental in the final design both of the missile and the proposed production version of the Tu-95MS.

On 28th January 1982, the Tu-95M-55 crashed during the course of departing the LII airfield at Zhukovsky. Ten crew members, including pilot N E Kulchitsky, were killed.

Tu-142 In Service

On 15th August 1969, the Commander-in-Chief of the Northern Fleet Air Arm signed an order forming the 76th Independent Long-Range ASW Air Regiment based at Kipelovo. The unit was equipped with brand-new Tu-142s – early production aircraft with 12-wheel main gear bogies, which were promptly dubbed 'centipedes'. The 76th's first commander was military pilot (1st class; a measure of pilot proficiency) Lt. Col. Vladimir I Dubinskiy.

The unit's personnel embarked on a theoretical training course in March 1970. The greater part of the aircrews and ground personnel took their training in Nikolayev on the Black Sea. On 15th April 1970, Lt. Col. Dubinskiy's crew made their first solo flight in a Tu-142.

The unit's first two aircraft, Red 40 and Red 41, arrived at Kipelovo air base on 21st March and 25th March. On 5th June, Lt. Col. Dubinskiy flew the first training sortie from Kipelovo. On 7th July, Lt. Col. V A Shamanskiy's crew flew the first real ASW training sortie, with the unit's commander flying as instructor. Other crews began flying at the end of July, and night flights started in September.

1971 was a special year for ASW aviation - it was then that the Tu-142 became operational. On 27th July 1971, a pair of Tu-142s (Red 40 and Red 41) flown by the 76th ASW Air Regiment's commander Lt. Col. Dubinskiy and the 1st Sqn commander Lt. Col. Shamanskiy flew over the Sea of Norway for the first time; the 13 hr 50 min sortie was more of a sightseeing ride for familiarization purposes.

The unit's second squadron was formed in February 1972 under military pilot (lst class) Lt. Col. Igor' A Yefimov. On 6th April of the same year the 76th took part in its first Northern Fleet exercise.

Gradually the long-range naval aviation made its mark. Indeed, the success of certain search operations was wholly attributable to the participation of long-range ASW aircraft. One such mission involving the tracking down and shadowing of a foreign submarine which had intruded into Soviet waters took place in the Barents Sea on 19th/22nd August 1974. Four Tu-142s piloted by Maj. V N Morozov,

Maj. V I Pavlov, Maj. A A Karpinchik and Lt. Col. I A Yefimov participated in it, mainly for the sake of training. Maj. Morozov's crew kept tailing the submarine for 2 hr 55 min before passing it on to ASW ships. A month earlier, on 11th July, Maj. V N Bulgakov's crew completed a first-of-a-kind mission for the Soviet Navy, successfully launching an APR-1 anti-submarine missile from a Tu-142.

In April 1975 the 76th Independent Long-Range ASW Air Regiment took part in the *Okean*-75 (Ocean-75) naval exercise. During the exercise two crews captained by Maj. V N Gabalov and Maj. N S Ostapenko detected a 'hostile' submarine on 17th April and shadowed it for 1 hr 7 min before passing it on to another pair of Tu-142 piloted by Maj. V I Pavlov and Maj. A A Karpinchik who stayed on the submarine for another 3 hrs 16 min.

On 29th June 1976, seven of the unit's aircraft were detached to the Pacific Fleet to take part in Operation *Rezonans*, operating from Khorol' air base. They flew 14 sorties before returning home on 17th July.

On 20th September 1976, Lt. Col. V G Deyneka was appointed as the new commander of the 76th ASW Regiment (he later went on to become C-in-C of the Soviet naval aviation.). That year the unit logged a total of 2,156 flight hours, including 940 hrs of night flight and 387 hrs of combat sorties.

On 10th October 1977, five of the unit's aircraft were again detached to Khorol' air base, flying four sorties against US Navy submarines in the Philippine Sea. In one of these sorties, Lt. Col. Deyneka's crew located a submarine and followed it for 4 hrs 5 min. In 1976 the unit accumulated 3,000 hrs of flying time.

Top: **The Tu-95MS prototype following modification and updating that included an inflight refueling probe.** Tupolev Design Bureau

Second from top: **A Tu-95MS shortly after takeoff; landing gear are beginning their retraction sequence.** Yefim Gordon collection

Third from top: **Propeller blade pitch angle of Tu-95MS in cruising flight indicates low rpm.** DoD

Left: **Tu-95MS on final approach to landing. Noteworthy is external fairing for electrical connectors.** Victor Drushlyakov

Top: **A Tu-95MS on final approach to Barksdale AFB, Louisiana.** Tom Copeland

Bottom: **Two Tu-95MSs during the course of an exchange visit at Barksdale AFB, Louisiana during 1995.** Tom Copeland

In 1978, 76th ASW Regiment Tu-142s patrolled the Northeastern Atlantic, locating 13 western submarines. That same year the unit began conversion training to the Tu-142M.

On 20th February 1979, Maj. Pavlov's crew made the first solo flight on a Tu-142M (Tu-142MK), followed on 1st March by Lt. Col. V A Kibal'nik. On 14th April, Lt. Col. V V Groozin's crew scored another 'first' for the unit, dropping an AT-2 torpedo after pinpointing the target with the *Korshun*-K radar. Twelve days later Lt. Col. Kibal'nik's crew flew the first combat sortie in which the *Korshun*-K STS was used, locating a Western submarine and shadowing it for 1 hr 10 min. Initially Tu-142Ms used old sonobuoys associated with the *Berkut* STS.

TYPE:	Tu-142	Tu-142M (Tu-142MK)
Year of First Flight	1968	1975
Powerplant	4xNK-12MV	4xNK-12MV
Shaft Horsepower (per engine)	15,000	15,000
Number of Crew/Passengers	9	11
Wingspan m (ft)	50.04 (164.1)	50.04 (164.1)
Wing Area m^2 (ft^2)	283.7 (3,120.2)	289.9 (3,120.2)
Length m (ft)	49.6 (162.7) w/probe	53.20 (174.5) w/probe
Takeoff Weight kg (lb)	165,154 (364,000)	167,877 (370,000)
Fuel Weight kg (lb)	(?)	(?)
Bombs/Armament kg (lb)	9,800/16,334 (21,600/36,000)	(?)
Empty Weight kg (lb)	(?)	(?)
Payload kg (lb)	(?)	(?)
Maximum Speed km/h (mph)	(?)	855 (531)
Cruising speed km/h (mph)	735 (456)	735 (456)
Service Ceiling m (ft)	(?)	(?)
Range km (miles)	12,300 (7,638)	11,800 (7,328)
Range w/Single Refueling km (miles)	(?)	13,800 (8,570)
Combat Radius km (miles)	(?)	(?)
Combat Radius w/Single Refueling km (miles)	(?)	(?)
Takeoff Run m (ft)	2,380 (7,806)	2,350 (7,708)
Takeoff Weight kg (lb)	(?)	(?)
Landing Run m (ft)	(?)	(?)
Landing Weight kg (lb)	(?)	(?)
Defensive Armament	AM-23 (2x23mm)	AM-23 (2x23mm)

Above: **A Tu-95MS being refueled, probably from a Ilyushin Il-78. Centerline position of refueling boom greatly facilitates inflight refueling process.** Tupolev Design Bureau

Below: **A Tu-95MS in cruising flight.** Tupolev Design Bureau

In 1979 the unit's crews flew 64 combat sorties, spotting 10 western submarines and accumulating 2,900 hrs total time. Same year the unit made a joint effort with the 392nd Maritime Reconnaissance Regiment (also based at Kipelovo and flying the Tu-95RTs) to evaluate the chances of air defence penetration near the Faroe Islands and Iceland, considering that the potential adversary would employ Boeing E-3A AWACS aircraft. On 15th October Lt. Col. Groozin became the unit's new commander.

In March 1980, 76th ASW Regiment Tu-142Ms took part in Operation *Svet* (Light) mounted by the Northern Fleet, flying 10 sorties and detecting two western subs. Same year the unit participated in the *Atlantika*-80 exercise. Next year the unit, which by then had been completely re-equipped with Tu-142Ms, joined the ready alert forces within the Soviet armed forces structure.

In 1982 the unit flew 90 combat sorties, detecting 18 submarines and accumulating 4,520 hrs total time. Next year it took part in the *Razbeg*-83 ('Running Start') exercise; till the end of 1983 the 76th Regiment flew 93 combat sorties and detected 31 western submarine.

In 1984 it was 79 combat sorties, 19 detected submarines and 4.171 hrs total time. On 20th January a new technique was used for the first time in the Sea of Norway: the Tu-142Ms dropped RGB-55A sonobuoys and UPLAB-50 bombs to scare off unfriendly subs. Next year it was 64 combat sorties and 14 detected submarines; in 1986 it was 84 sorties and seven submarines.

When the 76th ASW Regiment switched to the Tu-142M, the obsolete Tu-142s (including the early 'centipedes') were transferred to the Far East. Pacific Fleet pilots flew them over the Pacific and South-East Asia. In 1982, a mixed naval air detachment was formed at Da Nang air base in Vietnam. Its inventory included four Pacific Fleet Tu-142s (tasked with hunting US Navy subs in the Philippine Sea) and three Mi-14PL ASW helicopters. This was by no means the first attempt to establish a Soviet military presence in SE Asia; Tu-142s specially detached to the Far East overflew that region as early as 1975. Living conditions at Da Nang were horrendous, but the numerous complaints of air and ground crews hardly ever brought about a change for the better.

Originally the aircraft dispatched to Vietnam were to make 40 combat sorties, but on reflection this was reduced to 10, giving the crews more time for training. Besides snooping about the Philippine Sea the Tu-142s inspected the Aleutian Islands from time to time.

The late '70s and '80s were characterized by an alarming trend: in spite of the agreements concerning military aircraft flights over international waters, NATO fighters were becoming increasingly aggressive when intercepting Soviet aircraft. The fighters would often use the Soviet aircraft as practice targets, 'painting' them with their powerful radars and disrupting the operation of navigation systems, which was a flagrant breach of generally accepted rules. Tu-142s were often intercepted off Iceland when en route to the Atlantic.

392nd ODRAP Tu-95RTs reconnaissance aircraft were detached to Cuba on a regular basis, starting in 1970; detachments to Angola and other friendly nations followed soon afterwards. Gradually the AV-MF top command decided that Tu-142M crews had to master transatlantic flights, especially considering the fact that the Tu-142M's navigation suite was far better than that of the Tu-95 RTs. And, starting in 1983, Tu-142Ms began to put in an appearance at Cuban air bases.

On 14th March 1983, a pair of Tu-142Ms landed in Havana after crossing the Atlantic Ocean. After a week's rest the crews set to work looking for submarines in the Sargasso Sea. Judging by crew reports, all 10 sorties flown on that occasion were successful; total mission time exceeded 11 hrs. RGB-75 infrasonic buoys

Right: **A Tu-95MS being statically refueled prior to flight.** Yefim Gordon collection

Below: **A Tu-95MS during test and training operations at Zhukovsky.** Tupolev Design Bureau

were used for primary search and RGB-55As for pinpointing the submarine's position.

The Tu-142M seemed to be growing increasingly more effective in the Atlantic (76th Regiment aircraft kept operating from Cuba throughout 1985) and the Sea of Norway. The mission success figures exceeded all reasonable estimates, so gradually the AV-MF command grew suspicious - and with good reason. The only possible explanation was that the crews either mistook some 'innocent' signals for submarines (which was quite possible, since the *Korshun-K* system was notorious for giving false alarms) or deliberately embellished their scores. The latter was also possible, since data recorders used for debriefing were rather inadequate at the time. Therefore, a series of test flights was made in 1984 and an upgrade plan was made for search & targeting systems and ASW equipment.

The late '80s saw a change in the Soviet political situation. From 1989 on, the WS and AV-MP were forced to cut the number of sorties due to jet fuel scarcity. This caused the AV-MP Headquarters to address the problem by requesting a reduction in planned sorties. Transatlantic flights to the San-Antonio air base on Cuba were stopped, but Tu-142s stationed at Da Nang remained there for some time yet.

In 1992 part of the 76th Regiment's personnel was dispatched to Dabolim air base (India) to help Indian Navy pilots master the recently supplied Tu-142MK-E aircraft.

Currently (1996) Col. Gen. V G Deyneka is C-in-C of the Russian naval aviation. He has accumulated a wealth of experience in his days as commander of the 76th Long-Range ASW Regiment operating Tu-142Ms. Other people actively involved in improving combat tactics were Col. V N Kantsendahl (the unit's chief navigator) and Lt. Col. G A Khramtsov, who went on to become chief of the Northern Fleet's tactical planning division. They contributed hugely to the development of new tactics of detecting and tracking submarines.

Tu-95MS ('Bear'-H)

The first prototype Tu-95MS was built at the Taganrog factory utilizing documentation prepared by MMZ Opyt (Tupolev's design bureau). Production Tu-142MK, No.42105, was the aircraft modified to the new standard. The modification was initiated during 1978 and completed during September of 1979. Among the most significant changes were a totally revised nose configuration to accommodate the new cockpit and miscellaneous new missile-optimized systems.

Besides the new cockpit, there was a new radar fairing that covered the unit that was considered primary to the new targeting and navigation system complex. A fuselage shortening resulted from the new installation, this being due in part to cg. considerations and the small size of the new equipment.

The rotary launcher unit was also installed in the aircraft's enormous bomb bay. Other new on-board equipment was installed alongside the radar package and new communications and electronic countermeasures suites were added as well.

The four NK-12MV engines were replaced with more powerful NK-12MP engines. These offering improved performance and the attributed of more powerful electrical generators providing direct current for onboard systems.

The aircraft crew complement was reduced to seven including a commander, an assistant to the commander, a navigator, a second navigator, an engineer, an operator of on-board systems, and a tail gunner).

The Tu-95MS prototype flew for the first time during September of 1979. Production was initiated at the Taganrog factory following two years of flight testing and modification.

During 1983, the Kuibyshev aviation factory took over Tu-95MS production. Accordingly, production of Tu-95MS at Taganrog was terminated.

The Tu-95MS was built in two basic versions: the Tu-95MS-6 with six RKV-500A missiles in the bomb bay; and the Tu-95MS-16 which was capable of carrying not only the six missiles in the bomb bay, but an additional twelve missiles on ejection racks under the wings (six on each side). Two racks, mounting three missiles were mounted at the wing root in close proximity to the fuselage and two more were mounted aft of those also in close proximity to the fuselage.

Eventually, as a result of the OSV-2 disarmament agreement with the US which limited the number of nuclear warheads to be carried by a single bomber, all underwing pylons for the RKV-500A missile were eventually removed from the Tu-95MS-16 series aircraft.

Tu-95MS was upgraded several times during the course of its production run. Systems were improved and new equipment was introduced. Most notable of these was the installation of a new tail turret design. The old AM-23 cannons were replaced by an installation equipped with two GSH-23s (giving a total of four 23mm guns). This was the same unit that had been developed for the Tu-22M2.

By the beginning of 1991, the Soviet Union's long-range bomber arm was equipped with 84 Tu-95MSs. Over the years since, this figure has declined due in part to the disintegration of the Soviet Union and the Ukraine's claim on some of the remaining aircraft.

Regardless, as these words are written, the Tu-95MS remains the primary striking arm of Russian Strategic Aviation. At the beginning of 1993, a single production Tu-95MS was reconfigured as the prototype Tu-95MA. The latter, an advanced version of the former, is configured to carry a new air-to-surface missile of undisclosed designation. Two missiles can be carried on large pylons under the wings. As of this writing, the program is on hold. The prototype has been completed and flight tested, but the missile program has run into financial and technical difficulties.

OPERATING AND COMBAT FUNCTIONS OF THE Tu-95

The Tu-95 first entered operational service as a strategic bomber during April of 1956. The operational division was based in Uzin in the Ukraine. The first regiment was under the command of Col. N N Haritonov (who, during 1958, later became chief test pilot for Tupolev). The next division to receive the Tu-95 was based in Semipalatinsk in Kazakhstan.

Flight crews and maintenance personnel quickly mastered the new bomber. Underscoring this rapid integration of the type into the operational inventory was the display of a group of Tu-95s participating in the traditional airshow at Tushino during 1956.

In fact, the first three Tu-95s had come on line with a fair number of problems. The initial production version of the NK-12 engine, for instance, was equipped only with a manual propeller feathering system...and this proved insufficient to accommodate an emergency that quickly led to the loss of one of the first three operational machines. On 24th November 1956, Tu-95, No.310, lost an engine as a result of a turbine core failure. Because of the crew's inability to feather the propellers on that engine in timely fashion, the aircraft lost speed, stalled, and crashed. All aboard were killed.

Partly as a result of the accident, an automated feathering system was rapidly developed. By the end of the decade, all Tu-95s were equipped with NK-12V engines which had an automated propeller feathering system. This proved a critical device for use in emergencies and the system is credited with the saving of many lives.

As it was, the massive reduction gearbox of the NK-12 required a very efficient lubrication system with a high level of efficiency. Due to the notoriously cold Russian winters and the generally cool climate of the country, frozen oil was not an uncommon occurrence. Special heating systems were required to keep the oil in a fluid state and the engine and ground support systems were designed to accommodate this.

This pre-heating requirement impacted the Tu-95's combat readiness. Often, some three to four hours were needed to accommodate the pre-heating process. At operational airfields that lacked proper heating equipment, the Tu-95s had to go through an engine run-up and warm-up every three to six hours (depending on air temperature) in order the keep the oil at a proper temperature. When engines were shut down they were covered with thermal-insulation blankets. Besides the waste of time and energy, such cycling of the engines led to maintenance problems of their own, and impacted the time-between-overhauls numbers which were already unpalatably low. The oil problem eventually was solved by the development of a new formula that remained functional down to a temperature of minus 25° C.

Despite the numerous difficulties related to keeping the Tu-95 airworthy, flight crew transitions proved relatively easy. By the end of the 1950s, two Long Range Aviation regiments were fully equipped with the bomber. Concurrently, Soviet Strategic Aviation began setting up operational airfields in tundra areas around the North Polar region. Such facilities placed the bombers within practical striking distance of strategic US targets. Accordingly, within the context of training to attack such targets, Tu-95/Tu-95M Kupol aircraft were operated from snow covered runways in the Krainiy North. The width of those runways was only slightly more than the aircraft's wingspan.

Low-altitude as well as high-altitude penetration of supposed enemy air defenses was refined using Tu-95/Tu-95Ms during the early 1960s. Flights of single bombers and formations were undertaken at altitudes that oftentimes did not exceed 700 ft (213 m).

The Tu-95/Tu-95Ms later were modified to accommodate tactical as well as nuclear scenarios. Reviewing events in such remote areas as the Middle East had led to the conclusion that a tactical capability was desirable.

Top: **A Tu-95MR prototype at the Taganrog facility.** Beriev Design Bureau

Left: **One of two Tu-95MSs during the noteworthy Barksdale AFB exchange visit. The Tu-95MS made an interesting comparison to the B-52Hs that were on hand.** Tom Copeland

Long-range Aviation commanders eventually concluded that the aircraft should be modified for the tactical mission and accordingly, a system permitting the transport of up to forty-five x 250 kg (551 lb) iron bombs was introduced. The mission in this configuration was to destroy enemy airfields and runways.

The Tu-95 and Tu-95MRs routinely flew reconnaissance missions over US Navy aircraft carrier fleet operations in the Atlantic Ocean. This was initiated in the early 1960s during the course of what later became known as the Cuban Missile Crises.

The reconnaissance mission usually was conducted with Tu-95s flying in pairs. One was often a Tu-95KD/Tu-95KM and one a Tu-95MR for the actual reconnaissance role. The missile carrier was used to locate the US fleet using its radar. After that, the Tu-95MR overflew the ships and took detail photographs.

During the 1970s and 1980s, the Tu-95MRs generally flew their reconnaissance missions independently. These flights gave Soviet military commanders fresh information concerning the movements of US Navy ships in the Atlantic. This information, when coupled with data being generated by the rapidly-developing Soviet space reconnaissance capability, provided a considerable amount of data for use by military planners.

Tu-95Ks entered the operational inventory during late 1959. One regiment from the division based in Uzina became the first to receive the aircraft. During the early 1960s, the Tu-95K was introduced into the heavy bomber regiment in Mozdok (North Caucasus). As a result, Soviet Long-range Aviation began the task of getting the missile carrying variants of the Tu-95 up to fully operational status. From January to October of 1962, nineteen Kh-20 missiles were launched from Tu-95Ks in this unit. Fifteen of these missiles effectively destroyed their theoretical targets. This was considered a good record in light of the fact the missile and its associated transport and targeting systems were still new and effectively untried. Later, the first-generation Tu-95K regiments had little difficulty upgrading to the improved Tu-95KD and Tu-95KM-series aircraft. The Tu-95K-22 went into service with these same units during the 1980s.

With the improvements in targeting permitted by the newer intercontinental ballistic missile generations, Strategic Aviation targets assigned to the missile-carrying Tu-95s were slowly transitioned almost entirely to the US carrier fleets and their allies in the Atlantic and Pacific. The Tu-95K-22 proved the most suitable platform for this mission as it was equipped with the advanced Kh-22 air-to-surface missile. The conventional – not nuclear – warhead of the Kh-22 with its shaped charge was capable of doing serious damage to conventionally built ship hulls, and tests indicated that holes as large as 12 m (39.36 ft) in diameter were possible.

During the 1980s, the upgrade process to the Tu-95MS allowed the Tu-95K-22s to be transferred to the Ukrainka airfield in Baikal. There, the aircraft replaced the ZM bomber fleet, which was ageing rapidly.

During November of 1993, the newspaper *Red Star* published an excerpt from a Russian Federation of Military Forces General Headquarters message that described a typical operational scenario for the Tu-95K-22 attacking US Navy ships. It is as follows:

'On 18th July 1993, units of the US Pacific Ocean Navy Force (San Francisco) formed an aviation carrier-based multi-purpose group (AMG) headed by the nuclear aircraft-carrier 'Lincoln' in order to replace the aircraft-carrier 'Nimitz' on combat duty in the Persian Gulf zone.

'The transfer of responsibility from one carrier to the other was done under the protective umbrella of optical and electronic camouflage and while under complete radio silence. In order to detect the location and configuration of the carrier group, the Commander of Russian Long-Range Aviation decided to undertake aerial reconnaissance via a group of four strategic Tu-95K-22 aircraft.

'Two pairs of missile-carriers took off from the Far East airfield on 28th July at 18:03 Greenwich Mean Time. The aircraft crossed Kurilskya ridge and in 5 hours and at a distance of 1,400 km (869 miles) from the shore line, radar signals from the fleet were intercepted. Turning towards this source, the bomber crews discovered they were 220 km (137 miles) from the fleet …which consisted of six ships. As they approached the fleet, the bomber crews noted that, at a distance of 3 km (1.86 miles), there were four ships in a tight formation. The carrier was 140 km (87 miles) behind.

'The bombers then set their course at 190o and reduced their speed to 120 knots. The first pair of missile-carriers descended to 500 m (1,640 ft) altitude and flew their photography passes across the fleet. A pair of F/A-18 fighters (each with two Sidewinder air-to-air missiles) were launched to intercept the bombers following their second pass. The fighters came within 200 to 300 m (656 to 984 ft) of the bombers within a few minutes of takeoff. Thirty minutes later, two more fighters came up from behind the bombers on the right. These approached to within 100 m (328 ft). During that time the second pair of Tu-95K-22s located their target. At the same time, they discovered and photographed a supply ship which was sailing separately from group.

'Thus the assignment concerning detection of this US combat fleet at sea was successfully accomplished.'

The Tu-95MS entered service with regiments of the Soviet Union's Long-Range Aviation branch during 1982. A unit based in Semipalatinsk was the first to receive the aircraft. It was officially declared to be operational at the end of 1982.

During 1985 the Long-Range Aviation unit in Uzina was re-equipped with the Tu-95MS and during 1987, a unit at Mozdok also was so equipped. Concurrent with delivery of the type to these units they were perfecting the launching of the Kh-55MS missile, and coming to grips with inflight refueling technique.

During 1986, the Tu-95MS demonstrated its capabilities and the level of crew readiness that had been achieved to that point. Aircraft of the Uzin regiment, utilizing inflight refueling, flew around the perimeter of the Soviet Union. Integral to this mission, aircraft from Semipalatinsk flew from their home base, across the North Pole, and on to the Canadian border. These missions verified the Tu-95MS's ability to deliver weapons over intercontinental ranges.

The Russian Navy's initial version of the aircraft, given the identifier Tu-95RTs, became well known to US observers as a result of the many overflights of US Navy fleets during the Cold War era. Photographs of these large turboprops often were published in the western press. The aircraft eventually acquired the nickname Eastern Express as a result of the fact they were seen so often shadowing US Navy fleets.

Tu-95RTs were based on the northern edge of central Russia in the areas around Vologna and the Far East. During the 1970s and 1980s,

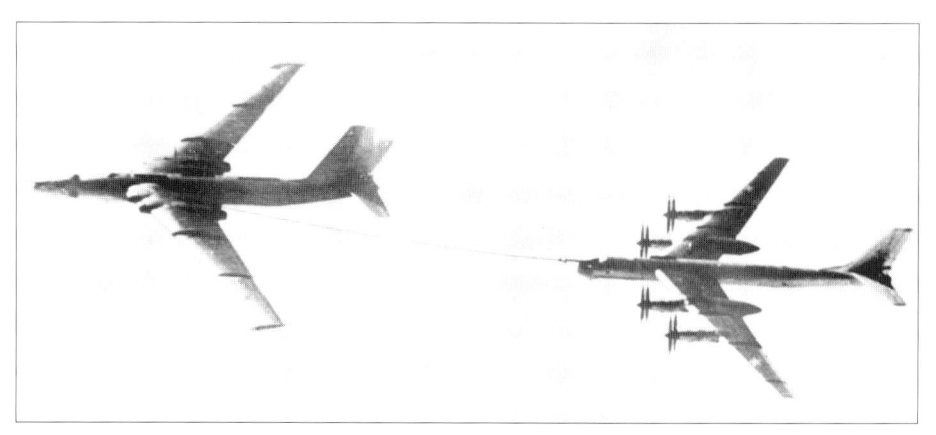

Right: **A Myasischev 3MS-2 refuels a Tu-95MS during tests. At one time these aircraft both were contending for the right to be Russia's future heavy bomber. The Tu-95, though less advanced, won out over its turbojet rival.** Yefim Gordon collection

Top: **A production Tu-114 following landing at New York's Idlewild Airport during a state visit to the US.** David Anderton collection

Left: **The prototype Tu-114 in front of the yet-to-be-finished TWA hangar at Idlewild Airport. Idlewild later would be renamed Kennedy International. A Bristol Britannia of Aeronaves de Mexico is in the foreground. The occasion for the visit was Premier N Khruschev's 1959 visit to the US.** Pete Bulban

Below: **The prototype Tu-114 upon arrival at Idlewild.** Pete Bulban

Bottom: **The prototype Tu-114 during flight testing at Zhukovsky.** Tupolev Design Bureau

these aircraft constantly flew mission from the Far East to Vietnam, operating into the former American military base at Da Nang. This facility accommodated basing requirements during the course of patrols in and around Southeast Asia.

Tu-95RTs remained on inventory until the beginning of 1991... at which time 37 aircraft were still operational. Active use had continued until the end of the 1980s, but this tapered off following the collapse of the Soviet Union several years later.

The Tu-142 in its various configurations was utilized by the Soviet Navy's aviation branch with the same intensity seen in the Tu-95RTs program. These aircraft, like the Tu-95RCs, operated constantly throughout the 1970s and 1980s from bases that oftentimes were outside Russian borders. Facilities in Angola, for instance, served as temporary bases for aircraft in need of fuel.

Interestingly, beginning in the early 1990s, the number and intensity of flights undertaken by the Tu-142 and Tu-95RTs fleets decreased significantly due to a shortage of fuel.

Until the actual collapse of the Soviet government, 147 Tu-95 bombers, missile carriers, and other variants were positioned at Aviation Industry Ministry airfields and attached to Long Range Aviation units. Of this number, 84 were Tu-95MSs, 63 were Tu-95Ks and Tu-95K-22s, and 11 were Tu-95Us. These aircraft were distributed as follows: in Uzina there were 21 Tu-95MS-16s, 1 Tu-95M, and 1 Tu-95K; in Mozdok there were 22 Tu-95MS-16s; in Semipalatinsk there were 27 Tu-95MS-6s and 13 Tu-95MS-16s; in Ukrainka there were 15 Tu-95Ks and 46 Tu-95K-22s; at the Kuibyshev factory's airfield there was 1 Tu-95MS-16; and at the training center for Long Range Aviation in Ryazan there were 11 Tu-95Us and Tu-95KUs. Additionally, there were some unidentified aircraft at the flight test facility at Zhukovsky.

Following the collapse of the Soviet Union, the disposition of the Russian strategic aviation inventory changed. Regiments in Uzina and Semipalatinsk remained out of country. Most of the Tu-95K-22 and Tu-95MS remained under the control of the Russian military and political powers in post-collapse Russia.

During 1993, a review of the status of Russian military aviation confirmed that most of the aircraft under Russian control were still in reasonably good condition. Renewed emphasis on training was underscored all over the country. Missions were flown to western borders and to the shores of the Pacific Ocean. Tu-160s and Tu-95MSs took part in the 1993 exercise, along with other front-line aviation aircraft. Later, Tu-160s and Tu-95MSs were transferred to operational airfields positioned many thousands of miles/kilometers from their normal home bases. During the course of the flights from home bases to their new assignments, the aircraft were repeatedly refueled by Ilyushin IL-78/IL-78M tankers. It later was determined the Tu-95 and Tu-142s were very dependable and suffered from only minor problems.

During the course of the 1993 training exercise, there were incidents that in retrospect only underscored the dependability of the big turboprop bombers. In one instance, a bomber collided with a ZMS-2 tanker and its vertical tail was severely damaged. This aircraft returned to base without further problems. During another refueling flight, a tanker's drogue assembly was accidentally lowered into the propellers of a Tu-95. Despite the fact that all eight blades on one engine were severely damaged (up to 40% of the blade length of select blades was severed) and the blades could not be feathered, this aircraft, too, returned to base safely.

In yet another incident, a bomber was hit by a lightning strike. The blast was severe enough to destroy a substantial part of the vertical fin and most of the electrical equipment on board, but the aircraft was also able to return to base without further difficulty.

Unfortunately, though flight crews had a great affection for the big Tupolev turboprops, they also were known to harbor some serious concerns about their safety. Some of the failings that were often mentioned included the absence of ejection seats for all crew members; the lack of a centralized ground refueling system; and the difficulty in taxiing the aircraft during ground operations.

On the positive side, the pilots were particularly fond of the ability to utilize the Tu-95's massive propellers in reverse pitch following landing. This shortened, by a considerable margin, the roll-out, and eliminated any need for a drag chute. Cases of over-run following landing were extremely rare.

CIVIL Tu-95 VERSIONS

The possibilities presented by a commercial version of the Tu-95 were not unfamiliar to Tupolev as the design evolved during the early 1950s. With its intercontinental range and large payload, it appeared to be an ideal candidate for a long-range passenger transport.

Eventually, the '114' design began to come together at Tupolev's facility near down-town Moscow. Similar in scope to the conversion of the Tu-16 jet bomber into the Tu-104 jet transport, the '114' evolved as a design variation of the bureau's new turboprop bomber.

Though on the surface making sense, the conversion of the Tu-95 to the '114' did have its detractions. Considerable money and effort could be saved by utilizing the basic wings, landing gear, engines, and horizontal and vertical stabilizers, but it was apparent there would be limitations to the expediency of using the bomber's slim fuselage and dense systems integration philosophy. Thus, a decision was made to design and manufacture an entirely new fuselage and mate it to the most usable parts of the bomber.

Tu-114 ('Cleat')

Work on what was to become the first civil version of the Tu-95 was initiated during 1955. One of the first major decisions, other than to create an entirely new fuselage, was to make the aircraft a low-wing - rather than mid-wing - design (as seen on the Tu-95). Accordingly, a new center section was developed as part of the new fuselage. The latter was a totally new configuration. Its diameter was increased dramatically, it was fully pressurized, and accommodations were provided for bathrooms and kitchens. Additionally, a new nose landing gear had to be developed and the nose gear well redesigned to accommodate it. The wing, horizontal and vertical tail surfaces, main landing gear, and engine packages all were retained in essentially

Right: **The prototype Tu-114 taxies in to off-load Khruschev at Idlewild.** Pete Bulban

Top: **A Tu-114 at Idlewild. The type was only rarely seen in the US.** Pete Bulban

Left: **A production Tu-114 shortly after takeoff. Aeroflot markings varied little from aircraft to aircraft.** Pete Bulban

Left below: **The prototype Tu-114 as it sits today at the famous Russian Air Force Museum at Monino outside Moscow.** Jay Miller

unchanged condition. In the cockpit, virtually all of the basic systems and instrumentation were the same as those found in the bomber...the only difference being the frequencies available on the radios; more emphasis was placed on commercial communication and less on military.

On 12th August 1955, the USSR Council of Ministers officially approved the documentation clearing the way for Tupolev and factory No.18 to begin development of aircraft '114' based on the Tu-95 bomber. It was to be completed and available for flight testing during the second quarter of 1957.

The new transport would have the following characteristics:

- maximum speed at an altitude of 7000 to 8000 m (22,960 to 26,240 ft) - 850 to 950 km/h (528 to 590 mph)
- cruise speed at an altitude of 10,000 to 12,000 m (32,800 to 39,360 ft) - 750 to 800 km/h (466 to 497 mph)
- takeoff run 1,400 to 1,500 m (4,592 to 4,920 ft)
- landing run 1,400 to 1,500 m (4,592 to 4,920 ft)
- maximum commercial payload weight - 27,223 kg (60,000 lb)
- maximum number of passenger seats - 170 to 180
- aircrew and flight attendants - 7 to 8
- operational range with max. commercial payload (w/one hour fuel reserve) - 3,500 to 4,000 km (2,174 to 2,484 miles)
- operational range with 13,612 to 13,838 kg (30,000 to 30,500 lb) payload (100 to120 passengers) - 7,500 to 8,000 km (4,658 to 4,968 miles)

The Council of Ministers resolution dictated that three prototypes of the new commercial transport be manufactured. The first of these would be built at Tupolev's factory in Moscow, and the second and third aircraft would be built at factory No.18 in Kuibyshev. Flight testing of the latter two was to be initiated during the third and fourth quarters, respectively, of 1957.

An engineering team under the direction of B M Kondorsky handled '114' preliminary design. As originally proposed, the new transport had a fuselage diameter of 4.6 m (15 ft), a wingspan of 52.25 m (171.4 ft), and a length of 54.85 m (179.9 ft). This was considerably larger than the original Tu-95 bomber.

The '114' was first designed as a double deck aircraft with upper and lower compartments. Both decks, along with the cockpit, were to be pressurized. The upper deck front cabin would accommodate 36 passenger seats behind the six-seat cockpit. Immediately aft of the front cabin were the toilets. Behind these were eight cabins configured to accommodate 24 sleeping bunks or 48 seats each. A middle cabin was positioned aft of that and equipped with 24 seats. The rear cabin was equipped with 50 seats. The upper deck also had several toilets. The lower deck accommodated the two galley/pantries, the baggage compartments, and the cargo holds.

Passengers entered the aircraft through two entries in the lower part of the fuselage by using extendible stairways which retracted into the bottom deck after boarding. It was possible, if necessary, for a passenger to change clothes in the lower deck area, check-in baggage, and then retire to a seat in the upper deck. Such comfort - afforded passengers as a result of the aircraft's extraordinary roominess - would not be realized again until the advent, two decades later, of such 'heavy' commercial transports as the Boeing 747 and the Airbus Industries A300.

Optimum configuration of the '114' had been determined by Tupolev's engineering staff to be a passenger cabin capable of seating up to 200 passengers in rows of 8 seats. Historically, this would set precedent for the entire family of wide-body transports that would not be developed until many years later.

Expeditious development of the '114' – dictated by a two year limit on the time needed to build a prototype as demanded by the Government resolution, curtailed actual development of the aircraft as a true wide-body transport. In fact, many of the afore-mentioned innovations and dimension issues eventually were set aside in order to meet the government's deadline. Accordingly, fuselage diameter was reduced to 4.2m (13.78ft), wingspan was reduced to 51.1m (167.6ft), and length was reduced to 53m (173.8ft). In this configuration, passenger entry was considerably more conventional, with doors positioned in their usual places on the fuselage sides. Only cargo was accommodated in the lower deck and only the kitchen/pantry area remained pressurized. Food prepared in this compartment was delivered to the upper deck via a special elevator.

Eventually it was decided to offer the '114', also now being referred to officially as the Tu-114 (all later Tupolev transports would utilize the number 4 as the last digit in the designation), in three versions.

The first of these, referred to as the basic version, was equipped with 170 seats or could accommodate a commercial load of 27,223kg (60,000lb). This configuration was optimized for routes such as Moscow-Khabarovsk or Moscow-Vladivostok. The second version was equipped with 120 seats and was optimized for non-stop intercontinental flights. The third configuration was referred to as the tourist version. It was equipped with 220 seats and was optimized for the relatively short flights such as Moscow-Sochi. Four compartments with three sleeping berths in each were stipulated for aircraft utilized on long-range routes.

The first Tu-114 (registered USSR-L5611), named Russia, was completed by Tupolev at their Moscow facility during mid-1957. The aircraft was transported to Zhukovsky and on 15th November, with test pilot A P Yakimov at the controls, successfully completed its first flight.

A year later, during late 1958, the first production Tu-114 was completed at factory No. 18 in Kuibyshev. Flight testing, in the hands of test pilot I M Suhomlinsky (highly experienced as a Tu-95 test pilot…and with considerable time at the controls of the first Tu-95s) progressed rapidly. Test-pilots V Dobrovolsky, I K Vedernikov, test-navigator K I Malhasyan, and many other Aviation Industry Ministry, Air Force, and GVF test pilots also participated in the flight test program.

An extensive flight test program spanning three years was undertaken. Finally, during July of 1960, official government trials were completed and the aircraft was cleared for preliminary commercial operation. Exploratory commercial flights were conducted between October of 1960 and March of 1961. On 24th April 1961, the first passenger flight, over the Aeroflot route between Moscow and Khabarovsk, was successfully flown.

During 1959, factory No.18 moved into full-scale production of the Tu-114. A total of 31 production aircraft eventually were completed (excluding the Tupolev-built prototype) over a period spanning from 1956 through 1964. Deliveries during those years were divided as follows: 1958, 2 aircraft; 1959, 6 aircraft, 1960, 3 aircraft, 1961, 6 aircraft, 1962, 6 aircraft, 1963, 4 aircraft, and 1964, 4 aircraft.

Both 170-seat and 200-seat versions of the Tu-114 were manufactured. The 170-seat configuration had 41 seats in the front compartment, 48 seats in the middle, 16 separate rows with three seats, then 24 seats (or 12 sleeping places), and finally 54 seats in the compartment farthest aft. The 200-seat aircraft were designed for in-country routes. The front passenger compartment was equipped with 47 seats, the middle passenger compartment had 60 seats, an interim aft compartment had 19 separate rows with three seats, and the rear passenger compartment had 49 seats.

The Tu-114 was successfully and regularly utilized on Aeroflot routes until 1976. It proved itself to be an exceptionally economical aircraft to operate on non-stop, long-range routes. Fuel consumption was 0.034kg (0.015lb) per passenger/kilometer (mile).

Tu-114s flew approximately 50,000 flights and carried approximately 6 million passengers during the course of the fifteen years they were in service. Only one Tu-114 was lost during the course of commercial operations (a takeoff accident occurred during February of 1966 at Moscow's Sheremetyevo airport).

Availability of the Tu-114 coupled with its exceptional range and payload capabilities for the first time permitted Russian commercial aviation to explore the options of international air service to virtually any spot on the globe.

During 1959, a Tu-114 was utilized to fly then-Soviet Premier Nikita S. Khrushchev to the US. The lengthy flight and the rarely-seen-in-the-west Tu-114 gave Khrushchev a grand and memorable arrival at what then was referred to as Idlewild Airport in New York.

On 10th July 1962, an exploratory route proving flight was flown from Russia to Havana, Cuba with an intermediate landing in Conakry. This flight pioneered the way for regular Cuban Tu-114 visits via the North Atlantic and an intermediate landing at Olenya airfield not far from Murmansk.

Further commercial operations were initiated on 19th August 1966, when Aeroflot began flying Tu-114s from Moscow to Tokyo, Japan on a regular basis. Two months later, similar connections were opened between Moscow and Montreal, Quebec, Canada.

The last production Tu-114s differed somewhat from their predecessors in being fitted with new and improved navigation equipment. Most notable of the changes involved the installation of *Course*-MP and *Way*-4 navigation devices. The second-to-last aircraft (Tu-114, No.471, registration USSR-76490) was completed during 1964.

Later all earlier Tu-114s were modified and upgraded via the installation of improved avionics at the GFB repair facilities.

Some production Tu-114s were delivered with 200-seat passenger cabins. By the end of the 1960s and early 1970s, almost all Tu-114s had been modified or delivered to this standard. These aircraft were known as Tu-114-200s.

During 1962, further modifications included the addition of fuel tanks under the passenger cabin area. These aircraft became Tu-114Ds and primarily were used over the long routes to Cuba. Fuel weight of these aircraft was 76,225kg (168,000lb). Because of the increase in fuel, passenger payload was significantly reduced.

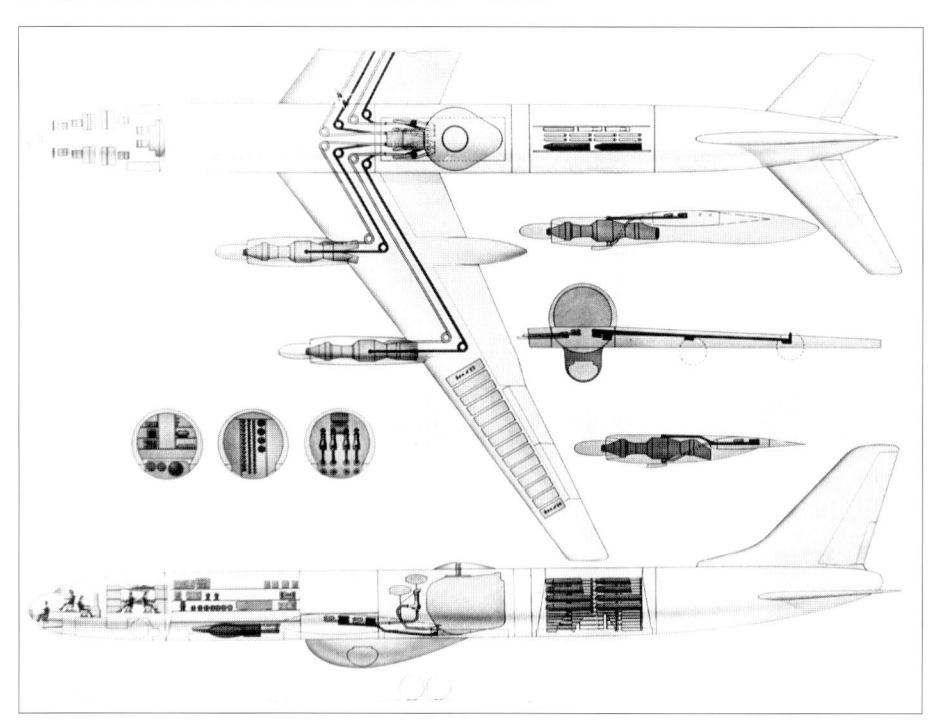

Right: **Nuclear engine testbed based on the Tu-114. The engines are experimental NK-14As (for Atomic).** Yefim Gordon collection

Left: **The prototype Tu-116 (also referred to simply as the '116') VIP transport.** Tupolev Design Bureau

Bottom: **The second Tu-116. These aircraft were equipped with special interiors and a comfort level far higher than anything seen by the average Russian during the course of his or her lifetime.** Tupolev Design Bureau

During the 1970s, fatigue cracks were discovered in structural components of some Tu-114s. As a result, the USSR Council of Ministers issued a resolution forcing the removal of the Tu-114 from operational service.

CIVIL AIRCRAFT PROJECTS UTILIZING THE Tu-114

A passenger airliner based on a Tu-114 with a redesigned wing that included a new airfoil section and improved high-lift devices such as slats and two-slotted flaps was offered to Aeroflot with the promise that range would be dramatically increased. Known as the Tu-114A, it had a wing with fixed torsion boxes for improved strength and rigidity and reduced weight. In its intercontinental form, it would have seated 98 to 102 passengers.

Engineering work on the Tu-114A was undertaken during 1963 and 1964, but no prototype was built. The program died when it was realized that Tu-114 production was soon to come to an end.

Another study during the 1960s proposed upgrading the standard Tu-114 via installation of new NK-8 turbojet engines. Six of these, suspended from pylons under the wings, would be required to propel the Tu-114. Estimated take-off weight of the proposed all-jet version would be increased to 172,958 kg (381,200 lb). Empty weight would be increased to 80,309 kg (177,000 lb) and fuel weight would be increased 81,942 kg (180,600 lb). Cruising speed was estimated to be 950 km/h (590 mph). With 100 passengers, operational range was estimated to be from 7,850 to 8,450 km4 (,875 to 5,247 miles).

The advent of the Ilyushin Il-62 and its successful Il-62M production version eventually ended any possibility the all-jet Tu-114 would be built.

Tu-116

At approximately the same time Tupolev received confirmation that it should undertake the design and development of the Tu-114, it received an order to modify two production Tu-95 bombers into high-speed passenger transports. These unique aircraft were to be optimized to serve as VIP transports for Soviet government officials and statesmen. They were to be designed to accommodate escort and security personnel as well and the interior appointments were to be deluxe in every way so that long-distance missions would not be fatiguing to the passengers.

The need for these aircraft had surfaced when it became apparent political tensions between the east and west might be easing. Existing Soviet VIP transports, including a small fleet of Ilyushin Il-14s, were out-moded and in need of a respectable replacement.

Though the Tu-114 was expected to be suitable for the VIP mission, its design, development, and flight test programs were predicted to take longer than the Soviet government was willing to wait. Tupolev was ordered to take two stock Tu-95s and modify them to meet the high-priority requirement. The '116' later would become known to the public as the Tu-114D, though in this case, the designation implied 'diplomatic', rather than 'long-range'.

On 12th August 1955, the USSR Council of Ministers released its order to Tupolev calling for the construction of the '116' aircraft. Actual modification was to take place at venerable factory No.18. The aircraft, when completed would be capable of carrying up to 20 passengers in comfortable conditions over routes spanning from 7,500 to 8,000 km (4,658 to 4,968 miles).

Flight testing initially was scheduled to get underway during September of 1956, but on 28th March, that date was revised to a later one in lieu of the fact Tupolev was being hard-pressed to meet its various military commitments. The required engineering drawings were not completed until April of 1956 and final approval was not granted by the Air Force until the following October.

When the modification program for the '116' was finally given a go-ahead, the aircraft was reconfigured to carry as many as 24 passengers and up to 400 kg (882 lb) of baggage. The list of support personnel for each flight included: a flight attendant, a cook, and a navigator-information officer who would provide relevant information to members of the government delegation during the flight. If the delegation was headed by a government person of high rank, ten to twelve armed guards would be part of the entourage.

The primary difference between the Tu-95 and the Tu-116 was the installation of the special pressurized passenger compartment in the area normally occupied by the bomb bay. The compartment had a displacement of 70.5 m^3 (2,489.6 ft^3) and was equipped with a limited number of windows for outside observation.

All defensive and bombing equipment normally found on the Tu-95 was removed. And from the forward end of the cargo compartment to the end of the second pressurized cabin everything was replaced by the new passenger cabins, a restroom, a wardrobe compartment, and an office.

The first passenger cabin was designed to accommodate from six to eight people; the second was designed to accommodate a 'senior passenger' and could comfortably seat three. Each cabin was equipped with couches and sofas. Interior design and quality was typical of that afforded only the upper echelons of Soviet government. The pressurized cabin had an entrance door at one end which exited into a vestibule. In turn, a stairway descended through a ventral hatch in the fuselage. This exit/entryway could be used for emergency egress if necessary. At the far end of the fuselage, in the empennage, flares and personnel parachutes were stored for emergency use.

The basic crew complement was the same as that for the Tu-95. It consisted of two pilots, a pilot-navigator, a navigation equipment operator, a flight engineer, a flight technician, and a radio-operator. An additional navigator, specializing in intercontinental missions, also was carried when necessary.

The Tu-116s also carried additional quantities of oil and hydraulic fluid in special tanks just aft of the pressurized cockpit. These were provided in consideration of the fact the NK-12 turboprop engines had high oil consumption rates and Tu-95 hydraulic system leaks were notoriously commonplace.

Fuel capacity of the Tu-116 was approximately 77,800 litres (20,539 gal), carried in 66 flexible rubber tanks. Maximum range was estimated to be up to 11,190 km (6,949 miles).

The Tu-116 was equipped with the most modern avionics then available in Russia. Included were a *Gelyi* short wave radio transmitter with an RPS receiver; a 1-RSB-70M radio station with a US receiver; three RSIU-4P radio station sets; two ARK-5 automatic radio compasses; PV-17 and RV-2 radio altimeters; and an SP-50 *Materik* blind landing system. Additionally, the *Rubidy*-MM 'panoramic radar' from the Tu-95 was retained. The passenger cabin had a *Mir* radio-phonograph system for entertainment. Communication with the crew was via a pneumatic mail system. In case of an emergency water landing, LAS-5 rescue boats and two SP-12 rafts were provided.

The first Tu-116, No.7801, underwent factory testing from 23rd April to 4th October of 1957. The second aircraft, No.7802 (completed on 3rd June 1957), was turned over for government testing during March of 1958. These static tests were effectively completed during late February, and finally, on 2nd March, the first Tu-116 became airborne for the first time, flying from Chkalovskoe to the GK-NII-VVS facility of the Air Force for further tests. These were conducted by a crew consisting of test-pilots V K Bobrikov and V S Kipelkin; test-navigators N S Zacepa and V S Pasportnikov; and radio-operator V S Popov. Test-pilot I K Vedernikov also participated. He later undertook many initial test flights of Tu-95 and Tu-142 production aircraft.

During the government test program, the Tu-116 flew a number of long-range test flights, including one over the Chkalovskoe-Irkutsk-Chkalovskoe route. This covered a total distance of 8,600 km (5,341 miles). Fuel remaining in the tanks following the flight indicated that another 1,500 to 2,999 km (932 to 1,862 miles) could have been flown. The average speed during the flight was 800 km/h (497 mph). Other routes flown included: Chkalovskoe-Vozdvigenka (Vladivostok)-Chkalovskoe; Chkalovskoe-Dikson-Cape Taigonos-Ukrainka; Chkalovskoe-Petropavlovsk-Kamchatsky-Tashkent;Tashkent-Dushanbe-Phrunze-Dikson-Velikie Luki-Chkalovskoe; and Chkalovskoe-Leningrad-Tallinn-Riga-Vilnius-Minsk-Kiev-Tbilisi-Erevan-Baku-Ashgabad-Rostov-on-Don-Chkalovsko. During one of these flights which required three intermediate stops for fuel, the total route distance (following the Soviet Union's border perimeter) reached 34,000 km (21,114 miles).

Special markings were provided for this aircraft. All military markings, such as the standard red stars, were removed and replaced with Aeroflot markings and the civil registration, USSR-76462.

Concurrent with the tests being flown using 76463, test pilot N N Haritonov (the last commander of a Tu-95 regiment) piloted Tu-116 No. 7801 on a non-stop flight covering the Moscow-Baikal Lake-Moscow route. His average speed was an impressive 740 km/h (460 mph). These ultra-long-range flights quickly verified the Tu-116 could accommodate the role for which it was intended.

Somewhat surprisingly, the Tu-116s were not to be utilized for their intended purpose as special government VIP transports. As they had been developed from Tu-95/Tu-95Ms equipped with the older NK-12 and NK-12M engines, the Tu-116s were not equipped with automatic feathering systems. When a similarly configured Tu-95 (No.310) crashed fatally on 24th December in Engels, government officials elected to curtail use of the Tu-116s until a fix was created. This in fact took place during the late 1950s, but by then, the Tu-114 had begun to enter operational service. As the Tu-114 was a much more commodious aircraft and was

Top: **Both Tu-116s were equipped with a special fold-down stairway on ventrally positoned in the aft part of the fuselage.** Tupolev Design Bureau

Right: **The second Tu-116 at takeoff. Markings of both Tu-116s were relatively colorful when compared to their bomber siblings.**
Yefim Gordon collection

Left: **The Tu-116s were exceptionally well suited for the high-speed VIP transport role.**
Tupolev Design Bureau

Below: **Unlike their bomber counterparts, the Tu-116s were equipped with fuselage windows for outside viewing by the passengers.**
Yefim Gordon

considered much more suitable for the VIP transport role, the Tu-116s languished without any legitimate mission.

Following government testing, the two Tu-116s were turned over to the Air Force which used them for transportation of high-ranking military personnel. They served in that role into the early 1990s. Today, Tu-116, No.7801, is at the Uzina air base in the Ukraine. Tu-116, No. 7802, based at the airfield in Semipalatinsk, was used for special transportation until April of 1991. It later was phased out of the operational inventory and cannibalized for parts.

It should be mentioned that two production Tu-95s, No.402 and No.409, also were converted to the Tu-116 configuration and used by high-ranking military personnel.

COMBAT AIRCRAFT DEVELOPED FROM THE Tu-114
Tu-115

While work got underway on the Tu-114, Tupolev also began studying a military transport version for the carriage of military equipment and crews. This configuration was referred to as the '115' and later was known as the Tu-115.

Unlike the Tu-114, the Tu-115 had an unpressurized cargo cabin. The revised aft section of the fuselage also was provided with a fold-down ramp which was designed to accommodate the loading of military payloads and personnel. At the very aft section of the empennage, an armed turret was installed for protection against attack from the rear. This unit was equipped with dual AM-3 cannons and a KRS-1 sighting radar.

Troops were transported in a pressurized compartment placed just aft of the cockpit. Total payload capacity was 36,298 kg (80,000 lb). The displacement of cargo and personnel could be carried in the following combinations:

- 4 x ZIS – 151 cars and 38 personnel
- 5 x GAZ – 63 cars and 38 personnel
- 13 x GAZ – 69 cars and 38 personnel
- 1 x T – 54 tank and 38 personnel
- 1 x 152 mm cannon and 1 AT-S tractor

Because the original Tu-114 configuration with the 4.6 m (15 ft) fuselage diameter was not pursued, all work on the proposed Tu-115 eventually ended and the project failed to reach the hardware stage.

Tu-114T

During 1963, Tupolev prepared a proposal calling for the modification of production Tu-114s into Tu-114T transports (also assigned the '115' designator). These aircraft would have their passenger cabins converted to cargo space and the lower deck area modified to accommodate heavy military equipment.

In addition to a hinged loading ramp/stairway positioned ventrally aft of the wing, the Tu-114T's aft fuselage also was hinged so that it could open completely for the loading of oversized cargo. Other modifications included wing slats and double-slotted flaps for improved landing and takeoff performance.

Work on the Tu-114T was stopped when the Antonov Design Bureau unveiled the An-22 'Anteus' heavy transport.

Concurrent with the work on the Tu-114T and Tu-115, Tupolev also had begun development of a dedicated transport/ambulance modification to accommodate staff officers and wounded personnel. This configuration was given the designation Tu-114TS. The first version, to carry troops, had pressurized upper and lower decks and could haul as many as 297 fully-equipped soldiers. The second version, optimized for the ambulance role, was designed to accommodate from 74 to 110 litters or could accommodate up to 184 injured personnel in the sitting position. Additionally, it could accommodate a medical staff of 15.

This project also failed to come to fruition and died on the drawing board. Somewhat ironically, at a later date, virtually all Soviet commercial and military transports were equipped with devices and systems that would permit their conversion to the ambulance mission in time of war or national emergency. Still later, during 1968, all Aeroflot aircraft had the conversion equipment removed in consideration of its impact on operating efficiency.

Tu-114PLO

The advent of practical nuclear propulsion systems for ocean-going ships and submarines, during the early 1950s, led to a strong interest in the potential of nuclear propulsion for aircraft. In particular, nuclear-powered long range patrol aircraft optimized for such things as anti-submarine warfare (PLO) and long-range bombing missions made nuclear power very appealing.

A nuclear-powered patrol aircraft was studied in Russia as late as 1975 (following the completion of the successful '119' aircraft program) with the intent that an operational version would be available by the early 1980s. This PLO aircraft would be based on the Tu-114 and powered by four NK-14A engines and a reactor providing 120,000 kV of energy. It was proposed that the NK-14As would work as conventional turboprop engines during takeoff and landing, but then would cruise using heat energy generated by the reactor.

The nuclear-powered Tu-114 would have generally been similar to early Tu-142s. The search radar was to have been ventrally positioned at mid-fuselage. The nuclear reactor(s) would have been positioned aft of the radar bay. The armament bay would have been positioned aft of the reactor(s). There were thirteen crew members in the pressurized forward cockpit and crew compartments. A radiation barrier and miscellaneous equipment would have been placed between the cockpit and the reactor bay.

Gross takeoff weight of the nuclear-powered Tu-114 was estimated to be 179,764 kg (396,200 lb). Flight duration was expected to be about 48 hours. The take-off run was estimated to be 3,350 m (10,988 ft). Patrol speed was esti-

Right and below: **Model of the prototype Tu-126 represented Russia's first foray into the world of airborne warning and control systems.**
Tupolev Design Bureau

mated to be 400 km/h (248 mph) and cruise speed to-and-from the target area was estimated to be 750 km/h (466 mph). The combat load (armament) was estimated to be 9,074 kg (20,000 lb). Weight of the NK-14A engines with their nuclear powerplant was estimated to be 88,748 kg (195,600 lb). The radiation shielding was estimated to weight 58,076 kg (128,000 lb).

Work on the nuclear Tu-114 and its special powerplant was terminated during the mid-1970s when it was determined that nuclear propulsion for aircraft was still an ill-defined and highly experimental science. It was simply too dangerous to pursue…and it was difficult to justify the extraordinary degree of risk.

Tu-126 ('Moss')

On 4th July 1958, the USSR Council of Ministers released an order calling for the creation of an aircraft-borne radar picket complex utilizing the newly-developed Liana radar and communications system. Liana was optimized to detect airborne targets at medium to high altitudes over great range. It was determined that an effective air defense system required such capability if it was to be effective. The difficult-to-defend northern borders of Russia were particularly vulnerable to attack, and it was proposed that the *Liana* system could close that hole in Russia's air defense network.

As the program progressed, it was decided to make *Liana* capable of detecting both airborne and surface targets. It was then determined that the mission would require long-duration flights, some in excess of 10 to 12 hours. Cruise altitude for the mission was to be between 8,000 and 12,000 m (26,240 and 39,360 ft). Detection range using line-of-sight computations was to be 100 km. (62 miles) for aircraft the size of the MiG-17; 200 km (124 miles) for aircraft the size of the Ilyushin Il-28; and 300 km (186 miles) for aircraft the size of the Myasischev M-4. Detection range below the horizon was limited to only 20 km (12.4 miles).

Communicating data to ground commanders was effectively accommodated by the transmitting range of the system, which was some 2,000 km (1,242 miles). Additionally, the system was compatible with all other communications and detection systems in the Soviet Union.

Initial studies calling for the modification of the Tu-95 to fill the picket role were quickly discarded in consideration of the bomber's lack of interior volume. The new Tu-114 proved a near perfect match for the Liana system and mission and as a result, the Council of Ministers passed a resolution during 1960 requesting Tupolev to review the Tu-114 and assess its suitability as a transport for the *Liana* system.

Tupolev concluded the following:
- the *Liana* system would fit into the Tu-114's pressurized cabin without difficulty and could be supported and maintained, even while the aircraft was in flight
- two full crews of 12 personnel each could be accommodated, thus allowing the *Liana* system to be manned around-the-clock
- heat dissipation requirements - always a major concern when a lot of avionics are involved - could be accommodated within the Tu-114's airframe and existing systems.

In its picket form, the new Tu-114 equipped with the *Liana* system was redesignated Tu-126 by the Tupolev bureau. Many difficulties were overcome in order to make the new system work, not the least of which was alleviating electromagnetic conflicts between the various components making up the *Liana* system.

One of the most challenging items during the course of Tu-126 development was determining the optimum design and location of the RLS radar unit's rotating antenna. Two options were explored by the Kuibyshev aviation factory (No.18) and Tupolev: one utilized a fixed dielectric fairing with the rotating dish positioned inside; the other utilized a rotating dielectric fairing with the antenna moving as an integral part of the the rotating unit.

It eventually was determined that the rotating option would be the most suitable. Accordingly, a rotating fairing large enough to accommodate the 12 m (39.4 ft) antenna was developed and mounted on top of a dorsally positioned pylon assembly. The antenna rotated at 10 rpm.

The original Tu-126 design studies called for the aircraft to have a tail gun turret with two AM-23 cannon and a *Cripton* sighting radar. This was shelved in favor of installing a powerful passive/active electronic countermeasures system. Additionally, the aircraft was equipped with a probe-and-drogue-type inflight refueling system which would thus permit it to stay on station for virtually unlimited periods of time.

On 30th January 1960, a draft proposal calling for hardware development of the new DRLO aircraft based on the Tu-114 passenger transport was approved. On 30th May 1960, the USSR Council of Ministers released the official resolution declaring the Kuibyshev factory (No. 18) to be the site where the prototype Tu-126 with its *Liana* system would be built. During August of 1960 confirmation was received and the following December, a mock-up review met with favorable results. It was projected that the prototype aircraft would be ready for flight test by the fourth quarter of 1961.

Work at Kuibyshev was supervised by A I Putilov, then chief of Tupolev's factory No. 18 operations. The first prototype was completed approximately on schedule and by the end of 1961, it was being readied for start of the flight test program. On 23rd February 1962, with chief test pilot I M Suhomlin at the control, the first Tu-126 took to the air for the first time.

Joint government tests of the Tu-126 and its *Liana* system were undertaken in two stages:
- The first was completed on 8th February 1964. It covered refinement of the *Liana* complex and testing of its compatibility with other Tu-126 systems and equipment.
- The second, completed during November of 1964, included testing of compatibility of the Tu-126 and the *Liana* system with ground- and ship-based systems and command centers. Of particular concern was

79

the ability of the aircraft to transmit data to surface receivers in high-countermeasures environments and in combat conditions. Nearly two years were required to verify the system's capabilities and limitations.

During August of 1963, even as testing proceeded, a decision was made to move ahead with Tu-126 production. However, because several important tests pertaining to the *Liana* system's viability had not yet been completed, the aircraft was not actually placed in production until early 1965.

Eight production aircraft (manufacturer's designation 'L') were manufactured from 1965 through 1967. During this period, improvements in electronic countermeasures systems were introduced and other changes were added to new aircraft as they rolled from the factory No.8 production line.

On 30th April 1965, the Tu-126 entered the operational PVO inventory as a result of a resolution of the USSR Council of Ministers. The Tu-126 squadron was based at an airfield not far from Shaulai (Latvia). The aircraft remained in front-line service until the early 1980s, when they were replaced with the Ilyushin A-50.

The advent of the Tu-126 gave PVO forces significant advantages over their predecessors:
- it was possible to detect fighters at a distance of 100 km (62 miles) and bombers at a distance of from 200 to 300 km (124 to 186 miles)
- at an altitude of from 2,000 to 5,000 m (6,560 to 16,400 ft) it was possible to detect fighters against background clutter at a distance of 100 km (62 miles) and ships of the cruiser class at 400 km (248 miles)
- early warning could be provided at ranges of up to 2,000 km (6,560 miles) from PVO command centers
- early warning times could be extended by up to 3 hours, depending on the distance to the patrol area and the cruise speed of the Tu-126
- mobility of the Tu-126 allowed the PVO to change early warning options in response to possible attack scenarios; this was particularly important in consideration of the size of the Soviet Union; Tu-126 transfer times to patrol sites were critical, however, as it could take many hours to get an aircraft on location under certain conditions (for example, moving the aircraft from the Kolsky peninsula area to the Vladivostok area took 10 hours)
- the Tu-126 was not easily impacted by weather…as it could fly over or around most inclement weather conditions; radar picket ships at sea did not have this luxury
- the Tu-126 could perform its mission in conditions as difficult as those found in the Arctic where land and ocean-based pickets often were incapacitated by adverse weather conditions

Top: **The Tu-126 prototype during the course of its flight test program, probably at Zhukovsky.** Yefim Gordon Collection

Left: **Another view of the Tu-126 prototype reveals its superior finish. Dark fuselage panel next to inboard propellers is probably a structural upgrade to accommodate fatigue concerns.** Yefim Gordon Collection

Below: **One of the few production Tu-126s, in flight.** Yefim Gordon

Overall, it was concluded the Tu-126's most notable attribute was its high level of dependability under all environmental extremes. Additionally, its electronic countermeasures suite, when coupled with its ability to detect enemy aircraft and other potential adversaries at great distance, was considered an excellent defensive system that made the aircraft difficult to detect and destroy.

The Tu-126 was found to be as effective against surface vessels as it was against airborne targets. The great range of its rotating radar permitted it to stand-off at great distance from aircraft carrier fleets while monitoring their movements and activities. This stand-off range also reduced the chances of interception by carrier-borne fighters.

Conversely, cooperative intercepts utilizing the Tupolev Tu-128S-4 long-range interceptor and its R-4R and R-4T air-to-air missiles in concert with the Tu-126 were investigated as the latter went into development. This had been instigated by the Air Defense units (PVO) of the Soviet Air Force and upon detailed study, had led to the conclusion that such a system could extend enemy aircraft interception ranges out to 621 miles (1,000 km) from Russia's borders. Western bombers such as the Boeing B-52 and the Avro 'Vulcan' could be neutralized as a threat if that buffer routinely could be provided by the Tu-126 and its early warning radar.

In connection with the cooperative Tu-126 /Tu-128 intercepts, an intercept officer was introduced into the Tu-126's crew. It thus became possible to integrate the fighter's capabilities with the long-range detection data from the Tu-126. This had not previously been considered an aspect of the Tu-126 mission. Once perfected, however, it worked well.

In general, the Tu-126 differed little from its Tu-114 predecessor. Other than the obvious rotating 'mushroom'-style PLS *Liana* antenna mounted dorsally at mid-fuselage, the Tu-126 incorporated only minor structural changes. Externally, the only other items of change were the readily visible communication and electronic countermeasures antennas and miscellaneous antenna fairings.

Fairings for the *Lira* antenna system were visible attached to the horizontal stabilizer tips. Additionally, a ventral fin was introduced on the Tu-126 in order to improve its directional stability in consideration of the destabilizing effect of the dorsally mounted rotating antenna. Virtually all other differences, including communications equipment, the cockpit configuration, and the *Liana* system operating panels were internal.

Two separate crews were provided. These consisted of the following: two pilots; two navigators; a radio operator and flight engineer; an intercept officer; three RLS panel operators; a radio-technical equipment operator; and an equipment repair engineer. The off-duty crew was provided a special rest area equipped with bunks and a restroom.

Special precautions were taken to protect the crew from the various electromagnetic energy sources in the Tu-126. Radiation absorbing insulation was applied where appropriate.

The Tu-126 remained viable as an early warning and control system until the end of the 1960s. By that time, the ability of NATO air forces to penetrate Soviet air space at low and very low altitudes had superseded the Tu-126's capabilities. As a result, a new system was initiated, this eventually resulting in the Ilyushin A-50 (based on the Il-76 transport). Much more capable than its predecessor, the *Shmel* detection system in the A-50 had special features that dramatically improved its ability to track aircraft operating at low altitudes while hiding in 'background clutter'.

Top and below: **Model of the advanced, all-jet Tu-156 which was never built.**
Tupolev Design Bureau

Tu-126 Specifications:

Wing span	51.4 m (168.6 ft)
Length (without refuelling boom	
	51.4 m (168.6 ft)
Height	15.5 m (50.8 ft)
Fuselage dia.	4.2 m (13.78 ft)
Wing area	311.1 m^2 (3,348.4 ft^2)
Max. take off weight	155,172 kg (342,000 lb)
Maximum speed	790 km/h (491 mph)
Cruise speed	650 to 700 km/h
	(404 to 435 mph)
Flight range	7000 km (4,347 miles)
Flight duration	10.2 hours
Service ceiling	10,700 m (35,096 ft)
Crew	24
Engines	4 x NK - 12MV turbo
props rated at	11,190 kW (15,000 shp) each

During 1966, the Scientific Research Institute in Moscow began developing a new airborne warning and control system for detecting targets operating at low altitude against complex background clutter. The scientific and manufacturing association, Vega-M, supervised by Chief designer V Ivanov, during 1969, started working on creation of new radar complex under the name *Shmel* that would accommodate this requirement.

Prior to the definitive development of the *Shmel* system, the Tupolev bureau began studying airframe options capable of carrying it. As *Shmel* grew, so did the carrier aircraft requirements. Among the less obvious concerns was the *Shmel* system's cooling needs...an issue of considerable importance in light of the fact that many kilowatts of energy would be consumed powering the radar...and energy meant heat. Two large air intakes thus were installed ventrally on the fuselage to accommodate the heat dissipation specification.

Regardless of the eventual successes realized by the Tu-126, by the end of the 1960s, it had outlived its usefulness and newer technologies had begun to supersede its onboard systems. Production of the Tu-126 and its Tu-114 commercial predecessor ceased at factory No. 18 and was replaced by Tu-154 and Tu-142 production.

Though out of production, existing Tu-126s were retained in service and utilized operationally. As *Shmel* development continued, a system was installed in Tu-126, No. 601, at the Taganrog Beriev factory. This was to serve as the *Shmel* system testbed.

Successful testing of *Shmel* resulted, during the early 1970s, in a USSR Council of Ministers order calling for Tupolev to develop a new platform to accommodate it.

Initially, it was thought the Tu-142M might suffice as a platform, but this did not prove to be the case. The Tu-142 it was quickly discovered, did not have the internal volume needed to accommodate all the various *Shmel* systems and hardware. The proposed aircraft, sometimes referred to as the Tu-156 (later, another DRLO aircraft was developed under this designation), was quickly discounted for the job as a result of the afore-mentioned space constraints. Eventually, Ilyushin won the airframe contract via a modification of their venerable Il-76 transport.

During a period spanning from 1960 through 1962, Tu-114s set 32 world records for class for distance-with-cargo, distance-without-cargo, altitude-with-cargo, and speed.

During 1989, a Tu-95MS set 60 world records for class including speed- and altitude-with-cargo. During 1990, a Tu-142MK set ten world records for class for altitude-with-cargo. And also during 1990, the Tu-142LL, No. 4243, set three world records for class for speed- and time-to-climb.

Left and below: **The Tu-95KMs are modernized K-20 and KD series aircraft equipped with upgraded defensive electronic warfare systems.** Yefim Gordon collection

Chapter Five

Tu-95 & Tu-142 in Detail

Tu-95 TECHNICAL DETAILS

Tu-95M

The Tu-95/Tu-95M bomber is an all-metal monoplane with a swept wing, conventional tail surfaces, and retractable tricycle landing gear.

Basic construction materials include D16 and D95 aluminum alloys, ZOHRSA and ZOHRSNA (for fastener and connecting part hard points), and ML5-T4 magnesium alloys.

Fuselage

Fuselage construction is semi-monocoque. It has an excellent fineness ratio, low frontal area, and a circular cross section with smooth stressed skin. The latter is conventionally fastened to frame rings and stringers using standard sunk rivets. Beefed-up structure is provided where necessary in the bomb bay, nose landing gear, and access hatch areas. The fuselage has production breaks as follows:
- forward canopy (F-1)
- nose section between the 1st and 13th formers including the front pressurized cockpit (F-2)
- unpressurized center section between formers 13a and 49 (F-3)
- unpressurized tail section between formers 50 and 87 (F-5)
- aft pressurized compartment between former 87 and the aft gun mount/cannon fairing

The canopy (F-1) and nose compartment (F-2) form the front pressurized cockpit section. There are working places provided for each of the crew members (commander; assistant to commander; navigator; second navigator; senior board technician; senior flight radio-gun operator; and ECM officer). The instruments, aircraft control panels, navigation equipment, high-altitude gear, and other miscellaneous equipment also are situated in this section.

The radar is mounted under the nose ahead of the nose landing gear bay between structural rings 6 and 13. Conventional and silicate glass materials are used in the cockpit transparencies. Most of the transparent panels in the nose and windscreen are electrically heated for deicing. For purposes of emergency egress, special hatches in the cockpit transparency sections permit egress. The senior radioman's transparent blister, found on top of the fuselage is located near structural ring 13.

Access to the cockpit area and forward section of the fuselage is via a hatch positioned in the nose landing gear bay. The hatch covering this entry is equipped with an emergency opening device powered by compressed air (it can be utilized only if the nose landing gear is extended). In concert with this is a release mechanism for the pressurized air in the forward cabin area.

The wing center section is attached to the fuselage center section (F-3) between structural rings 19 and 28. The bomb bay is positioned between structural rings 28 and 45. Target flares and fire retardant bottles are positioned aft of the bomb bay. Bays containing flexible fuel cells N.1, N.2, N.3, N.6a, and N.6b occupy most of the aft fuselage (F-3) past the bomb bay. The LAS-5-2M inflatable rescue boats are mounted in two containers and are installed on the left side between structural rings 14 and 17.

Below: **The unsophisticated but highly practical cockpit of a Tu-95MS. Noteworthy are analog instruments and center throttle quadrant.**
Tom Copeland

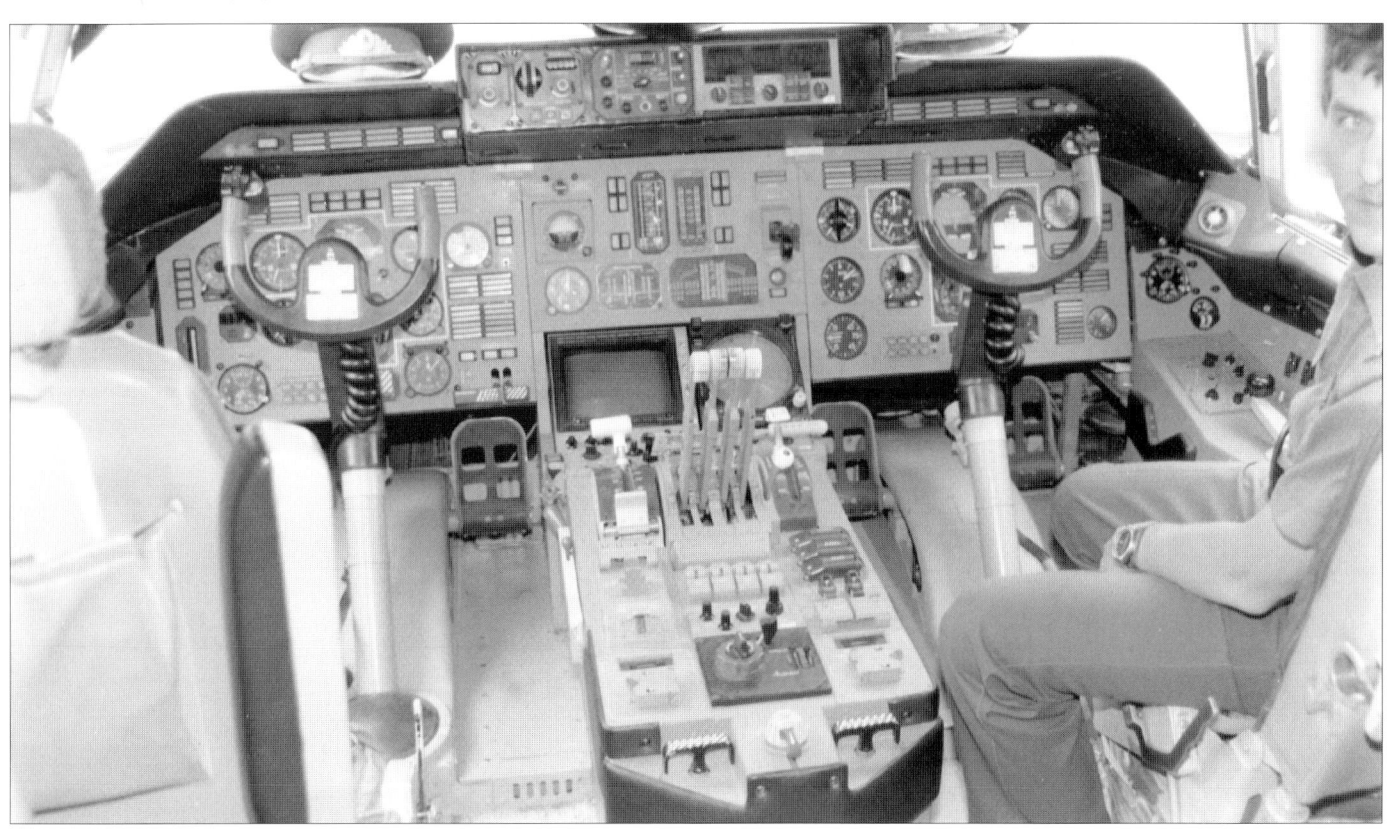

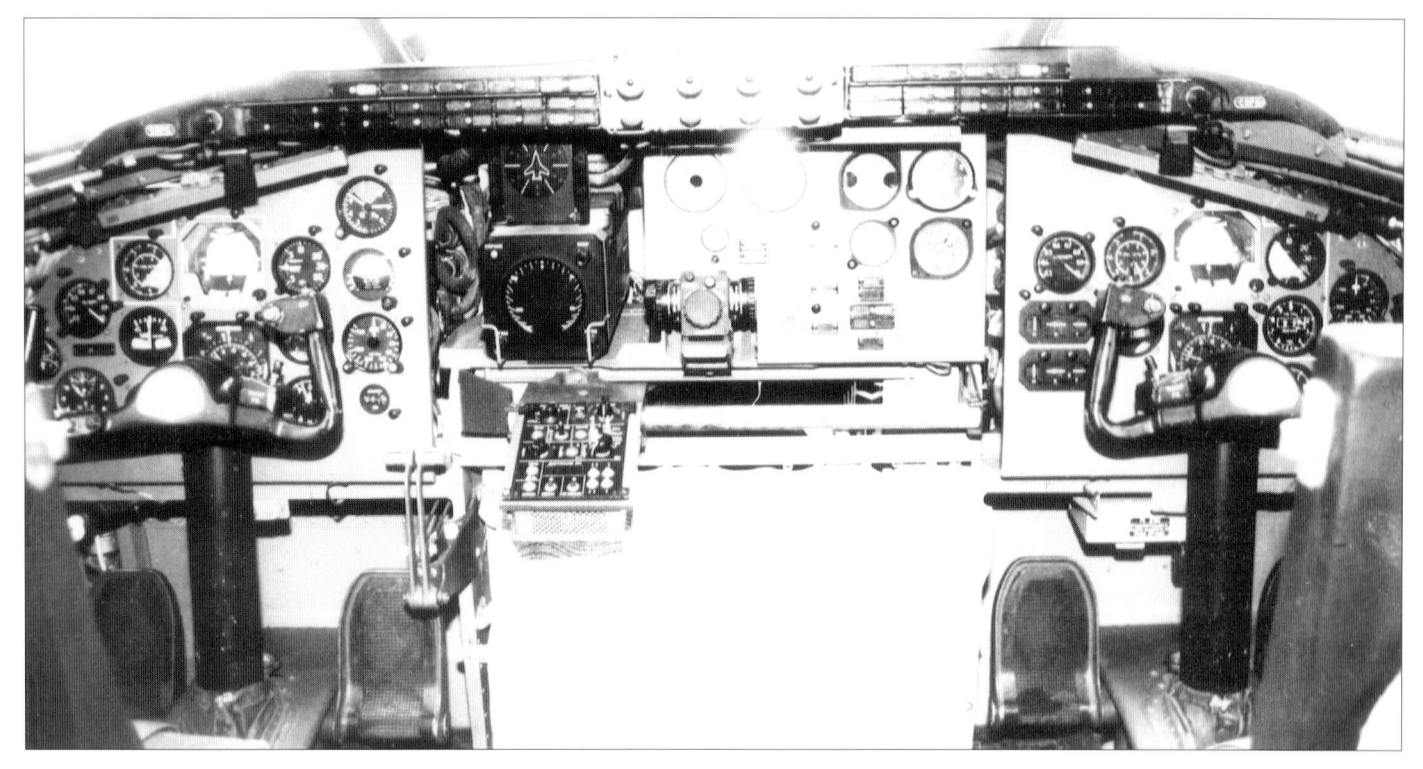

Above: **Main instrument panel of Tu-95MR.** Yefim Gordon

Left: **Engineer's panel of Tu-95MR.** Yefim Gordon

The fuselage framework is strengthened by two beams in the space formed by the bomb bay. Cluster bomb racks are fastened by nodes to the vertical walls of the bomb bay. The bomb bay doors are attached via hinges to the bottom edge of the bay walls. The cluster bomb racks (at the top part of bomb bay) are fastened to the horizontal longerons which are connected with the bomb suspension unit slung between structural rings 30 and 33.

Some pieces of equipment, including control cable runs and other miscellany are mounted on both sides of the fuselage. The bomb bay is winterized and equipped with electrical heating.

The rear compartment, tail unit, and tail bumper are positioned at the far aft end of F-4. The top part of the aft fuselage forms a dorsal fin which is positioned between structural rings 69 and 81. This section also includes: flexible cell-fuel tanks (N.4, N.5, and N.5a); top and bottom gun mounts; nitrogen bottles; hydraulic system gear; oxygen bottles; and other miscellaneous equipment for maintenance and support. A special hatch is provided for access.

Framework for the tail surfaces includes two longerons which run from the ventral part of the aft fuselage. The vertical stabilizer is attached to the two main structural frames (81 and 87) of the section. The work stations for the radioman-gunner; the commander of the tail gun positions; the gun sighting stations (including the PRS-1 sighting system); and the tail gun equipment are all in the aft pressurized compartment.

The access hatch to the aft cabin can be opened and closed by pressurized air during flight, if necessary. Glass blisters for observation of side hemispheres are provided just forward of the gun compartment. Gun compartment transparencies are of armor-plated glass. A glass emergency hatch is located on the left side of the transparency section. The left transparency panel has an observation port.

The cantilever wing is swept and utilizes a torsion box construction technique. Construction materials include aluminum and magnesium alloys. It consists of a center section with two separate cantilever panels attached on each side.

The basic load-bearing part of the wing torsion box is formed by front and rear longerons with top and bottom panels consisting of thick stressed skin.

The fuel tanks are placed in the torsion box between two ribs. Electrical heating elements for the anti-icing system are positioned inside the wing leading edges. Three stall fences are positioned on the top surface of each wing.

The wing center section is attached to the fuselage just over and ahead of the bomb bay. A central rib assembly divides the wing center section into two parts. Fuel tanks are positioned in each of these halves.

The load-bearing torsion box serves as the mounting point for the three outer wing panels and the three-section leading edge which is fas-

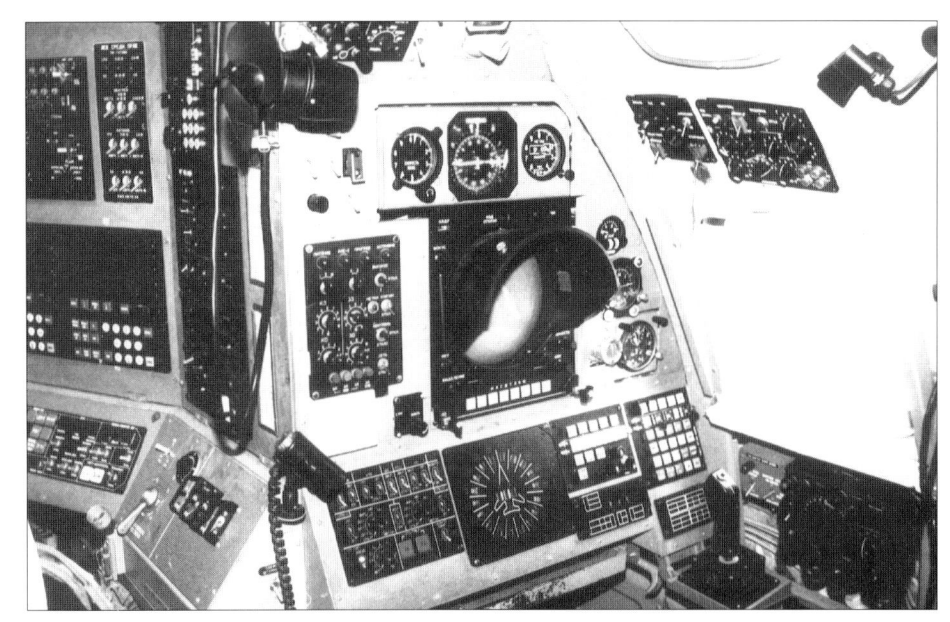

Above: **Aft radar panel panel of Tu-95MR. Electronic countermeasures also were accommodated from this position.** Yefim Gordon

Above right: **Communications system panel of Tu-95MR.** Yefim Gordon

Right and below: **Right (top) and left engineer's and navigation system panels of Tu-95MS.** Tom Copeland

tened by screws to the front longeron. A trailing edge section also is attached to the torsion box. The main landing gear loads also are passed to this at two points and are attached to the rear spar.

Two of the aircraft's engines are mounted on the first, inboard wing section. The landing gear legs, in turn, are attached to the wing structure just aft of these engines and are accommodated in the engine aft fairings which, in turn, contain main gear wells. These are insulated from exhaust heat with formed titanium panels.

The wing panels are attached conventionally, with the carry-through structures being attached using flanges and nut and bolt fasteners. The outer wing panels, attached similarly, consist of a load-bearing torsion box fastened to the front spar. The leading edge is a separate structural member and is removable. The trailing edge pieces are attached directly to the rear spar. A tip fairing accommodates the wingtip configuration and associated BANO-45 navigation flying lights positioned on the tops and bottoms of each fairing.

Additional fuel tanks are located in the torsion box. The trailing edge panels have ribs to accommodate structural load requirements. The panels are connected to each other by brackets and the aileron load-bearing pieces. The latter form cut-outs and serve to support the aileron hinge assemblies.

The top and bottom panels of each wing section have hatches for access to the control cables, the fuel pressure pump, and the fuel level indicators. There also were fuel fillers and hatches for access to the fuel jettison valve.

The ailerons and flaps are positioned conventionally on the trailing edge of the wing. The ailerons are of all-metal construction and positioned on the outer wing section. Each aileron is divided into three separate parts to avoid binding as a result of wing deflection. The ailerons have internal mass and aerodynamic balances. The electrically-actuated trim-balance tab (the control unit for which is fixed on the wing rear spar's back wall) is attached to the inboard aileron section.

Ribs on the inboard wing sections are evenly spaced until the 25th rib. At that point, the landing gear fairing is forced to split. The flap guides for this inboard wing section are suspended by two internal mounts and three external.

Each flap section is actuated by screw jacks. These are positioned in the flap actuator fairings and are faired using rubber gap fillers which are riveted to the trailing edge of the bottom surface of the wing.

The swept, cantilever tail unit is of all metal construction. The leading edge sweep of the vertical and horizontal tail surfaces is 40°.

The torsion box-type horizontal stabilizer consists of two halves connected to each other along the fuselage centerline. Originally, a device for changing the angle-of-incidence was to be installed, but this never actually took place. The angle-of-incidence is fixed at 2.5° relative to the fuselage centerline. Each stabilizer half consists of a torsion box formed by two longerons and associated panels, a removable leading edge with electrical heating, a trailing edge assembly, and a tip fairing. Each stabilizer is fastened to the fuselage by four bolt assemblies. Hinged bearing assemblies attached to the rear spar support the elevators.

The vertical fin consists of a torsion box, a rib assembly, a three-part leading edge with electrical heating, and a tip fairing. The rear spar serves to support the hinged bearing assemblies required for the large rudder.

The elevator has a 30% axis aerodynamic balance and a mass balance with 3% overbalancing. Both halves of the elevator are mechanically interconnected by shaft assemblies. The control tubes are attached to the shaft assembly. The shaft bracket serves as a sixth support point.

Elevator construction consists of a longeron, a set of ribs, top and bottom skins, and a leading edge. The knife-edge type trailing edge is constructed of magnesium.

Top left: **Dual navigator stations in nose of Tu-95KU.** Yefim Gordon collection

Middle left: **Upper cockpit transparencies of Tu-95K-22.** Yefim Gordon

Left: **Detail of forward fuselage section of Tu-95K-22.** Yefim Gordon collection

The manually and electrically actuated trim surface is attached via six brackets on each elevator half near the surface's root. The rudder also is made with a 30% axis aerodynamic balance and a mass balance with 2% overbalancing. It is mounted using four brackets which are installed on the fin structure. Rudder movement is accomplished by turning the shaft via its pin-with-rudder post.

Rudder construction consists of the rudder post, a set of ribs, top and bottom skins, and the leading edge assembly. The knife-edge trailing edge is manufactured of magnesium. The trim-balancing tab and its electric drive are mounted on six supporting brackets at the tip of the rudder.

Landing Gear

The aircraft has conventional, retractable, tri-cycle-type landing gear. A tail bumper is provided for over-rotation protection.

The main gear assemblies are electro-hydraulically actuated and when retracted are housed in extended engine nacelle fairings which are attached to the inboard wing sections. The main gear trucks rotate a full 180° during the retraction process. Each truck has four wheel assemblies and each of these is provided a conventional tire of 1,500 x 500 mm V type (49.2 x 16.4 in). Tire pressure is 9.5 kg/m^2 (0.01 lb/in^2). Each wheel also is equipped with a hydraulically-actuated disk brake assembly.

An air-oil shock absorber is provided to improve load distribution at touchdown. The strut is charged with AMG-10 fluid and nitrogen. Nitrogen pressure is 40 kg/m^2 (0.06 lb/in^2). When the landing gear is in the extended position, the truck is angled 4° front-wheels-down.

There are two brake cylinders attached to each wheel. The braking system is controlled automatically.

The aft part of the inboard engine nacelle where the landing gear wells are located is built primarily of aluminum with conventional framing and longeron construction. The gear well has two large doors at the rear and a smaller, single-piece door at the front. A smaller fairing covers the main gear primary drag strut assembly. Mechanical links to the struts and gear close or open the doors sequentially with gear retraction or extension. The main gear well doors close after extension.

The nose undercarriage strut is attached conventionally to the front part of the fuselage and has two 1100 x 330 mm V (33.5 x 10 in) wheels. The shock absorber is the same as that found on the main gear struts. Nose gear strut nitrogen pressure is 27 kg/m^2 (0.03 lb/in^2 and pressure in the wheel tires is 9 kg/m^2 (0.01 lb/in^2).

All three: **Three different views of a Tu-95MS nose. Radar fairing has been widened to accommodated enlarged antenna. Wiring to interface with aft-mounted avionics runs through long tunnel fairing attached externally to fuselage.** Tom Copeland

The nose gear, like the main gear, retract aft via an electro-hydraulic ram. The nose gear well has mechanical linkages that open and close the doors. When extended into the slipstream, the doors are held open by two pneumatic shock absorbers. The rear gear well door is held in position by a mechanical locking device.

Nose gear steering is via the rudder pedals in the cockpit and associated hydraulic actuators. The over-rotation bumper on the aft end of the fuselage is equipped with an air/oil shock absorber. It is equipped with two wheels and inflatable 480 x 200 mm (14.6 x 6.1 in) tires.

Powerplant
The initial Tu-95 production series aircraft were powered by four NK-12 turboprop engines. Each of these was rated at 8,952 kW (12,000 shp). All following Tu-95 variants were powered by the NK-12M or the later NK-12MV turboprop engine. All modifications to the early production Tu-95, including the Tu-95M were equipped with the NK-12M or later, the NK-12MV turboprop engine.

Each engine was equipped with a counter-rotating AV-60-type propeller assembly. Later, these units were changed to the AV-60N or AV-670K.

The NK-12 consists of the following basic parts: differential planetary reduction gearbox; axial-flow compressor; annular combustion chamber; turbine; and a fixed jet nozzle assembly. Auxiliary equipment is attached to the main engine assembly. Each engine is mounted via four attachment points to the support truss assembly. A vibration neutralization unit is provided.

A reduction gearbox serves to deliver the engine's power to the contra-rotating propeller unit. Gear reduction is 0.088 (equivalent to an engine turbine speed of 8,300 rpm and a propeller speed of 736 rpm). Power transfer to the propellers is not divided evenly. The front propeller receives 54.4% of the power and the rear propeller receives 45.6%. The reduction gearbox consists of three different units as follows: camshaft casing for the rear propeller; a gearbox casing with drive; and the actual reduction gearbox. The camshaft casing of the rear propeller is an element of the actual engine. This accommodates both the propeller thrust loads and the structural loads.

The 14-stage engine compressor is of standard axial flow design. At maximum power, the compressor's pressure ratio is 9.5 units at an airflow rate of 55.2 kg/sec (121 lb/sec).

The welded, annular combustion chamber is constructed of high-temperature steel. Fuel is delivered to the combustion chamber through fuel nozzles with twelve orifices in each. The five stage turbine section provides about one-third

Above: **Left side ventral view of Tu-95MS nose with taxi light and various communication system antennas visible.** Tom Copeland

Below: **Nose of Tu-95RTs.** Yefim Gordon collection

of its total power output to the propellers. Propulsive force generated by the conventional jet reaction generate the rest of the power required to propel the aircraft. The titanium exhaust pipe is attached to the rear flange of the turbine casing.

The exhaust pipe system consists of a tail exhaust pipe (attached to the stub extension off the turbine casing and then bifurcated so that two exhaust ports are provided for each engine). The exhaust pipes are suspended from the aircraft structure by two rigid brackets. All four exhaust systems are essentially similar in construction, with differences applied where necessary to accommodate wing structural considerations.

Each engine nacelle is divided into three basic parts: front, middle, and rear. Oil tanks (of which there are three for each nacelle) are positioned at the bottom front of each nacelle. Engine oil is heated via hot air ducting which runs from the 14th stage compressor of each engine. The middle part (formally called the nacelle) is the basic power element of the engine nacelle. The rear part is a fairing (the rear part closest to the fuselage engine nacelles is used as a fairing for the main undercarriage strut assemblies).

The following auxiliary systems are installed on each engine: two GSR-18000M dc. generators; an SGO-30U a.c. generator; an AK-150NK air compressor; a KTA-14N fuel control unit; a 450UK high-pressure fuel pump; a 1007K low pressure fuel pump; an R-60DA rev regulator; an oil unit; a 437F hydraulic pipe; an intake guide vane assembly control unit and an AU-12 inter-compressor air bleed valve; a pressure oil pipe and scavenge oil pipe; a centrifugal breather; and DT-2 and DT-33 tachometer transmitters. Engine starting is accommodated using a TS-12M turbine starter.

The engine's fire-extinguishing system includes a number of fire-retarding dividing walls which separate the engine nacelles from the rest of the airframe and the fire-extinguishing system.

The propellers consist of two contra-rotating (the front rotates clockwise; the rear rotates counter-clockwise) units utilizing four-bladed AV-60, AV-60N, or AV-60K blade sets with variable pitch capability. The blade airfoil is a NACA-16. Pitch change is accommodated by a hydraulically controlled rev governor. The propellers can be feathered or unfeathered upon pilot command.

Top and second from top: **Noses of Tu-95K-22 and special Tu-95N.** Tom Copeland and Jay Miller

Third from top: **Another view of the ventral antenna array under the forward nose of a Tu-95MS. Faceted unit is a multi-spectrum receiver warning antenna.** Tom Copeland

Right: **Inflight refueling boom of Tu-95MS. Design of this unit is quite similar to that of US Navy aircraft.** Tom Copeland

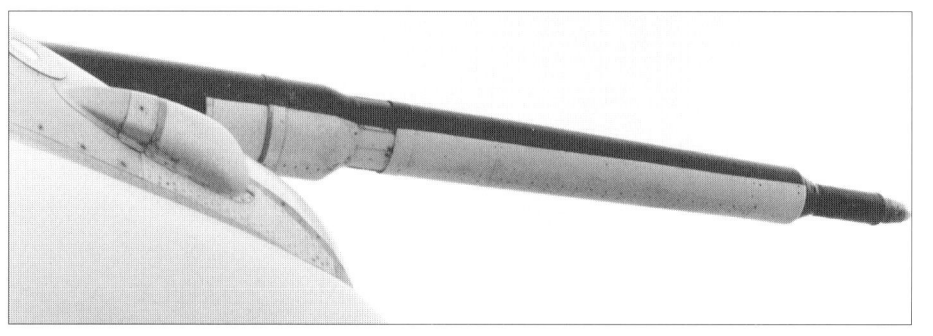

In the event of an engine failure during take-off or in flight, the NK-12MV engines are equipped with an automatic feathering system activated by a torque monitoring device. All propellers are equipped with a deicing system consisting of electrical heating elements imbedded in tape and attached to the blade leading edges. Power for deicing is provided by an SGO-30U generator.

The fuel (aviation kerosene T-1, T-2, TS-1 type) is contained in a series of flexible rubber fuel tanks mounted in the fuselage, the center wing section, and the outer wing panels. The Tu-95 carries its fuel in 71 separate fuel tanks and the Tu-95M carries its fuel in 74 separate fuel tanks. The tanks are interconnected by plumbing that forms four independent fuel systems... with one allocated to each engine.

The fuel tanks are strategically positioned to accommodate structural load and cg. limitations. An SAT-80A system for monitoring fuel load displacement and consumption rates is integral with the fuel system. An emergency dumping system also is provided.

Armament
Free-falling bombs are carried in the lengthy bomb bay. Bomb weights of from 1,500 to 9,000 kg (3,306 to 19,836 lb) are normally carried in the combat configuration. When used as a trainer, bomb weights vary between 50 and 4,500 kg (110 and 9,918 lb). A normal bomb load is 5,000 kg (11,020 lb).

Bomb suspension units consisted of the following options:
- one MBD6-95 beam-type carrier with Der6-5 locks for bomb's ranging in size from 5,000 to 9,000 kg (11,020 to 19,836 lb);
Der6-4 locks for 1,500 to 3,000 kg (3,306 to 6,612 lb); or Der6-3 locks for bombs weighing from 250 to 500 kg (551 to 1,102 lb).
- one BD5-95M beam-type carrier with Der5-48 locks for bombs weighing 5,000 kg (11,020 lb) or Der5-4 locks for bombs weighing 1,500 to 3,000 kg (3,306 to 6,612 lb).
- two cassette-type KD4-295 carriers with Der4-49 locks for bombs weighing 1,500 to 3,000 kg (3,306 to 6,612 lb).
- two cartridge-type KDZ-695 carriers with Der3-48 locks for training bombs weighing from 50 to 500 kg (110 to 1,102 lb).

Also positioned in the bomb bay are ASO-95 and ASO-2B radar chaff dispensers.

The OPB-11RM (OPB-112) optical vector

Top three left: **Miscellaneous fuselage details of Tu-95MS including cooling intakes, venturi tubes, receiver antenna fairings, and wing root section leading edge.** Tom Copeland

Left: **Ventral view of Tu-95MS fuselage looking aft from the forward weapons bay.** Tom Copeland

90

synchronous sight, which interfaces with the autopilot, is provided for bombing in daylight conditions. The sight automatically calculates aircraft flight parameters and targeting data for improved bombing accuracy.

Bomb aiming normally is accommodated via the RPB-4 (or R-1D) radar sighting unit which in turn is interfaced with the OPB-11RM (OPB-112) optical sighting system.

The aircraft's defensive armament includes a complex of mechanized gun installations connected to remote aiming stations and computer units. There are three articulated dual gun installations positioned as follows: dorsally (DT-B12); ventrally (DT-N12); and at the tail (DK-12). The guns are AM-23s of 23 mm with a muzzle velocity of 680 m/sec (2,230 ft/sec) and a firing rate of 1,250 to 1,350 rounds per minute. Normal ammunition complement is 2,500 rounds allocated as follows: DT-B12/700 rounds (350 per barrel); for DT-N12/800 rounds (400 per barrel); and for the DK-12/1,000 rounds (500 per barrel).

The dorsal DT-B12 installation is retractable. It can be extended into firing position at any time. Aiming equipment consists of PS-153 optical aiming stations, PRS-1 radar sighting and automatic control units for aerial shooting. An ABS-153 unit is integrated with an ADP-153 for automatic parallax control. There are four remote aiming stations for the guns: top (PS-153VK); right (PS-153BP); left (PS-153BL); and aft (PS-153K).

Remote control is accommodated in the form of a transforming selsyn tracking system. Mismatching between the selsyn pick up (aiming station) and the selsyn receiver (cannon installation) takes place in the form of electrical signals transmitted to a SU-3R servo-amplified and from there to a DV-1100 electric motor connected with the gun's vertical and horizontal guidance channels.

Equipment

(Refers to Tu-95 and Tu-95M aircraft after their modernization during the 1970s.) Aircraft instrumentation includes the following flight and navigation instruments: KUS-1200 combined speed indicators; VD-20 height finders; VAR-30 vertical speed indicators; MS-41Mach meters; SSN-8 warning indicator of velocity head; AGD-1 gyro horizon, UUG pitch angle indicator; AUP-53 electric turn indicator; GPK-52 gyro direction indicator; AP-15 autopilot; BC-463A star tracker; DAK-DB-5 remote astrocompass; AK-53P astrocompass, SP-1M aviation periscopic sextant; and a 13-20HP aviation chronometer.

Top right: **Looking forward along top fuselage of Tu-95K-22.** Yefim Gordon collection

Right, both lower photos: **Two views of Tu-95MS lower fuselage.** Tom Copeland

Ancillary equipment includes the following: UVPD-15 height indicator and differential pressure indicator; RVU-46U airflow indicator; TNV-15 and TNV-45 outside air thermometers; TUA-48, TV-45, 2TUA-11 air thermometers; AM-10 g-meter; KI-13 magnetic compass; VS-46 altitude warning unit; UZP-47 trailing-edge flaps position indicator; K3-63 flight recorder; and a AHS-1 clock.

The following engine instruments are provided: 2TVG-366 exhaust gas temperature gauges; 2TUA-11 oil temperature gauges; 2ADMU-3 fuel pressure gauges; 2ADMU-10 oil pressure gauges; 2TA9-1M electrical tachometers and MT-50 thrust manometers; UPRT-2 fuel lever position indicator; MA-95D electrical remote oil contents gauge; IH-61 engine operating time meter; and a U-03-4 oil cooler shutter position indicator. There also is a MSRP-12-96 (MSRP-12B) flight data recording system onboard.

An AFA-42/100 aerial camera system is installed in a stabilized platform on both the Tu-95 and Tu-95M between fuselage rings 67 and 69. These serve the purpose of acquiring reconnaissance imagery and can also be used for post bomb damage assessment. In concert with the camera installation the aircraft also are equipped with FOTAB or SAB illumination flares.

The radio complement provides long-range and short-range radio communication with ground receivers. Additionally, there is an internal communication system for crew use. All communications can be recorded using a tape-type recording unit.

The R-837 and R-807 radio stations are used for long-range radio communication in the middle and shortwave bands. An R-802 command radio set is provided for use in the ultrashort wave band. An R-861 radio station is provided as an emergency back-up.

Radio communication inside the aircraft is provided by a SPU-10G system. The crew's conversations are recorded on a MS-461 tape recorder.

Top two left: **Tu-95MS wing root sections from leading edge, aft. Lower airfoil curvature is readily apparent.** Tom Copeland

Left two: **Aft views of wing root section; upper photo is from inboard engine nacelle, outboard, looking forward, and lower photo is at fuselage intersection.** Tom Copeland

Facing page, top: **Top view of Tu-95MS wing provides detail of wing fence positions, flaps, and ailerons.** Tom Copeland

Facing page middle: **Wing trailing edge aft of engine nacelles is skinned in titanium for protection from hot engine exhaust.** Tom Copeland

Facing page bottom: **Tu-95MS wing trailing edge and wingtip. Note break in wing fences to accommodate flap movement.** Tom Copeland

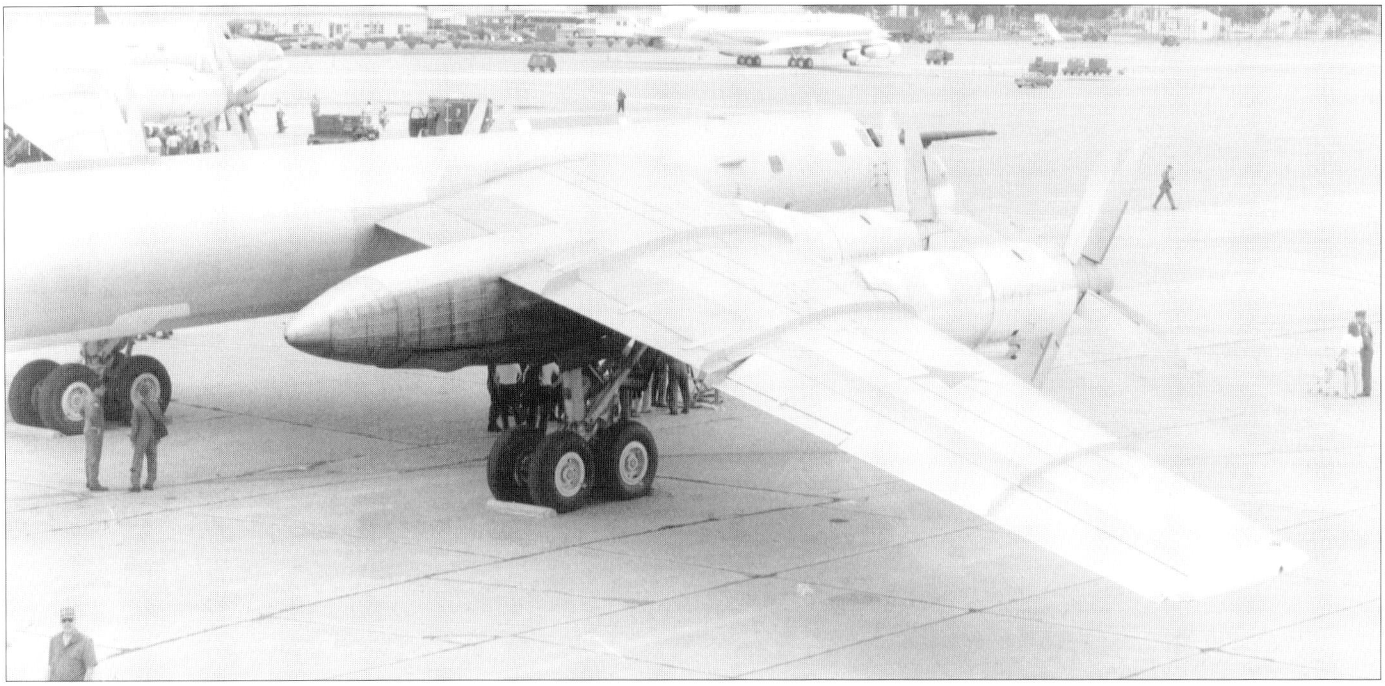

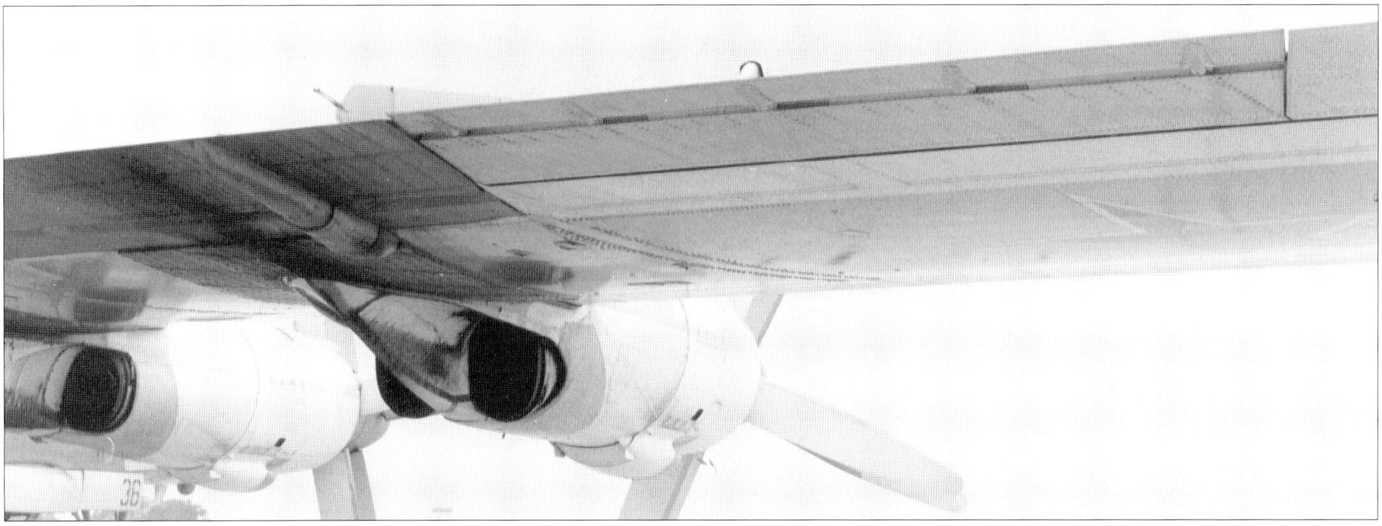

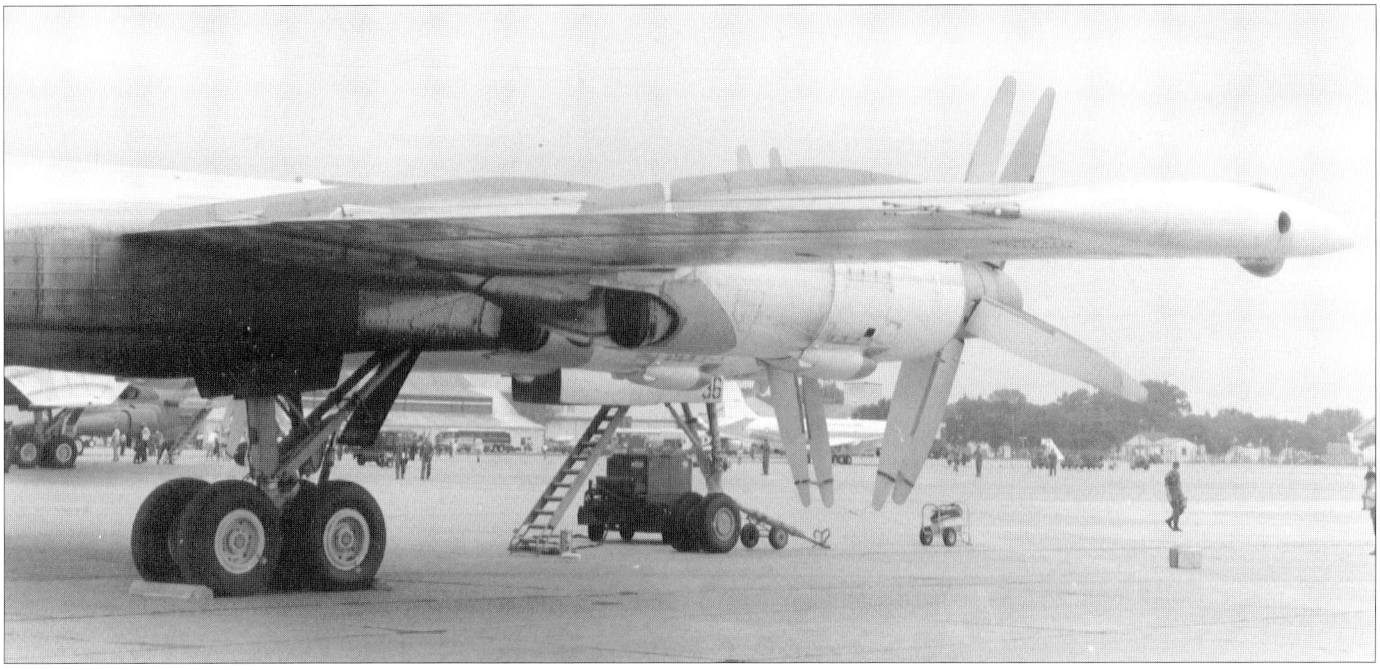

The radio-navigational equipment consists of an ARK-5 (or ARK-11) automatic radio compass; RV-UM (or RV-5) low-altitude radio altimeter; RV-25A high-altitude radio altimeter; SP-50 blind landing equipment which is combined with a GRP-F course radio receiver; GRP-2 glide path receiver; MRP-56P marker receiver and a SD-1 radio rangefinder; DISS-1 Doppler speed and drift meter; A-327 position and formation flight equipment; RSBN-2SV radio-technical system for short-range navigation and ADNS equipment for long-range navigation with a PKC-type digital coordinating convertor.

The following radio and other equipment are installed on the Tu-95 and the Tu-95M: RBP-4 *Rubidyi* MM-2 (or R-1D *Rubin*-1D) radar bombing sight connected with the OPB-11RM (OPB-112 optical vector synchronous bomb sight); SR30-2M interrogator; SRO-2P and SO-69 responders for the PRS-1 *Argon* radar sight station; SPS-1 (SPS-2) ECM equipment; SPO-2 (*Sirena*-2) receiver unit; and a DP-3 radiation monitoring instrument.

Electrical System

The aircraft has power sources of alternate and direct current. There are eight GSR-18000M generators (two on each engine) for alternating current needs. Twelve SAM-55 batteries are used as buffers and an emergency power source.

Aluminum and copper wiring is utilized. A single SGO-30U d.c. generator is installed on each engine. For systems requiring a stable power supply, there are two single-phase PO-4500 and three three-phase PT-70 (PT-125) and PT-600 series units installed.

Top left: **Left wing trailing edge, wingtip, and aft inboard engine nacelle.** Tom Copeland

Middle: **Outboard wing panel leading edge detail.** Tom Copeland

Left: **Left wing undersurface root section (inboard engine nacelle) with detail of flap leading edge and flap actuator fairing.** Tom Copeland

Equipment requiring alternating current includes the wing and tail surface leading edge deicing heaters and some remotely controlled equipment elements.

Direct current is utilized for propeller deicing units, and the navigator and pilot window deicing systems. Other dc. requirements include the communication radios and the radar navigation system.

Flight Control System

Control of the aircraft is accommodated via the two control columns and two pairs of rudder pedals. Part of this is interfaced with the stability and control system.

A low-pressure hydraulic system with a reversible hydraulic actuator is included in the rudder and aileron control system. This reduces pilot effort in actuating control surface movement.

When the aircraft is sitting statically, the ailerons and controls are locked by a special cable restraining unit. The ailerons, rudder, and elevators are all equipped with adjustable trim/balancing tabs. The elevator has both manual and electric trim available. The rudder and ailerons are electrically trimmed only.

The servo units are hooked up to the elevator and aileron control channels in order to ease pilot effort.

Extension and retraction of the flaps is accommodated by a MPZ-12 electric system that is controlled either by the pilot or an in-flight engineer. Flaps can be extended or retracted from either position.

Hydraulic System

The aircraft has two independent hydraulic systems for high and low pressure needs. The high-pressure hydraulic system has 120 to 150 kg/sm^2 (54.4 to 68 lb/sm^2) and is worked from electrical pump drive station 465A. It provides power to the following systems: normal and emergency braking; retraction and extension of nose landing gear strut; control of nose wheel steering; extension and retraction of forward gun installation; windshield wipers; and other miscellaneous actuator drives.

The low-pressure hydraulic system 75 kg/sm^2 (34/sm^2) works from two 437F hydraulic pumps and is used for feeding the reversible hydraulic actuators which are integrated into the aircraft's control system.

Top right: **Tu-95MS right wingtip fairing with night flying lights and associated transparencies.** Tom Copeland

Middle two: **Static discharge lines attached to Tu-95MS left (upper) and right wingtip fairing trailing edges.** Tom Copeland

Right: **Empennage, vertical tail, horizontal tail, and tail gun of Tu-95MS. Tail of Boeing B-52H, in background, represents the Tu-95's western counterpart in every way.** Tom Copeland

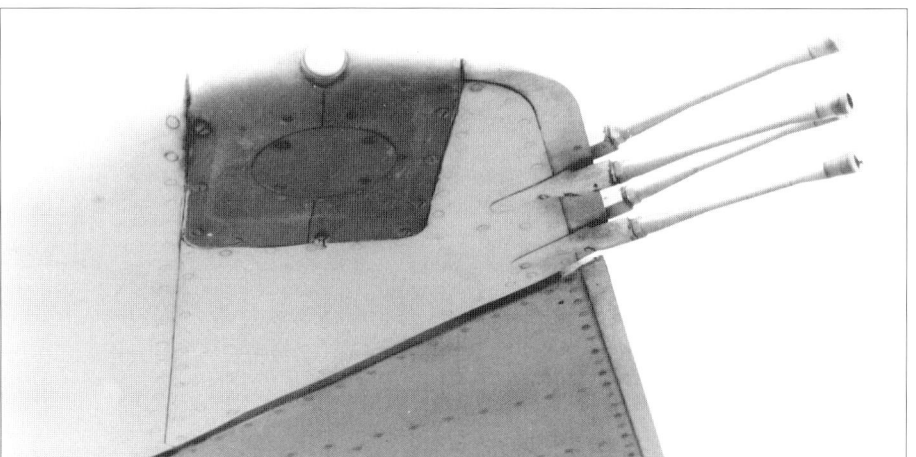

Pneumatic System

Pneumatic system pressure is 150 kg/sm² (68 lb/sm²). AK-150NK air compressors provide compressed air for the pneumatics. Items utilizing compressed air include:
- emergency nose landing gear extension
- emergency opening of the front cockpit hatch
- fuel dumping control system
- cabin pressurization system
- the 'charging system' for the RBP-4 (R-1D) and PRS-1 radar station equipment bays; the RV-25A radio altimeter; the R-837 radio station; and the Doppler velocity and DISS-1 drift meters.
- generator cooling system flap actuators
- cannon recharging system

De-icing System

Consists of:
- an alarm system with CO-4A sensors placed in the engine nacelles
- electrical deicers on the wing, tail unit, propeller blade leading edges, and the propeller cuffs
- de-icing system for the intake guide vane assembly and engine cowling leading edges; hot air from the 14th stage of each engine compressor serves as the heat provider
- electrical heating of full pressure pick ups and front glass of pilots' cockpit.

High-Altitude Equipment

High-altitude equipment includes:
- cabin pressurization, heating and ventilation
- additional electrical heating
- pressure control system in cockpit
- emergency cockpit depressurization system
- pressurization of hatches and windows
- cockpit thermal insulation
- loss of pressurization alarm system in cockpits

Cockpit pressurization and heating is achieved using air taken from the 9th stages of each inboard engine. Air for the front pressurized cockpit is cooled in advance by a heat exchanger; air for the rear compartments is cooled by a 'turborefrigerator'.

Cockpit pressurization is achieved automatically by an ARD-54 pressure regulator. During the ascent to 6,560 ft (2,000 m), the cockpits are automatically ventilated and pressurized to a static condition. At 7,000 m (22,960 ft), cockpit

---

Top left: **Tail of standard production Tu-142MR.** Yefim Gordon

Middle: **Tail of standard Tu-142. Noteworthy are horizontal tail tip antenna fairings.** Yefim Gordon

Left: **Tail of Indian Navy Tu-142MK-E.** Beriev Design Bureau

pressurization remains constant at an equivalent altitude of 2,000 m (6,560 ft).

A constant drop in pressure between the cockpit and the outside atmosphere, equal to 0.4 kg/sm² (0.18 lb/sm²) is maintained for the rest of the aircraft's ascent to cruising altitude. The pressure drop is reduced to 0.2 kg/sm² (0.09 lb/sm² at combat altitude) to reduce the potentially catastrophic effects of explosive decompression at high-altitude. In an emergency, the pressure in the cockpit and cabin areas can be quickly reduced via a pressure relief valve.

Oxygen System

The aircraft's oxygen system consists of a KP-24M stationary dilute-demand oxygen unit with KM-32 oxygen masks for every crew member, KP-23 parachute oxygen sets, four liquid oxygen converter sets, KAP portable oxygen equipment and a KAB-16 on-board oxygen fixture.

Inert Gas System

Inert gas is utilized to reduce a fire hazard in the fuel tanks in partially empty or empty conditions. The inert gas is provided by dioxide-acid bottles.

Fire-extinguishing System

The fire extinguishing equipment includes the following:
- pressurized compartment system consisting of a OS-8M fire extinguisher with freon
- engine fire extinguisher system
- SSP-2A fire extinguishing system alarm
- Eight OSU-5 dioxid-acid bottles containing inert gas used in addition to the standard aircraft fire extinguishing system
- Five hand-held OUT-type fire-extinguishers in the cockpits

Rescue System

In the event emergency egress is required, the following items are provided:
- an extendible slide from the cockpit hatch to the ground
- special emergency opening systems for hatches at the front and rear of the cockpit
- other emergency hatches strategically placed at various positions throughout the aircraft crew compartments
- inflatable survival boats

The extendible slide section is made in the form of a locked ribbon positioned in the central aisle next to the navigator's station adjacent to the access hatch. The extendible slide is hydraulically actuated.

Top: **Ventral antenna fairing found on aft fuselage of Tu-95MS.** Tom Copeland

Middle and right: **Tu-95MS horizontal tail root detail.** Tom Copeland

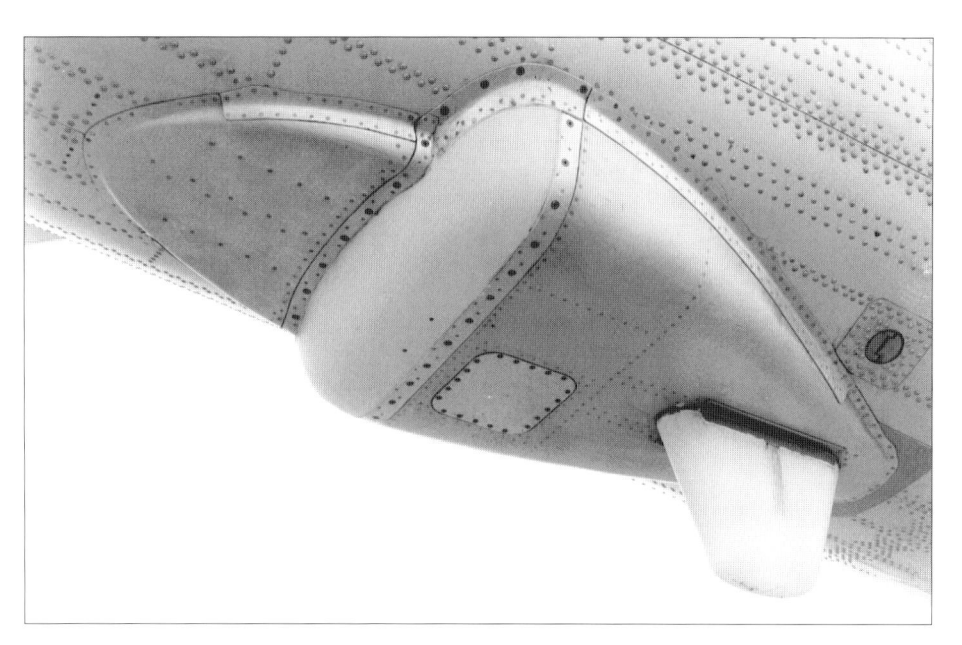

97

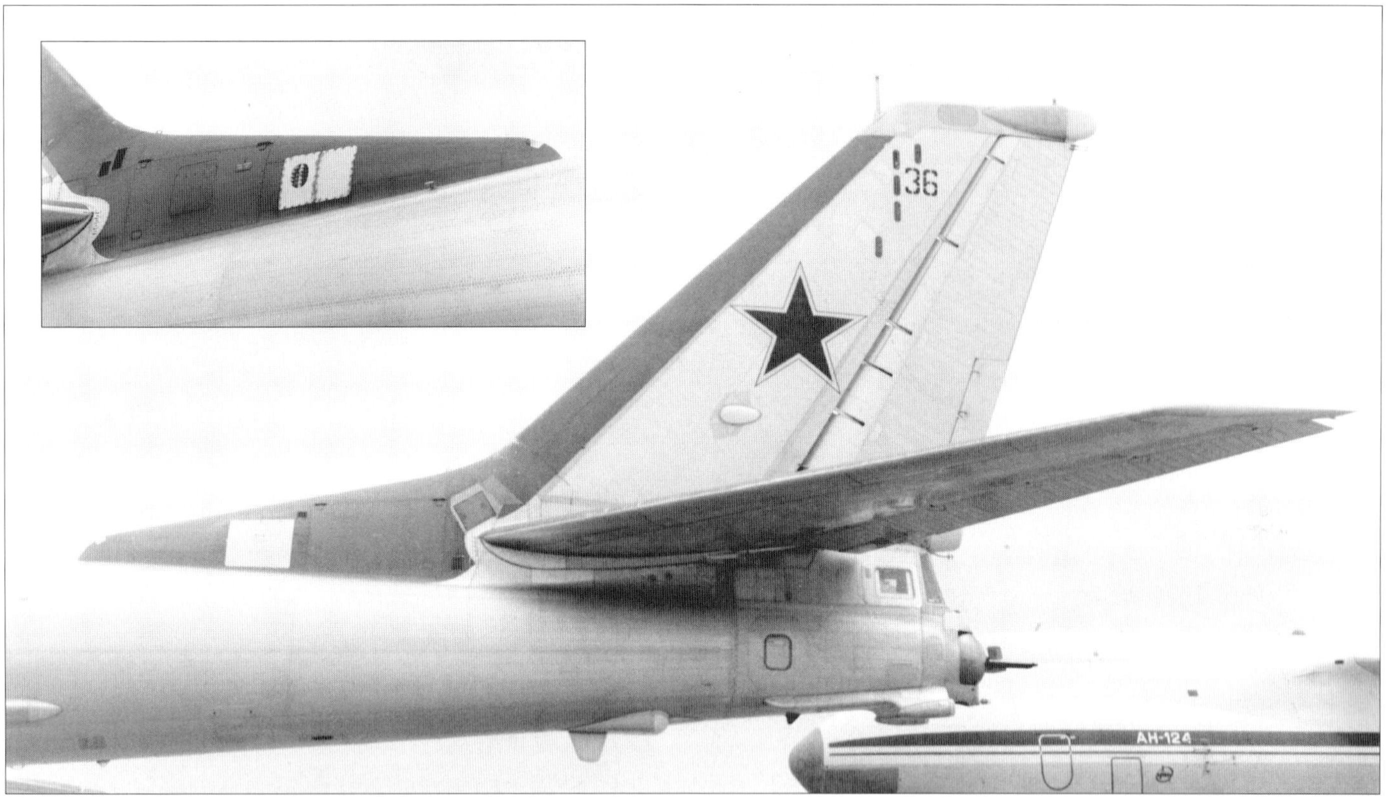
36
АН-124

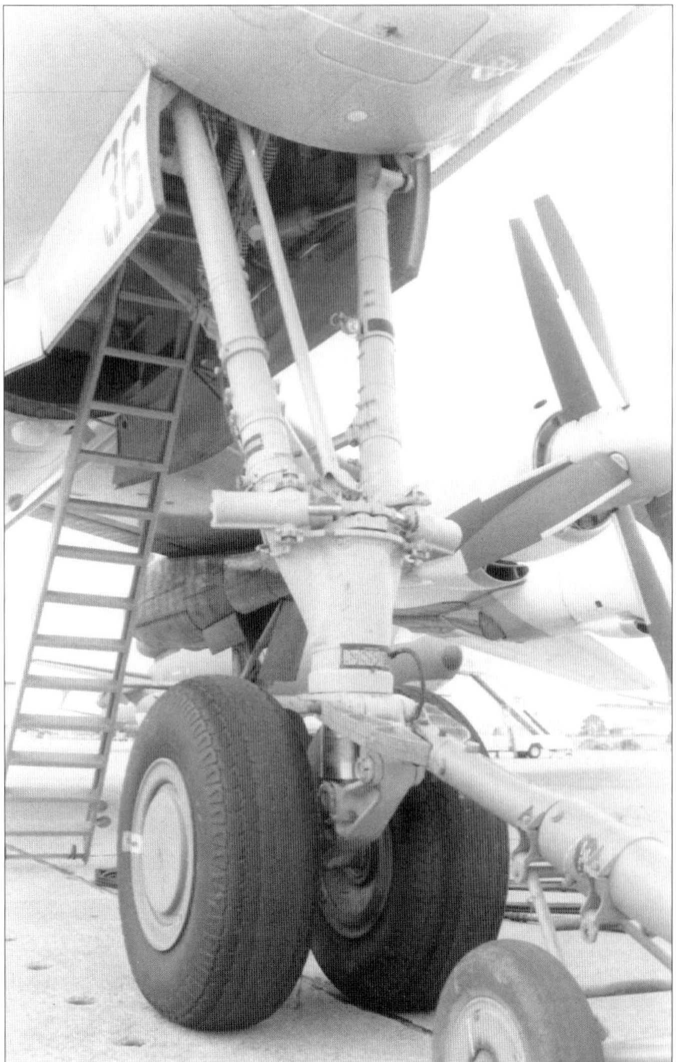
36

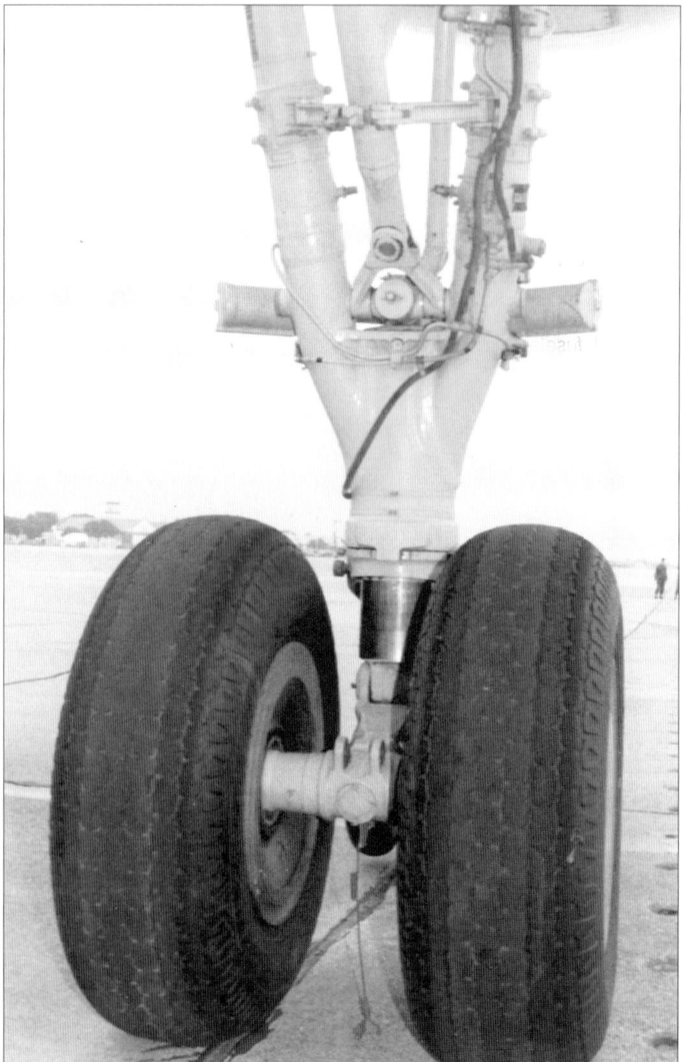

Emergency opening of the forward access hatch is accomplished via compressed air in coordination with emergency extension of the nose landing gear strut. Egress is by sliding down the extended flooring.

The opening of the aft hatch of the rear pressurized compartment is accomplished via two air cylinders. The hatch concurrently serves as an air dam, protecting escaping crew members from the initial wind blast if the aircraft is still airborne.

Safe egress is limited to speeds no greater than 630 km/h (391 mph) and an altitude of no less than 200 m (656 ft). In the event of a water landing with gear retracted, the crew can egress the aircraft from the front cockpit via a hatch positioned at the senior technician's and second navigator's positions and also through the pilots' windows. The crew occupying the aft stations can abandon the aircraft through the right emergency hatch in the rear canopy area. Inflatable LAS-5-2M raft-type boats are provided for flotation in the event of a water landing.

TU-95MR RECONNAISSANCE AIRCRAFT AND TU-95M BOMBER DESIGN DIFFERENCES

The Tu-95MR strategic reconnaissance aircraft was derived from the Tu-95M bomber. Differences are subtle, but notable and include a nose mounted telescoping in-flight refueling probe.

A dielectric fairing for the SRS-1 electronic reconnaissance station is positioned in the middle ventral fuselage section in the area of structural rings 13 and 22. Additional photographic cartridge holder brackets and trusses are mounted on the beams and top keel. In place of the bomb bay doors, a 90 mm (2.95 ft) extended fuselage section to accommodate the camera bay door transparencies is installed. The right side of the bay contains four camera windows to accommodate AFA-40, AFA-42/20, AFA-42/100, and AFA-41/20 cam-

---

Facing page top and inset: **Left and right views of vertical tail and dorsal extension of Tu-95MS.** Tom Copeland

Facing page bottom left and right: **Front and rear views of Tu-95MS nose landing gear.** Tom Copeland

Top (left): **Tu-95MS nose landing gear detail.** Tom Copeland

Top (right): **View of Tu-95MS nose landing gear well looking forward.** Tom Copeland

Right second from bottom: **Tu-95MS nose landing gear well doors. Noteworthy is bulged aft door panel to accommodate nose gear tires.** Tom Copeland

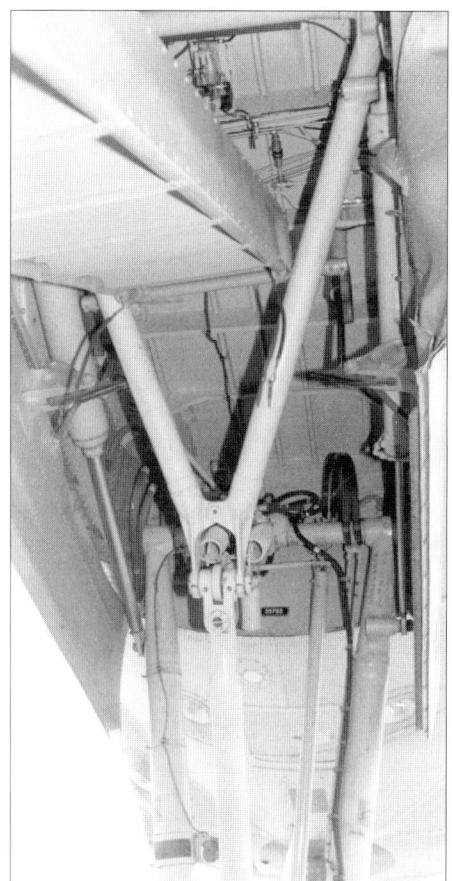

Bottom: **Tu-95MS gear retraction strut assembly with hydraulic actuators.** Tom Copeland

eras with a TAU topographic installation. The left side of the bay contains three camera windows for AFA-40, AFA-42/20, and AFA-42/100 cameras.

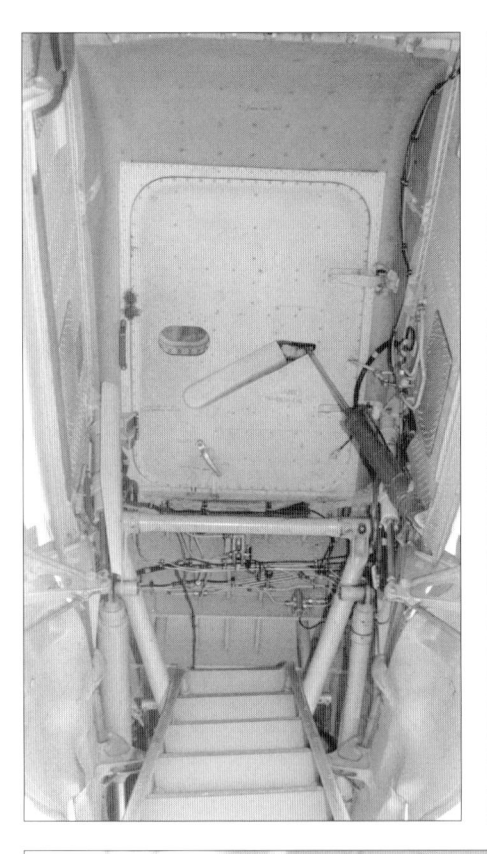

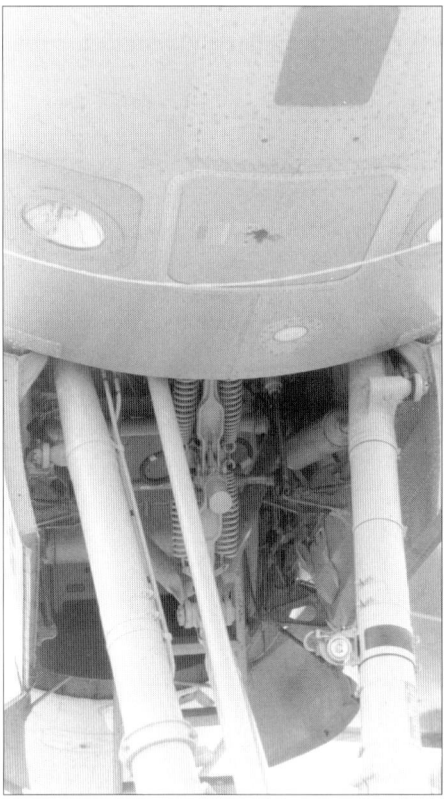

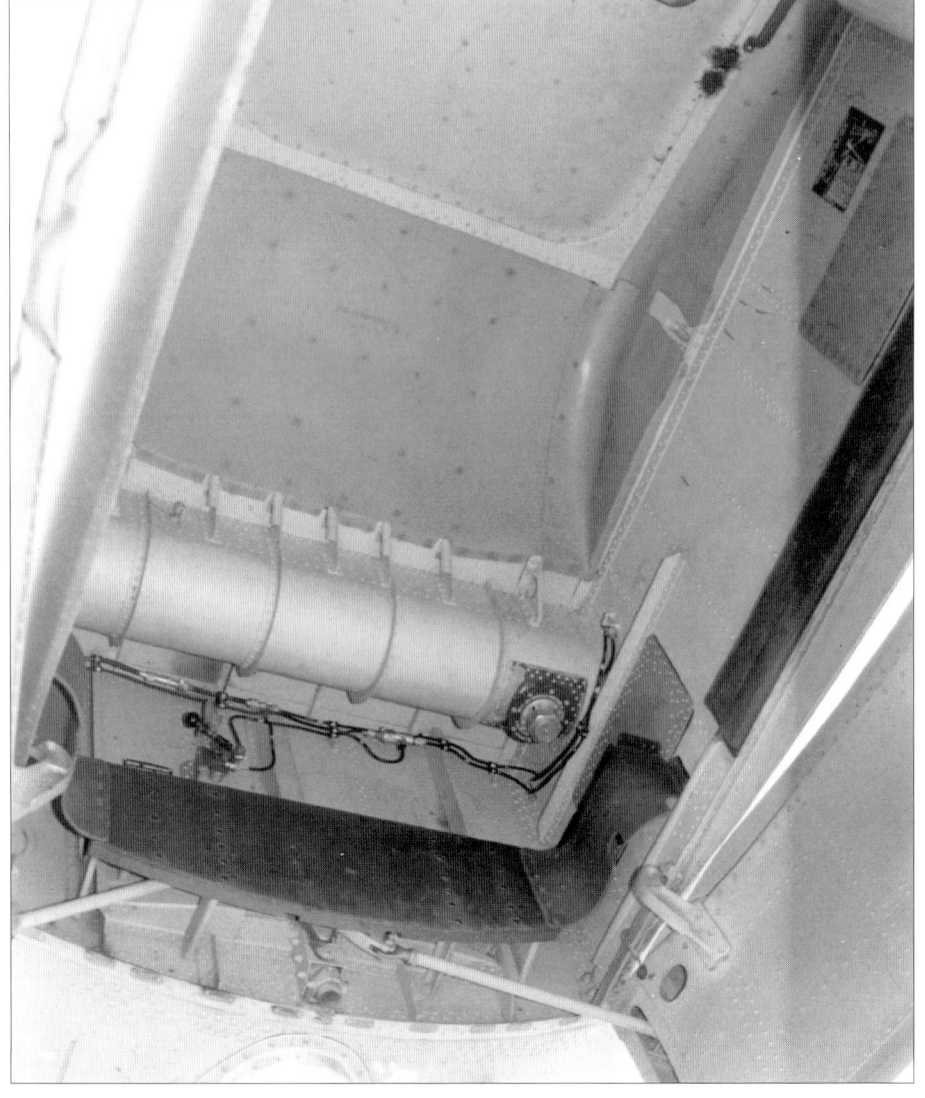

The camera bay doors provide frames for the protective, optical quality glass. Each glass panel is equipped with a protective, mechanically actuated cover that slides back and forth via electric drive motors as required.

The aft bay serves as the mounting point for a series of receiving antennas. Additionally, photo flare dispensers are positioned in this area and provided a hatch-like cover similar to the sliding units provided for the photo equipment. The DISS-1 Doppler speed and drift system antenna is mounted on this cover.

The fairing for the SRS-6 (*Romb*-4A) and SRS-7 (*Romb*-4B) electronic reconnaissance systems are set up between structural rings 65 and 72 on both the right and left sides of the aircraft.

The Tu-95MR's fuel is carried in no less than 72 tanks. The centralized *Konus* refueling system is standardized on the Tu-95MR. The fairing for the fuel plumbing is positioned on the right side of the fuselage. The refueling probe extension and retraction actuator is pneumatically powered.

The ARK-U2 *Istok* ultra-low-frequency system has been integrated into the radio navigation equipment complex with the Tu-95MR. The AKR-US in combination with the R-802 radio station is designed to accommodate the positioning requirements for coordinating inflight refueling sessions.

The Tu-95MR is equipped with the following electrical reconnaissance systems and equipment: SRS-1 with FRU-1 photorecorder, SRS-6 and SRS-7 and also radar sight R-1D with FARM-2A photo-attachment. The electrical equipment suite also has PT-1000CS converters.

The Tu-95MR has both daytime and nighttime photographic capability and is equipped accordingly. A bay between structural rings 67 and 70 serves as the mounting point for the following:

Daytime photography version 1:
- two AFA-42/20 cameras in fixed photo-installation
- four AFA-42/100 cameras in two dual swinging photo-installations
- AFA-41/20 in topographic photo-installation TAU
- AFA-42/10 camera in mobile oblique photo-installation
- ASHAFA-5 in fixed installation.

Top left: **Tu-95MS nose landing gear well detail. Entry hatch is closed.** Tom Copeland

Top right: **View of Tu-95MS nose landing gear upper strut assembly.** Tom Copeland

Left: **Tu-95MS nose landing gear well looking aft. Contoured upper roof section for tires is noteworthy.** Tom Copeland

Daytime photography version 2:
- two AFA-40 cameras and two AFA-42/20 cameras in fixed installations on two trusses
- AFA-41/20 camera in topographic installation TAU
- AFA-42/100 camera in mobile oblique photo *f* installation
- ASHAFA - 5 in fixed installation

Nighttime version:
- two night cameras NAFA-MK-75 joint in one container on swinging photo-installation
- ASHAFA -5 in fixed installation
- AFA-42/100 in fixed oblique installation FOTAB or SAB lighting flares are mounted in a cassette holding bay in the night version.

STRATEGIC MISSILE CARRIER DESIGN DIFFERENCES
Tu-95KM and Tu-95M

The Tu-95KM strategic missile carrier was designed to carry the Kh-20M stand-off missile and was different from the Tu-95M in the following ways:
- transmitting and receiving antennas and associated equipment for the Yad radar station were positioned in the nose radar compartment (with the guidance antenna mounted on top under a dielectric fairing; the target acquisition and tracking antenna was mounted under a ventral fairing under the nose)
- the inflight refueling boom was positioned over the nose, similar to that of the Tu-95MR
- the Kh-20M missile was carried partially retracted in the bomb bay and mounted on a pylon suspended between structural rings 21 and 23; a pneumatically actuated three-part fairing smoothed the airflow around the missile during cruise to launch point; the top half of the missile and its vertical fin were thus enclosed

During launch, the missile was lowered from the bay a distance of 950 mm (3.04 ft) while still attached to the pylon assembly. Once extended into the slipstream, the Kh-20M's engine was ignited and run up to cruise thrust. Once all systems were cleared for launch, the missile was released for the flight to the target.
- fuel was carried in 74 fuel tanks. An additional fuel tank was carried to accommodate the Kh-20M's launch requirements; this tank was mounted between structural

Top: **Tu-95MS nose landing gear strut detail from rear looking forward. Steering actuators are mounted on the front of the strut and interface with the lower strut assembly.**
Tom Copeland

Bottom: **Tu-95MS main landing gear assembly. Front of aircraft is to the right.** Tom Copeland

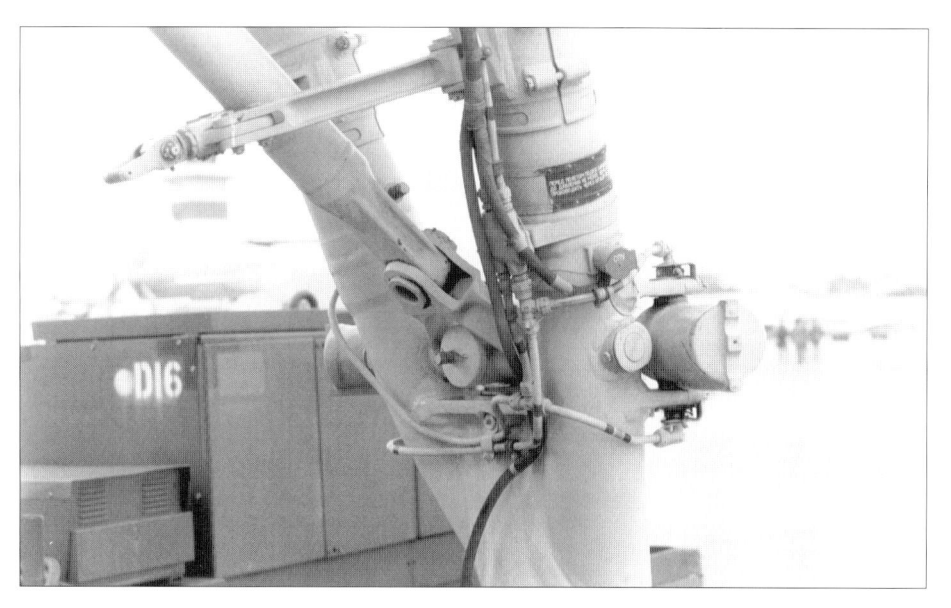

rings 45 and 51; it could carry up to 500 kg (1,102 lb) of fuel; the Tu-95KM, like the Tu-95MR, was equipped with an all-purpose fuel loading system
- the additional PO-4500 converter was installed for providing power to the Yad equipment. Low-powered PT-70 and PT-125 converters were replaced using the PT-500C and PT-1000CS (PT-1500C).

The radio communication suite was basically unchanged except for the installation of a R-832M radio unit. Additionally, the radio navigation equipment complement was enhanced via the installation of an RV-17 radio altimeter in place of the RV-25, and the installation of an ARK-U2 automatic radio compass.

Other radio and radar related changes included the installation of a *Yad* radar station, replacement of the PRS-41 *Argon* sighting station on the PRS-4, replacement of the SPO-2 station (*Sirena*-2) with the SPO-3 (*Sirena*-3), replacement of the SPS-2 with the SPS-3 electronic countermeasures unit, and installation of the *Romb*-4 reconnaissance system as installed on the Tu-95MR.

The *Put*-1B flight and navigational system was installed in the Tu-95KM. This provided semi-automatic control of the aircraft and eased the pilot's workload. ANU-1A auto-navigation and KS-6D compass systems also were installed.

The Tu-95KM was equipped with an ASO-2B passive jamming device. It was installed on two KDS-16-28 cassette holders between structural rings 62 and 63.

The Tu-95K-20 air-launched cruise missile aircraft carried the guidance systems for the K-20 and Kh-20M.

The *Yad* radar station for the K-20 system was designed for target acquisition and tracking and also for Kh-20M missile guidance to the target in conjunction with the *Yar* radar station and the *Yak* system as installed on the Kh-20M. The *Yad* system consisted of three basic parts: target acquisition and tracking equipment, guidance equipment, and control equipment.

Kh-20 guidance utilized a conventional line-of-sight guidance system. Control was maintained via transmissions from the carrier aircraft. The carrier aircraft, of necessity, had to remain in the general vicinity of the target in order to control the missile.

Kh-20 launch could be undertaken using either of two *Yad* options: using radar location or navigation location. Data from either could be input to the K-20 onboard systems. Both range and targeting data were included.

Top: **Tu-95MS right main landing gear detail.** Tom Copeland

Bottom: **Tu-95MS main gear strut assembly. Hydraulic lines and truck configuration are easily discerned.** Tom Copeland

After missile launch (via autopilot command), the Kh-20M's cruise-to-target would take placed at an altitude of about 15,000m (49,200ft). Once the missile was within striking distance, the carrier aircraft, at a distance of about 16km) would command (via the Yar system) the missile to begin its dive. Target contact would take place shortly afterwards.

The Kh-20 winged flying bomb was an all-metal monoplane with a swept cantilever wing and tail unit and a circular nose intake. The engine was an AL-7F (AL-7FK) turbojet with afterburner. The fuselage was essentially cylindrical in cross-section and served as the mounting point for the various guidance system components, the warhead (either conventional or nuclear), and the engine and fuel tanks. A PVD-7 air data sensor was mounted under the air intake. Operational weight of the Kh-20 was between 11600 and 11800kg (25,566 and 26,007lb). Empty weight was 5,878kg (12,955lb). Wingspan was 9.03m (29.62ft). Wingspan without the PVD-14 was 6.0m (19.68ft) - with PVD-15 it was 4.15m/13.61ft. Height was 3.015m (9.89ft), and maximum fuselage diameter was 1.805m (5.92ft).

Anti-Submarine Aircraft

The appearance of US nuclear submarines armed with Polaris ballistic missiles caused the Soviet anti-submarine warfare forces to extend their submarine detection range far enough out to sea to take into account the extraordinary range of these new weapons.

During the early 1960s, one aspect of this new thrust surfaced in the form of an initiative calling for the development of an aircraft with the range and armament needed to detect and destroy submarines at great distances from Russia's borders.

TU-142 TECHNICAL DETAILS

The Tu-142 is an all-metal cantilever mid-wing monoplane with a conventional tail unit, four turboprop engines, and a tricycle landing gear.

The airframe comprises the fuselage, wings, four engine nacelles and tail unit.

The fuselage is a stressed-skin monocoque structure with frames and stringers. Crew compartments are located forward and aft of the wings, the aft fuselage incorporates a tail gun barbette. Fuselage length is 46.4m (152ft 2¾in), maximum diameter is 2.9m (9ft 6in). A fixed refueling probe is installed in the fuselage

Top (left): **Tu-95MS main landing gear from front. Disk brakes are fully capable of stopping the aircraft on short, rough runways.** Tom Copeland

Top (right): **Tu-95MS main landing gear from rear. Noteworthy is static discharge drag line.** Tom Copeland

Right: **Tu-95MS main landing gear with retract strut assembly and gear well doors.** Tom Copeland

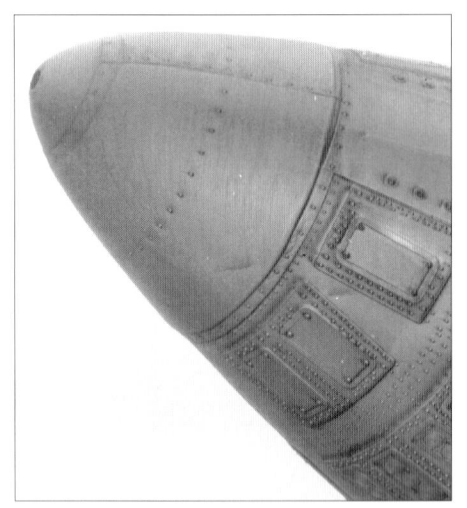

Top left: **Tu-95MS man landing gear strut assemblies. Massiveness dictates a robust unit.** Tom Copeland

Top right: **First production Tu-142s had twelve wheels and tires on each main gear assembly.** Yefim Gordon collection

Far left: **Aft section of main gear well fairing which is essentially a continuation of the inboard engine nacelle.** Tom Copeland

Left: **Tailwheel for over-rotation.** Tom Copeland

Below: **Aft section of main gear well fairing accommodates only the gear and its retraction/extension actuators. Engine exhaust, visible to the right, generates considerable heat around the gear well, thus dictating the use of titanium skin.** Tom Copeland

nose. Anywhere from 28,007 to 35,009 kg (61,728 to 77,160 lbs) are transferred during a single refueling, depending on mission radius and distance from base.

In an emergency the crew bails out through the entry hatch located in the nosewheel well. The sequence is initiated by opening an air cock, after which the nose gear unit is extended and the entry hatch is pneumatically opened. The flight deck floor incorporates an hydraulically-driven conveyor belt; the motor of the latter is powered by pressure from three hydraulic tanks, which allows it to run for 100 seconds even if all four engines and all electrics fail. The tail gunner bails out via the ventral entry hatch.

In the event of ditching the crew evacuates via three dorsal emergency exits in the forward crew compartment and a portside emergency exit in the tail gunner's compartment. There is a container with two PSN-6A inflatable rescue rafts in the forward crew compartment and with an LAS-5M inflatable rescue dinghy in the tail gunner's compartment.

The centre fuselage incorporates two payload bays for bombs, ASW torpedoes and sonobuoys.

The wings are made up of five sections (centre section, inner and outer panels). The inner and outer wing panels have integral fuel tanks divided into four bays each side; two bag tanks are located in the centre section and one more in the aft fuselage, giving a total fuel load of 91,024 kg (200,617 lb). The wingspan is 164 ft (50 m), leading-edge sweep is 33° 30'. The wing employs sections utilized on the Tu-95 and other Tupolev aircraft; however, the sections have been modified by 'bending' the leading edge downwards to improve the lift/drag ratio. This markedly reduces the fuel consumption per mile; thus, the Tu-142 has a very similar fuel consumption to the basic Tu-95, despite the increased drag produced by the large ventral radome.

The powerplant consists of four Kuznetsov NK-12M turboprops rated at 15,000 eshp and driving AV-90 four-bladed contra-rotating propellers.

Tests showed that, at a takeoff weight of 182,048 kg (401,234 lb), the aircraft has a 12,300 km (7,687 miles) range with a 5,500 kg (12,125 lb) payload and a 5% navigational fuel reserve. Cruising speed is 700 to 750 km/h (437 to 468 mph).

Top right: **Main gear retract aft into gear well.** Tom Copeland

Right (center): **Titanium is a difficult metal to work. To accommodate heat expansion, the titanium panels are overlapped vertically and ribbed horizontally.** Tom Copeland

Right: **View of right pair of Tu-95 Kuznetsov NK-12 engines and their enormous contra-rotating propellers.** Victor Kudryavtsev

The Tu-142 is equipped with a *Berkut* search radar (originally developed for the Ilyushin Il-38) slightly modified for better integration with the airframe and other systems. The radar set is almost unchanged, except that the TsVM-264 computer is replaced by a TsVM-263 unit, causing some software changes.

Unlike the Il-38, the Tu-142 carries only two types of sonobuoys (RGB-I and RGB-2), no MAD sensor is fitted.

The *Berkut*-95 radar is linked with the airspeed sensor, altimeter, compass and gyro. Major changes to the electric wiring had to be made, since the Tu-142's flight data sensors and flight controls have rather different parameters from those of the Il-38.

The number of automatically computed and performed tactical tasks was reduced to nine: flying to the search area, setting up a straight barrier of sonobuoys, monitoring a straight barrier of sonobuoys, offset dropping of RGB-2 buoys, setting up a circular barrier of sonobuoys, flying in parallel tacks, dropping bombs or torpedoes as directed by RGB-2 buoys and dropping torpedoes as directed by RGB-I buoys' beacons.

It is obvious that some tactics which were no longer current were deleted. These included all tasks associated with the RGB-3 sonobuoys which the aircraft did not carry; automatic search based on radar inputs was also dismissed as an outdated tactic. Besides, operational experience showed that crews would not return and drop an extra buoy to replace one that went unserviceable (as originally envisaged), and this task was deleted as well.

The designers made good use of the operational experience accumulated with the Il-38 and equipped the Tu-142 with the ANP-3V automatic navigation system without waiting for aircrews to request this. This eased crew workload a good deal and increased combat efficiency, especially when tracking a sub.

Like the Il-38, servicing was rather difficult. It took ground crews 7 to 8 hours to prepare the aircraft for a sortie; it was not until much later that this time was drastically cut. Of the forty-odd payload configurations that could be carried by the Tu-142 the most effective by far was the search/strike weapons fit comprising 176 RGB-1 sonobuoys, ten RGB-2 buoys and two different ASW torpedoes was regarded as the most effective. In pure search (maritime patrol) configuration the aircraft could carry 396 or 440 sonobuoys, which was completely unnecessary from a tactical standpoint; only top brass with little knowledge of the Tu-142's missions could be delighted by this monstrous payload.

Receiving an aircraft with twice the range of the Il-38 then in service with the AV-MF improved its ASW capabilities no end. The Tu-142 could easily reach the North Atlantic; however, in so doing it had to pass close to the Faroe Islands and Iceland, and high-flying Tu-142s were habitually intercepted by USAF and RAF fighters on the way out and home. More than once they were also shadowed by Lockheed P-3A 'Orions' and BAe 'Nimrods' which would occasionally try to stop the Soviet aircraft from accomplishing their task.

However, the desire to get an aircraft with long range and great endurance finally led to a loss of quality: the avionics fit was outdated and the aircraft was much more costly to operate than the Il-38. Therefore, the Tu-142's production run was very modest. As the Tu-142M equipped with state-of-the-art avionics entered service, the AV-MP top command had no idea what to do with the initial production Tu-142s and in 1978 the aircraft were transferred to the Pacific Fleet Air Arm which had no further use for them. Thus, by 1978 the early Tu-142 became - 'an aircraft without a cause'.

Opposite page top: **Tu-95K-22 outboard engine nacelle.** Victor Kudryavtsev

Opposite page middle: **Outboard NK-12MP engine and nacelle on Tu-142MR.** Yefim Gordon

Opposite page bottom: **Inboard NK-12 engine and nacelle from Tu-95MS.** Tom Copeland

Right: **Tu-95MS outboard engine nacelle.** Tom Copeland

Below (left): **Rear view of forward nacelle fairing and root sections of contra-rotating propellers.** Tom Copeland

Below (right): **Intake for NK-12 is positioned ventrally.** Tom Copeland

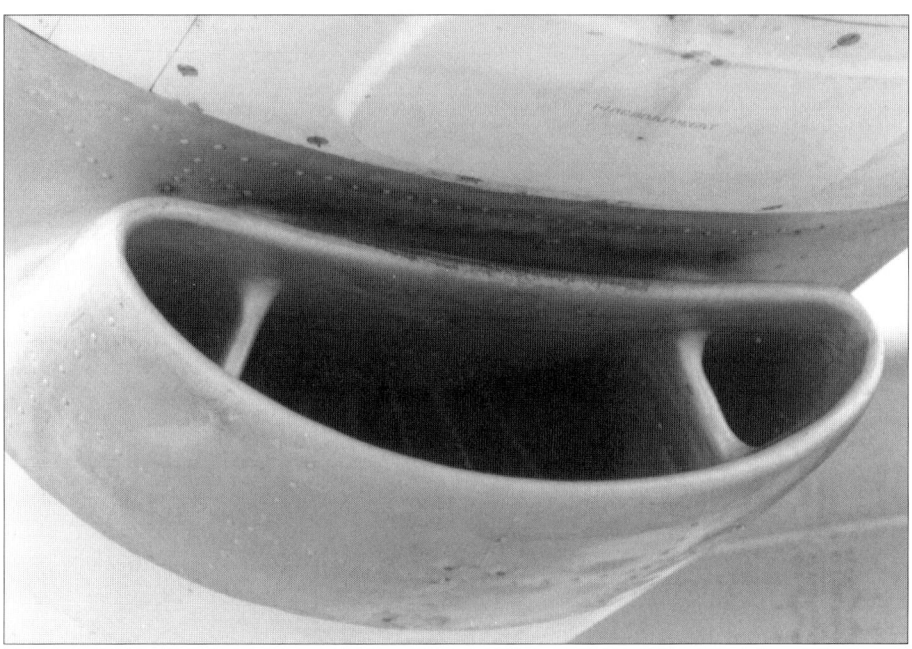

Left: **Each of the Tu-95's four Kuznetsov NK-12 engines is equipped with a massive contra-rotating AV-60 propeller unit consisting of two four-bladed propellers. This design innovation provided two distinct advantages over any other configuration: (1) it permitted efficient and complete utilization of the NK-12's massive torque output; and (2) it permitted a smaller diameter propeller disk, thus permitting the installation of smaller and lighter landing gear.** Tom Copeland

Below: **All four blades on each propeller unit are featherable and their pitch angle is manually set by the pilot. Blade pitch angle plays a critical role in all aspects of the Tu-95/Tu-142's performance including takeoff and landing distances, maximum speed, cruising speed, rate-of-climb, range, and fuel consumption.**
Tom Copeland

Top left: **Inboard Kuznetsov NK-12 exhausts are bifurcated and exit on each side of each engine nacelle aft fairing (which serves as the main landing gear bay).** Tom Copeland

Top right: **Aft fairing behind NK-12 exhausts is constructed of titanium for heat resistance.** Tom Copeland

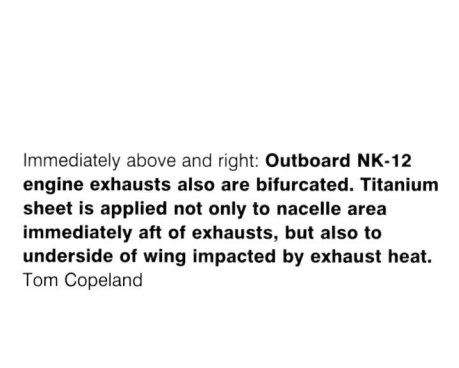

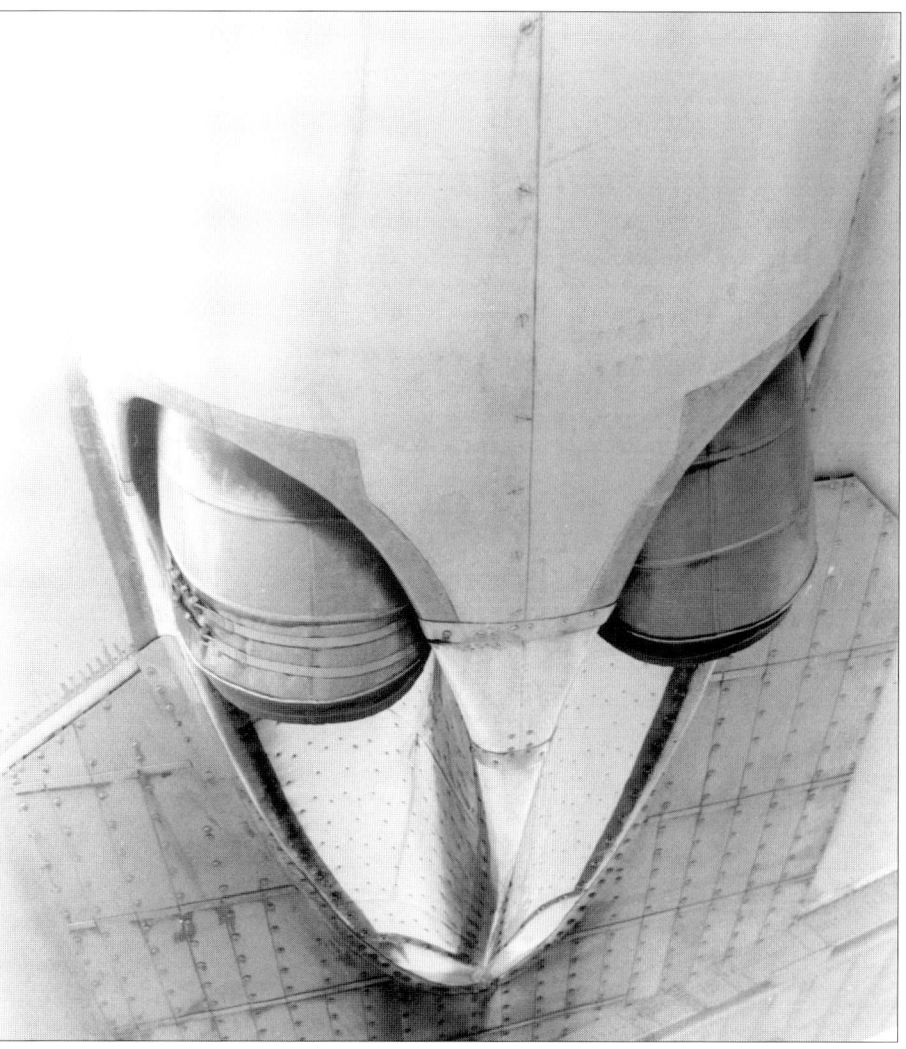

Immediately above and right: **Outboard NK-12 engine exhausts also are bifurcated. Titanium sheet is applied not only to nacelle area immediately aft of exhausts, but also to underside of wing impacted by exhaust heat.** Tom Copeland

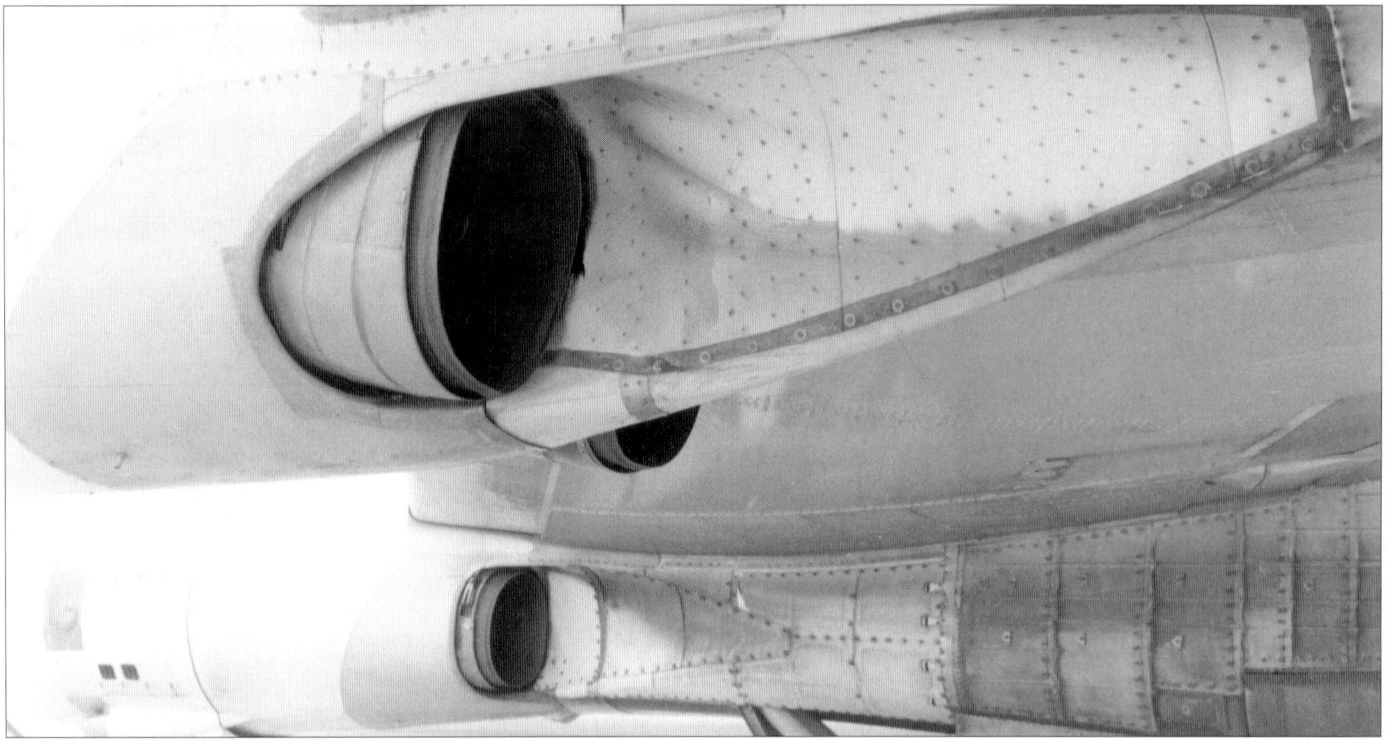

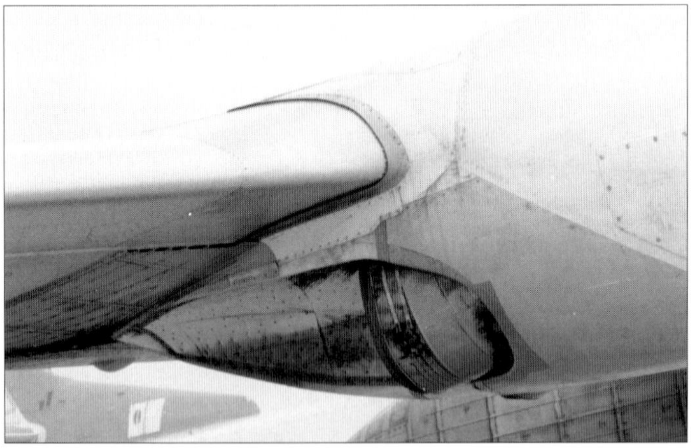

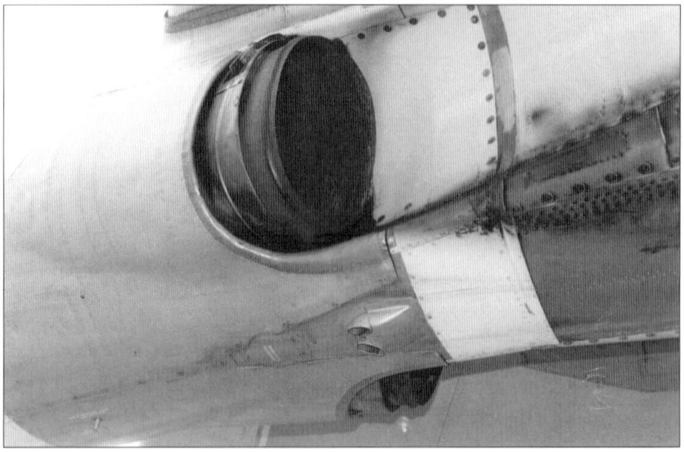

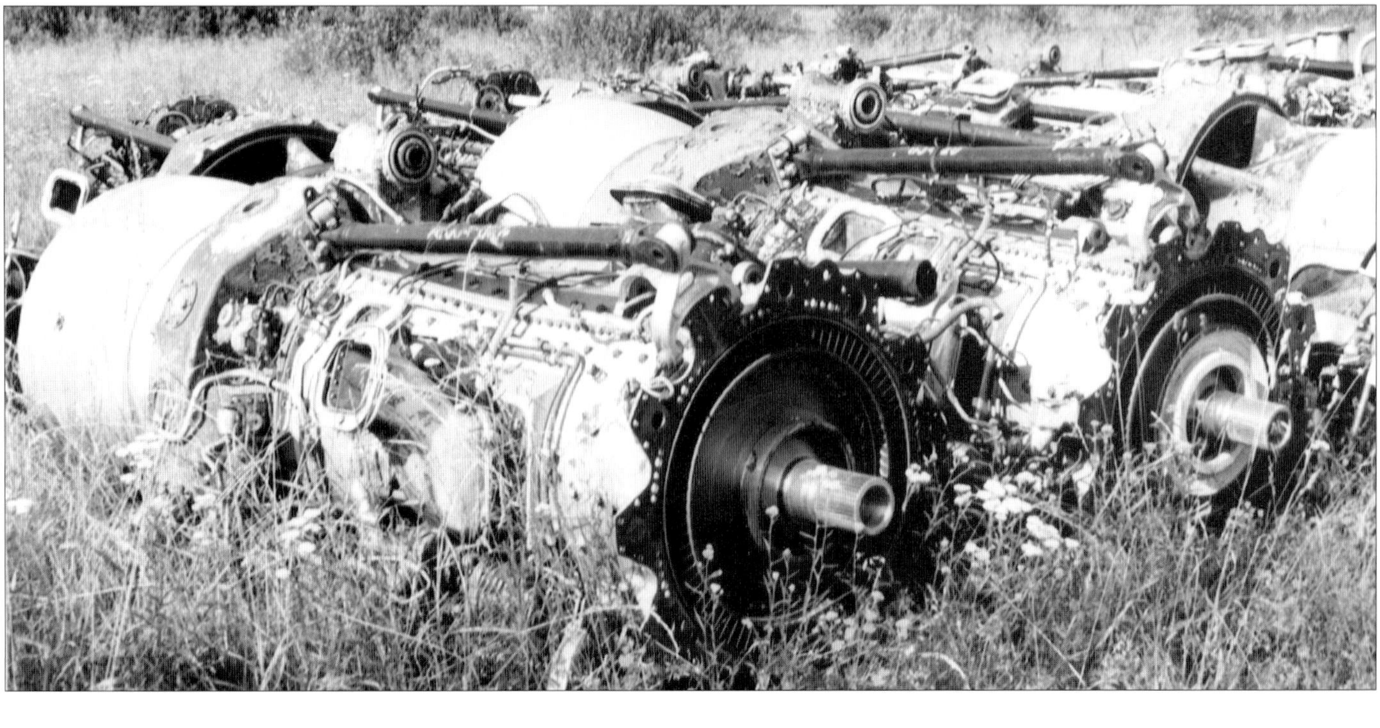

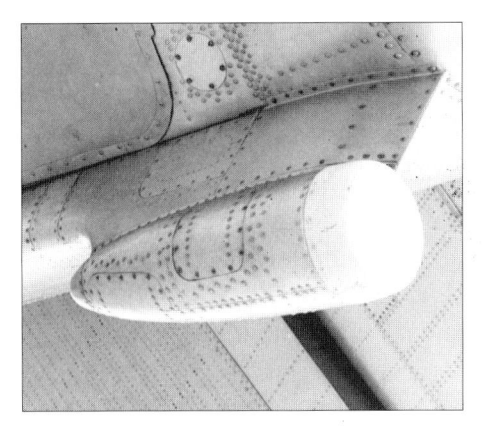

Opposite page top: **Differences in outboard (foreground) and inboard engine exhaust configurations is readily apparent in this view.** Tom Copeland

Opposite page middle left: **Outboard NK-12MP exhaust is abbreviated when compared to the inboard nacelle exhaust. Leading edge root fairing is noteworthy.** Tom Copeland

Opposite page middle right: **Inboard NK-12 engine exhaust and associated fairing.** Tom Copeland

Opposite page bottom: **Discarded NK-12s resulting from the down-sizing of the Russian Air Force and the subsequent decision to scrap older Tu-95s.** Yefim Gordon

Directly above: **Aft facing warning sensors and their associated fairings are positioned on each side of the empennage, just below the tail gun installation.** Tom Copeland

Above right: **Tu-95MS-16 with wing pylons for carrying the Raduga Kh-55MS cruise missile. Six missiles can be carried in the bomb bay and 10 can be carried on the pylons.** Tom Copeland collection

Right, second from top: **Sonobuoys being prepared for loading into a Tu-142.** Yefim Gordon collection

Right: **Radar-directed, remotely-controlled gun turrets, equipped with two 23 mm cannon, are usually retracted and faired cleanly with the rest of the fuselage.** Yefim Gordon collection

Below: **Special wingtip-mounted camera for Tu-95N.** Jay Miller

Bottom right: **View of the rear-facing under fuselage turret.** Yefim Gordon collection

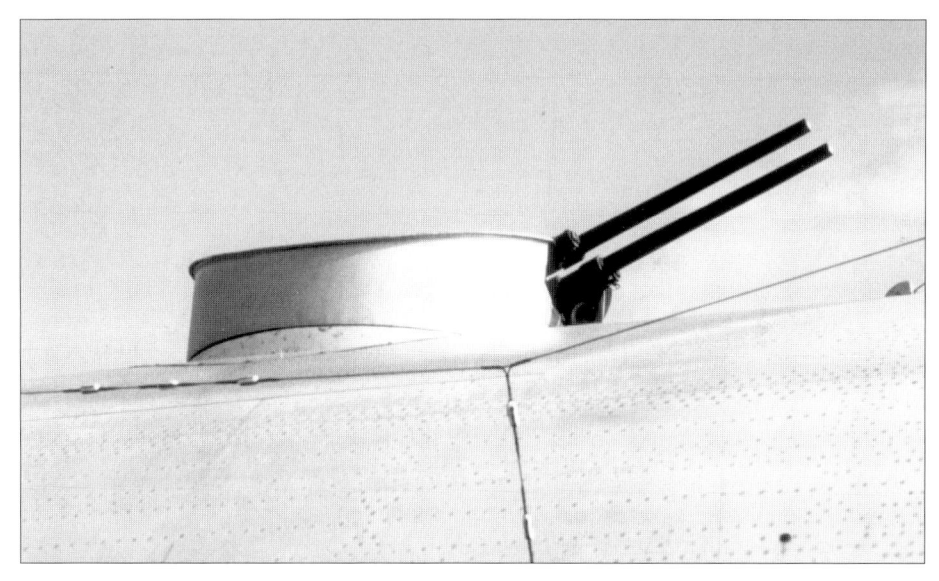

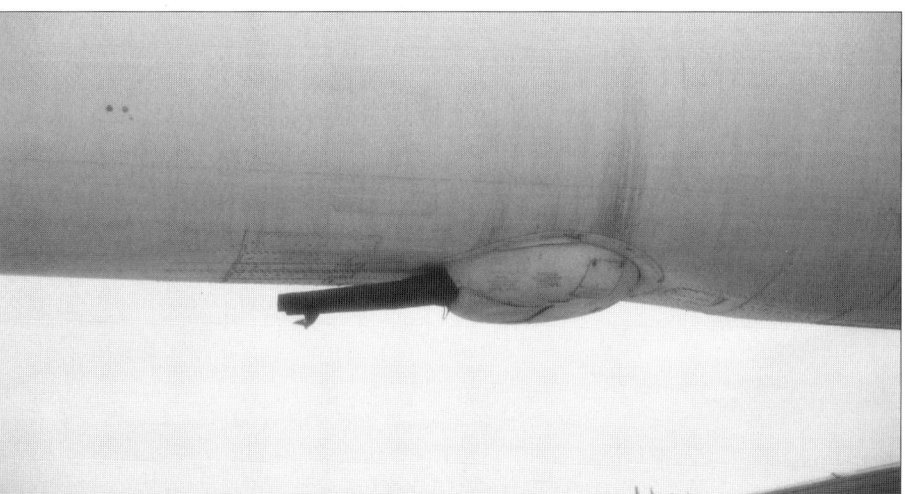

Top left: **Tail turret is manned and equipped with two 23 mm cannon.** Tom Copeland

Top right: **PRS-4 radar for tail gun is mounted above turret.** Tom Copeland

Middle left: **Special fairing in Tu-95K-22 bomb bay accommodates missile.** Yefim Gordon

Above: **Tail guns are articulated horizontally and vertically.** Yefim Gordon

Left: **Trailing wire antenna unit for VLF transmission/reception is mounted in aft bomb bay of Tu-142MR.** Yefim Gordon

Below: **Atmospheric sampling unit of Tu-95RTs is seen mounted above wing and aft of outboard engine nacelle.** Jay Miller collection

Design Study for '64' Bomber
(One of many)

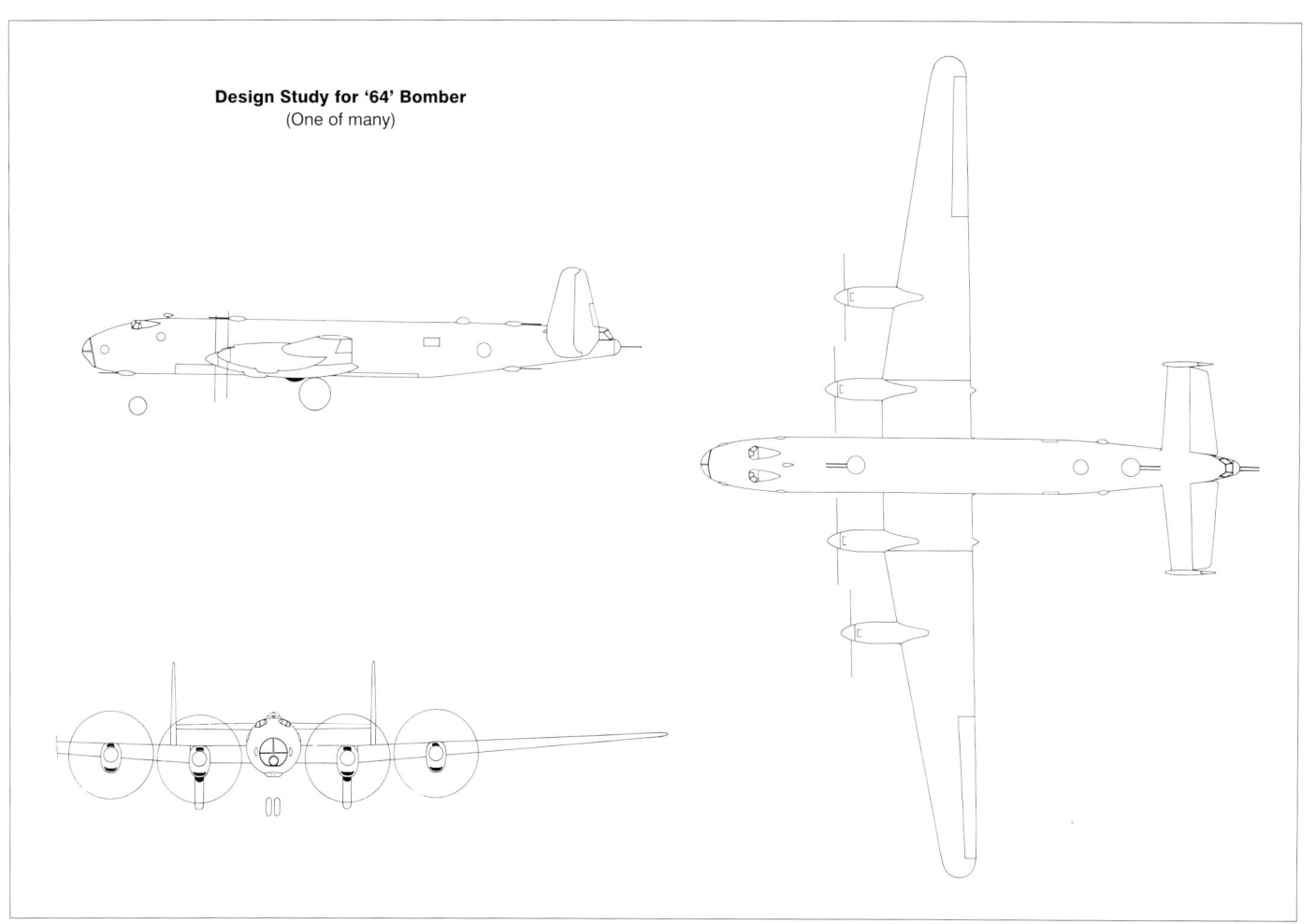

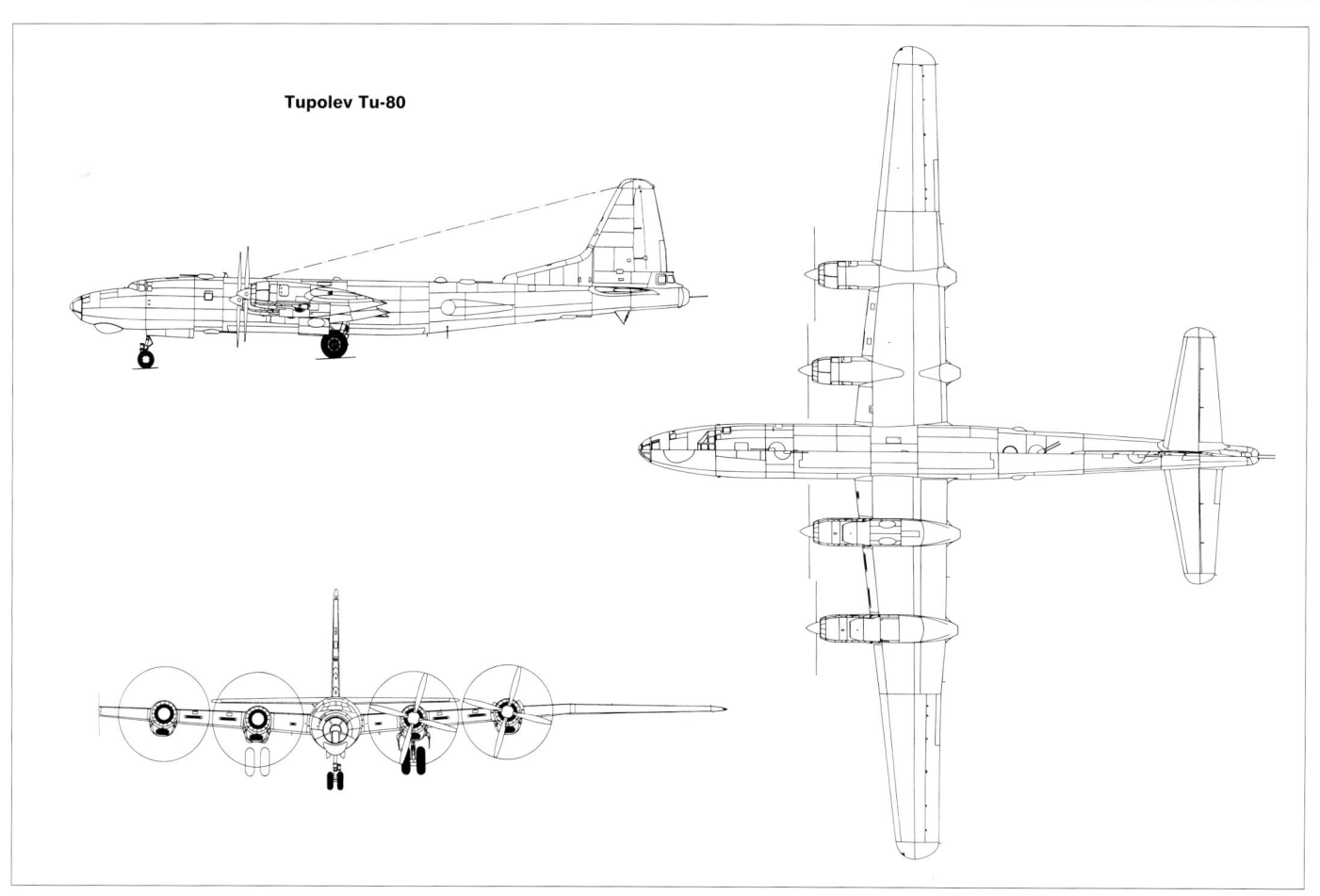

Tupolev Tu-80

Tupolev 95-1 Prototype

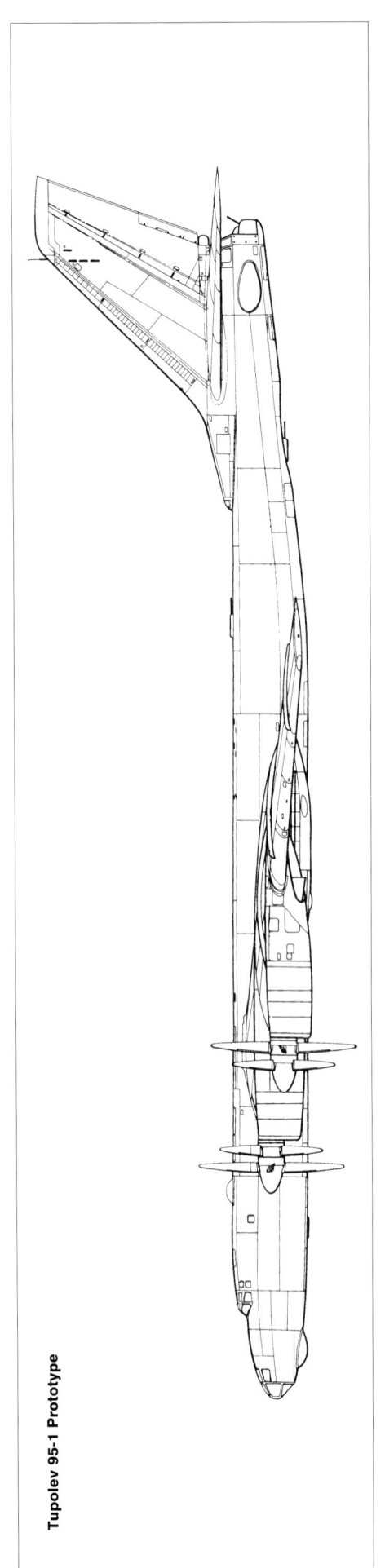

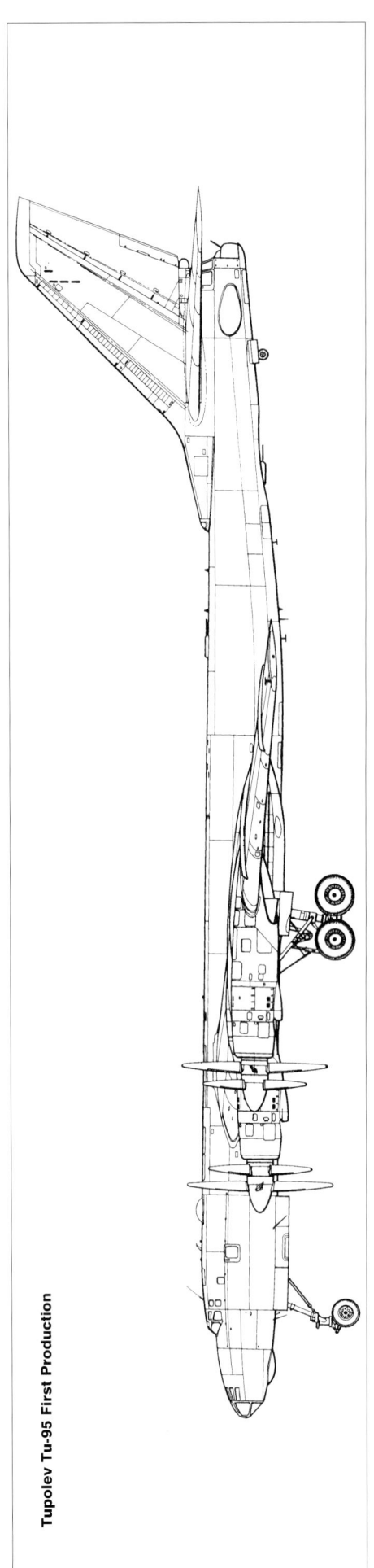

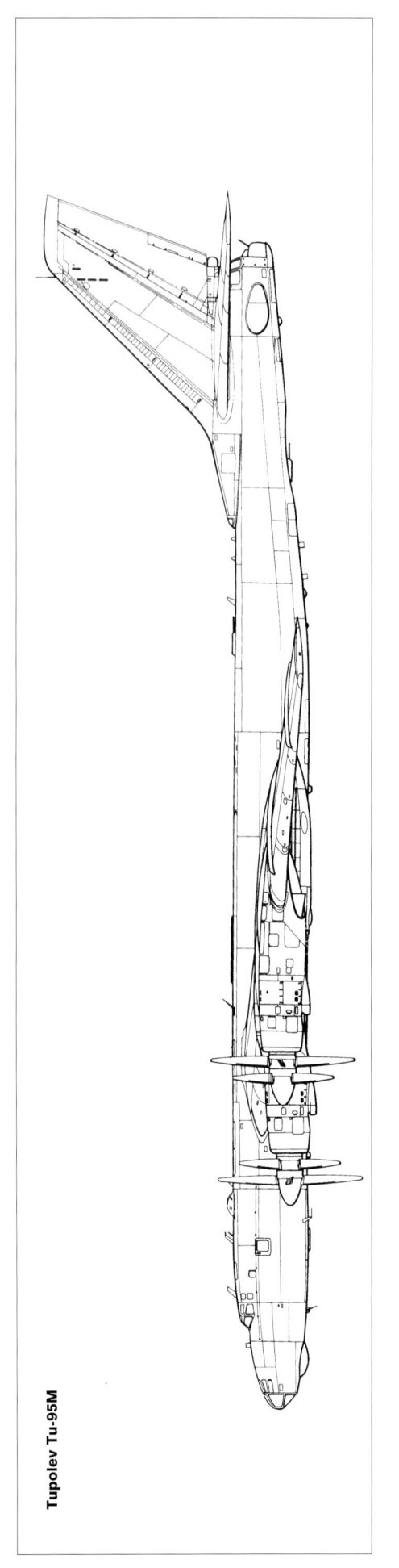

Tupolev Tu-95 First Production

Tupolev Tu-95M

Tupolev Tu-116

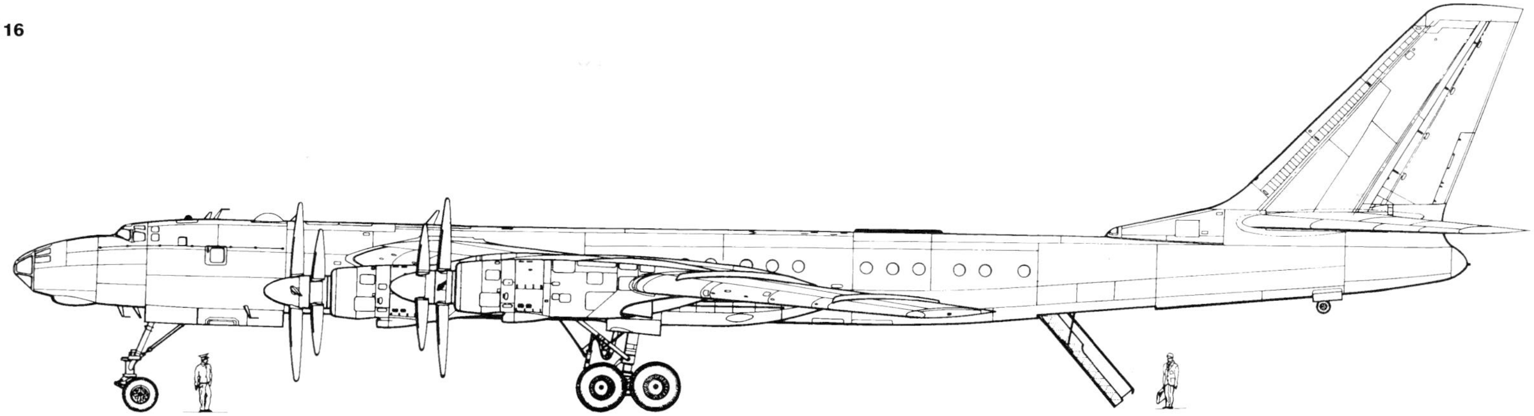

Tupolev Tu-95M-5

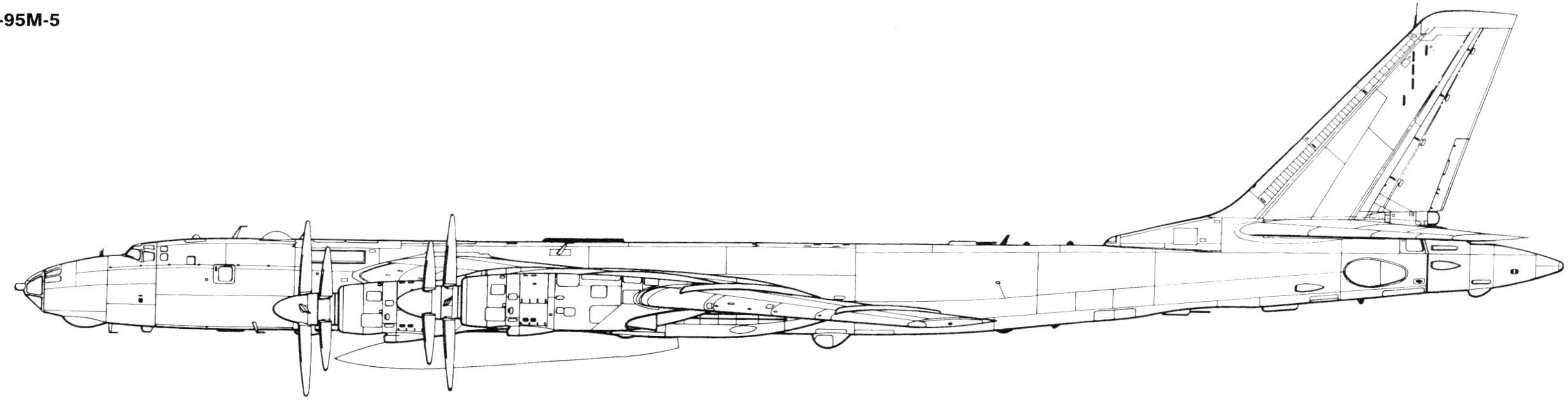

Tupolev Tu-95K

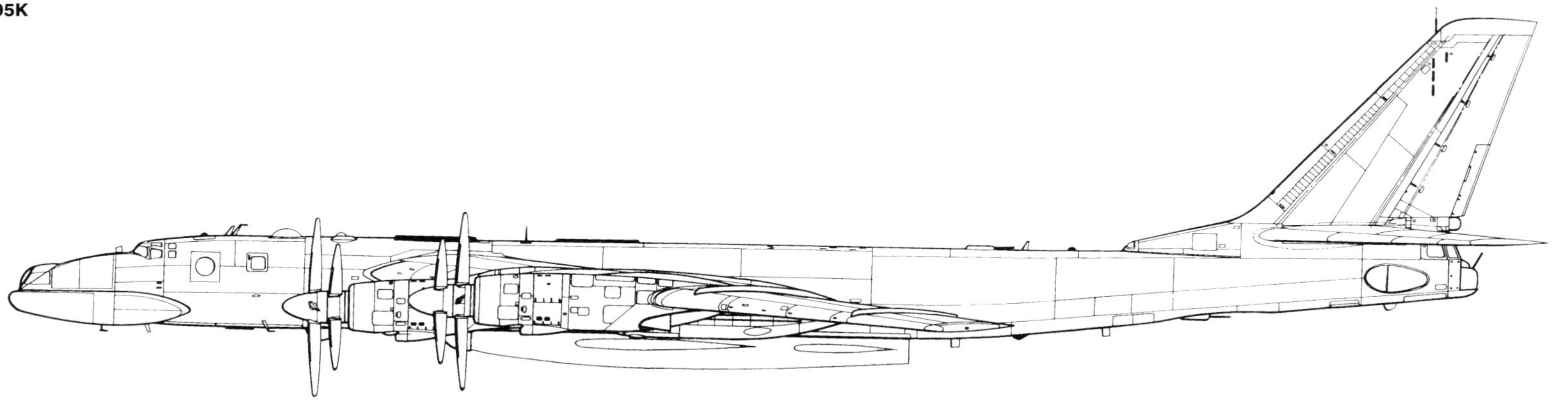

115

Tupolev Tu-95KD

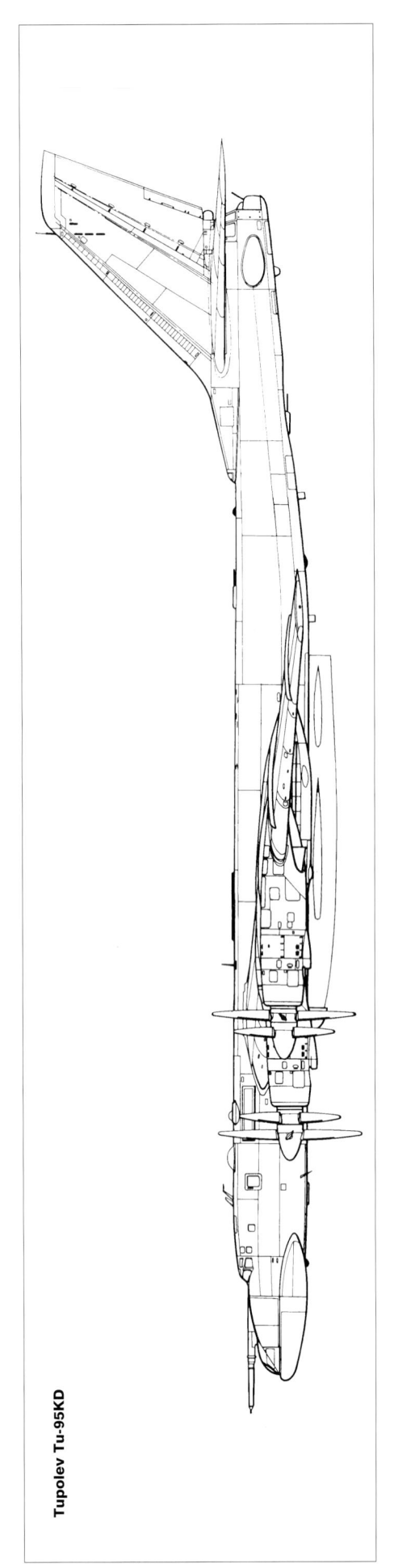

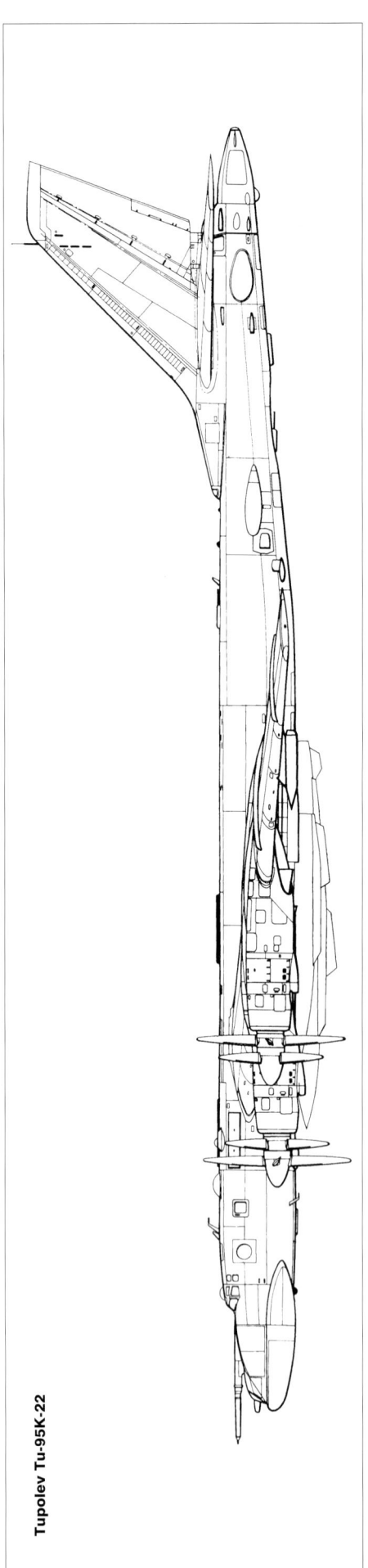

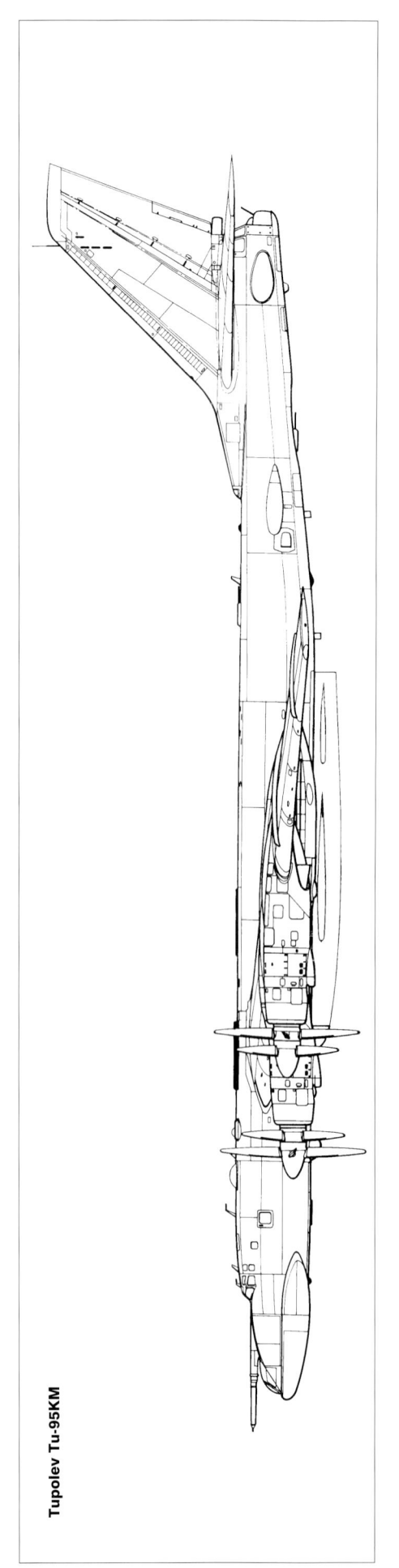

Tupolev Tu-95K-22

Tupolev Tu-95KM

Tupolev Tu-95M-5 (without missile)

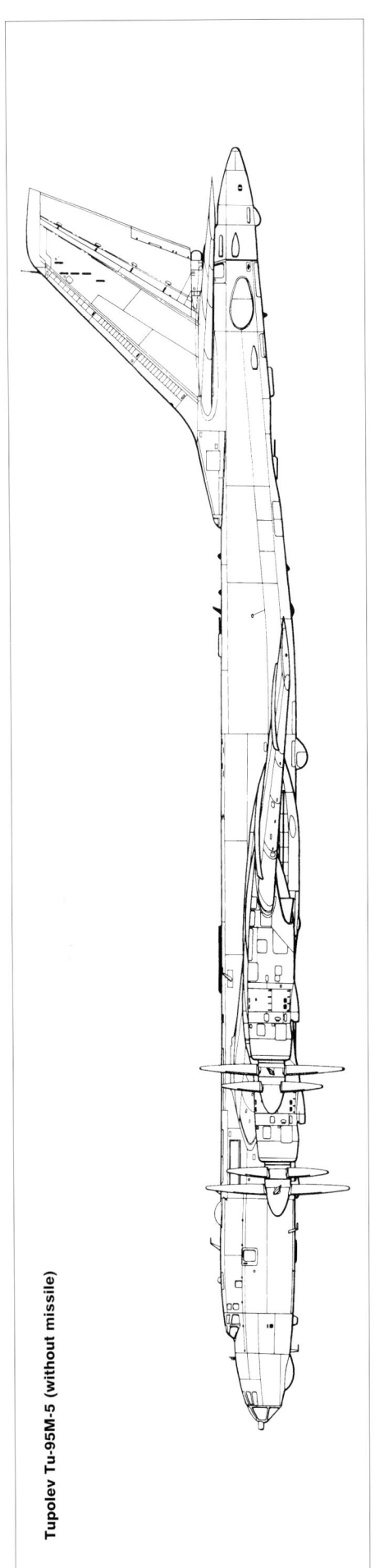

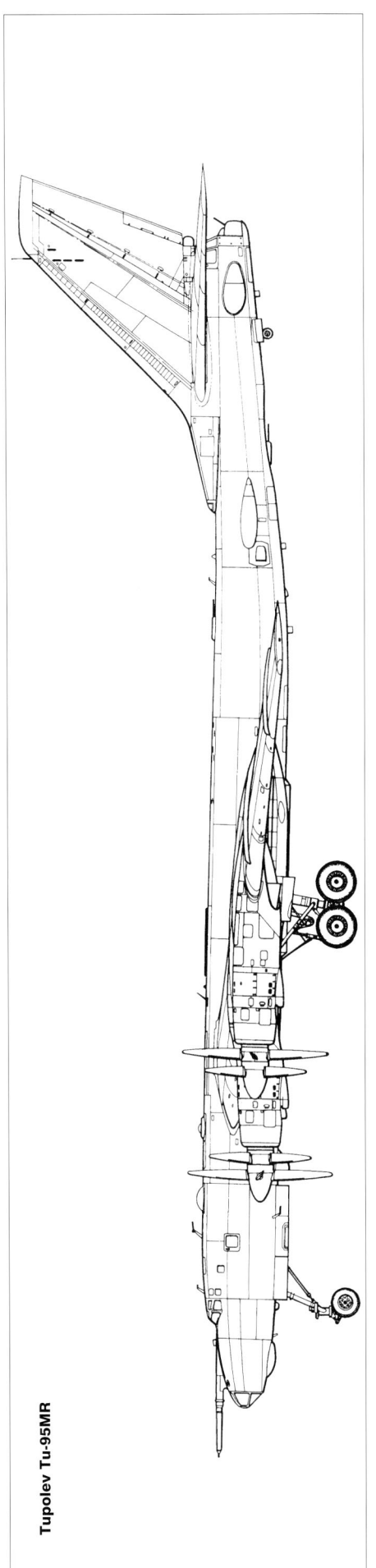

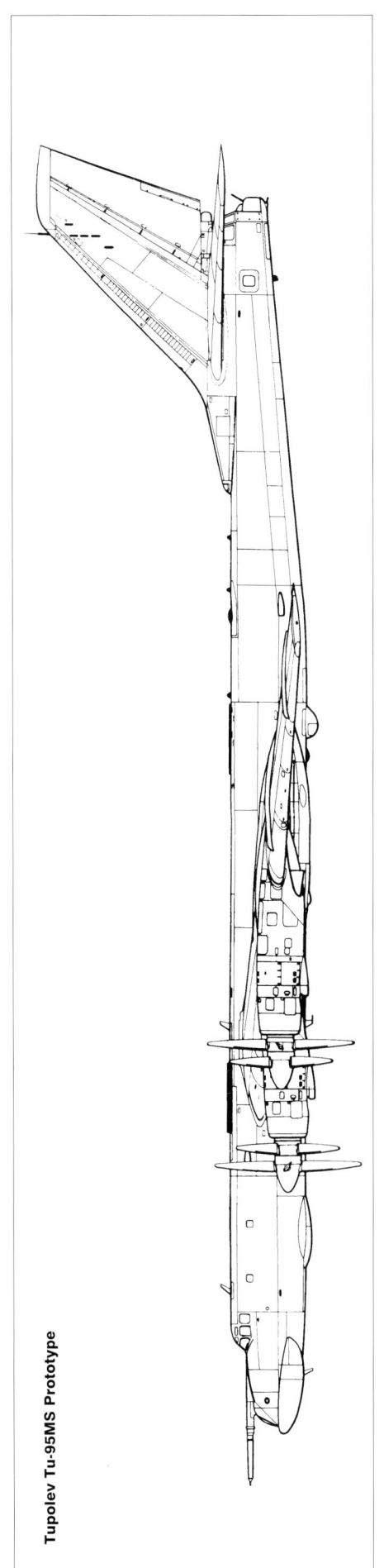

Tupolev Tu-95MR

Tupolev Tu-95MS Prototype

Tupolev Tu-95MS

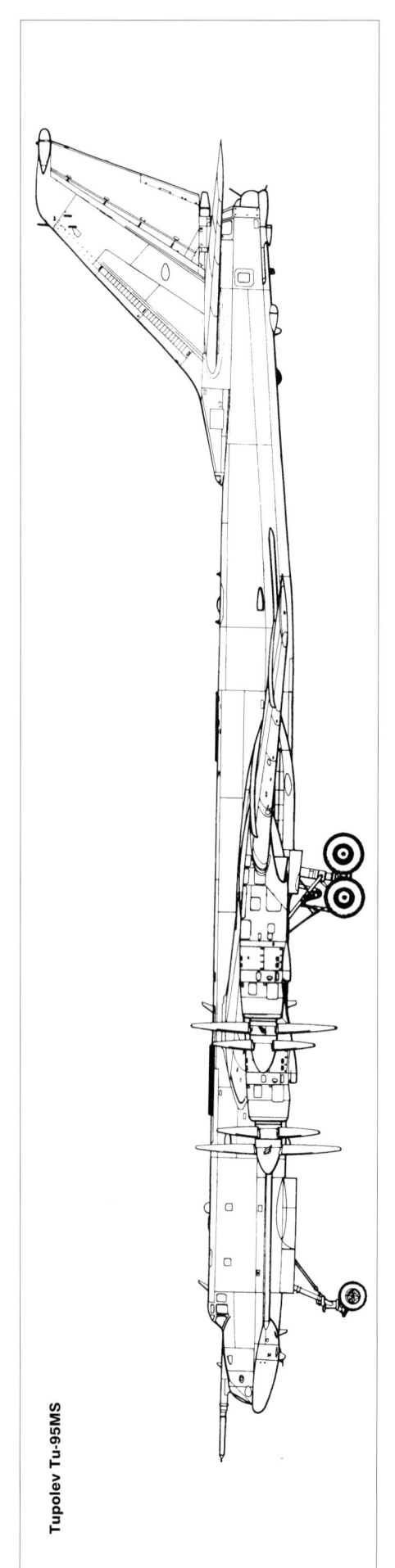

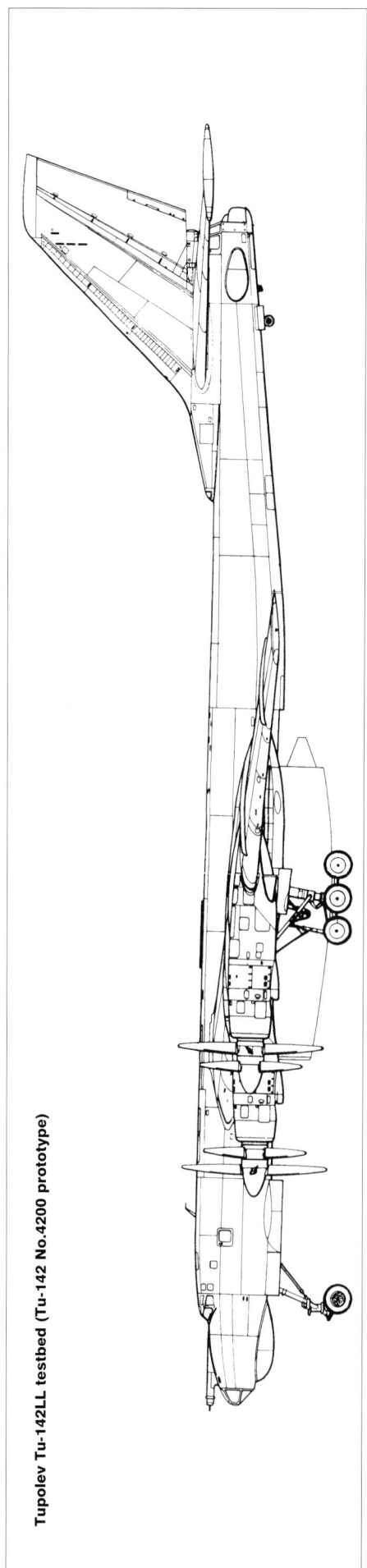

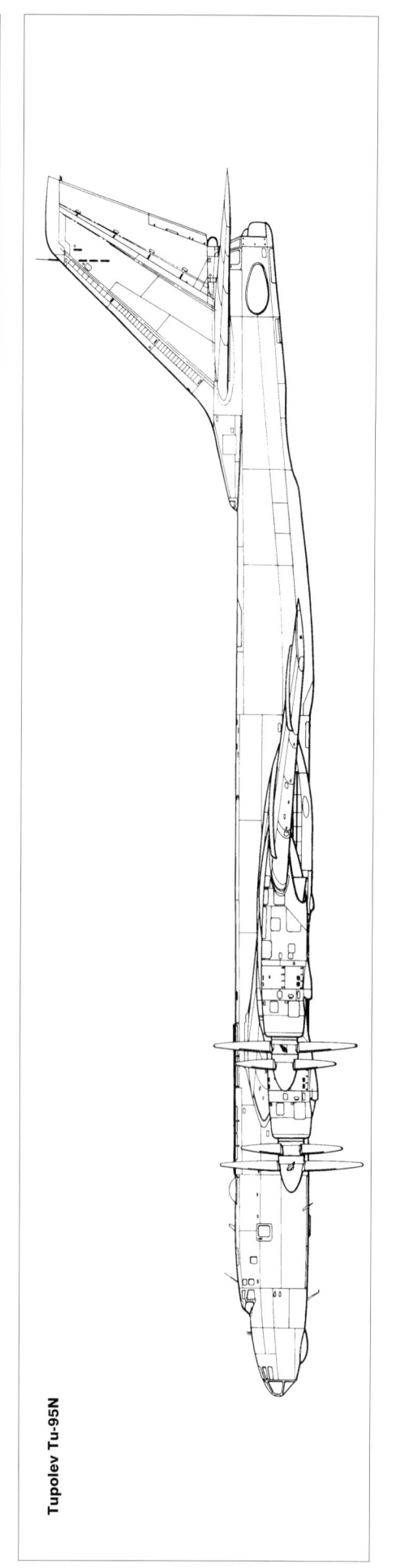

Tupolev Tu-142LL testbed (Tu-142 No.4200 prototype)

Tupolev Tu-95N

Tupolev Tu-95LAL testbed

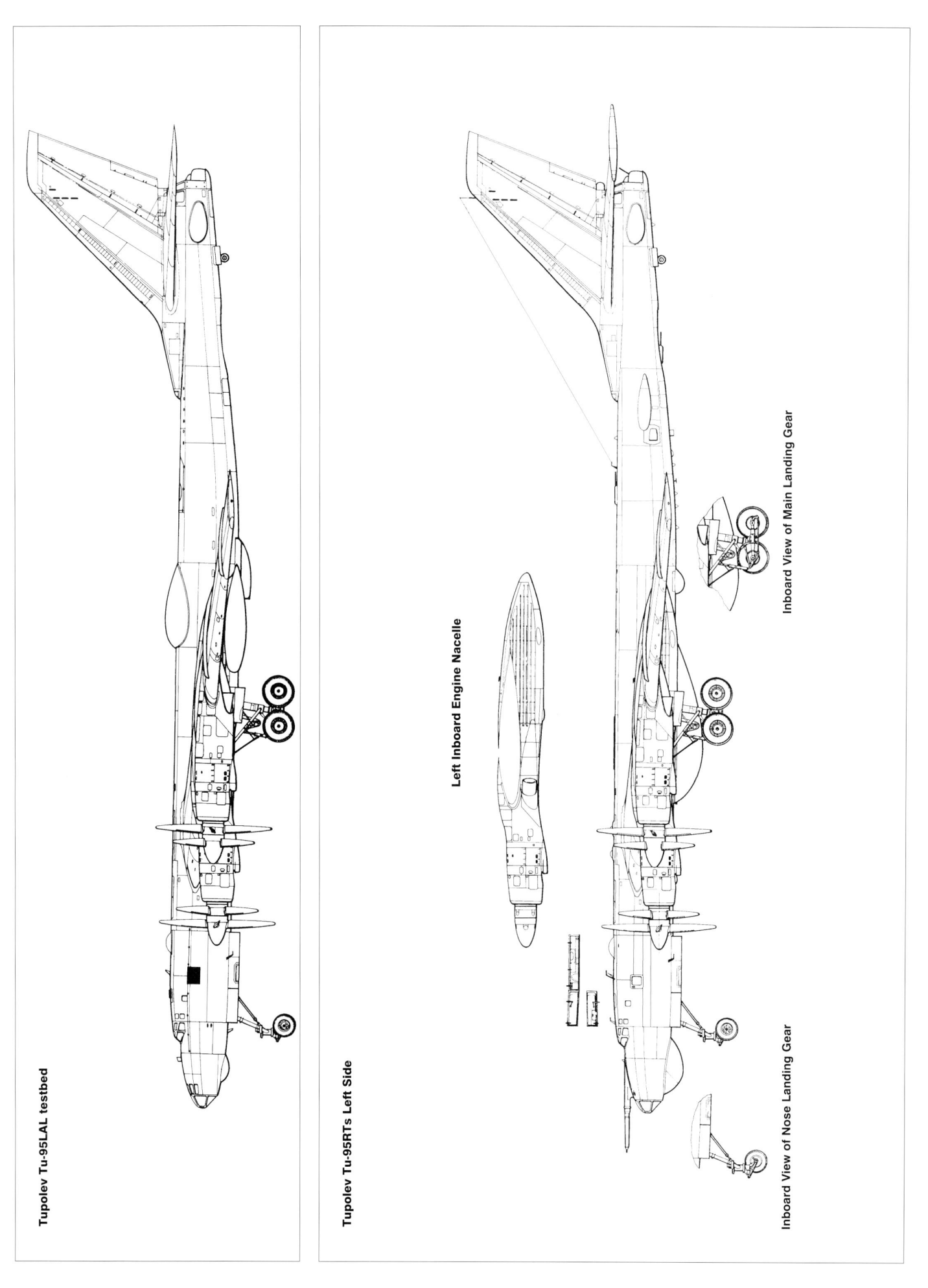

Tupolev Tu-95RTs Left Side

Left Inboard Engine Nacelle

Inboard View of Main Landing Gear

Inboard View of Nose Landing Gear

Tupolev Tu-95RTs Right Side

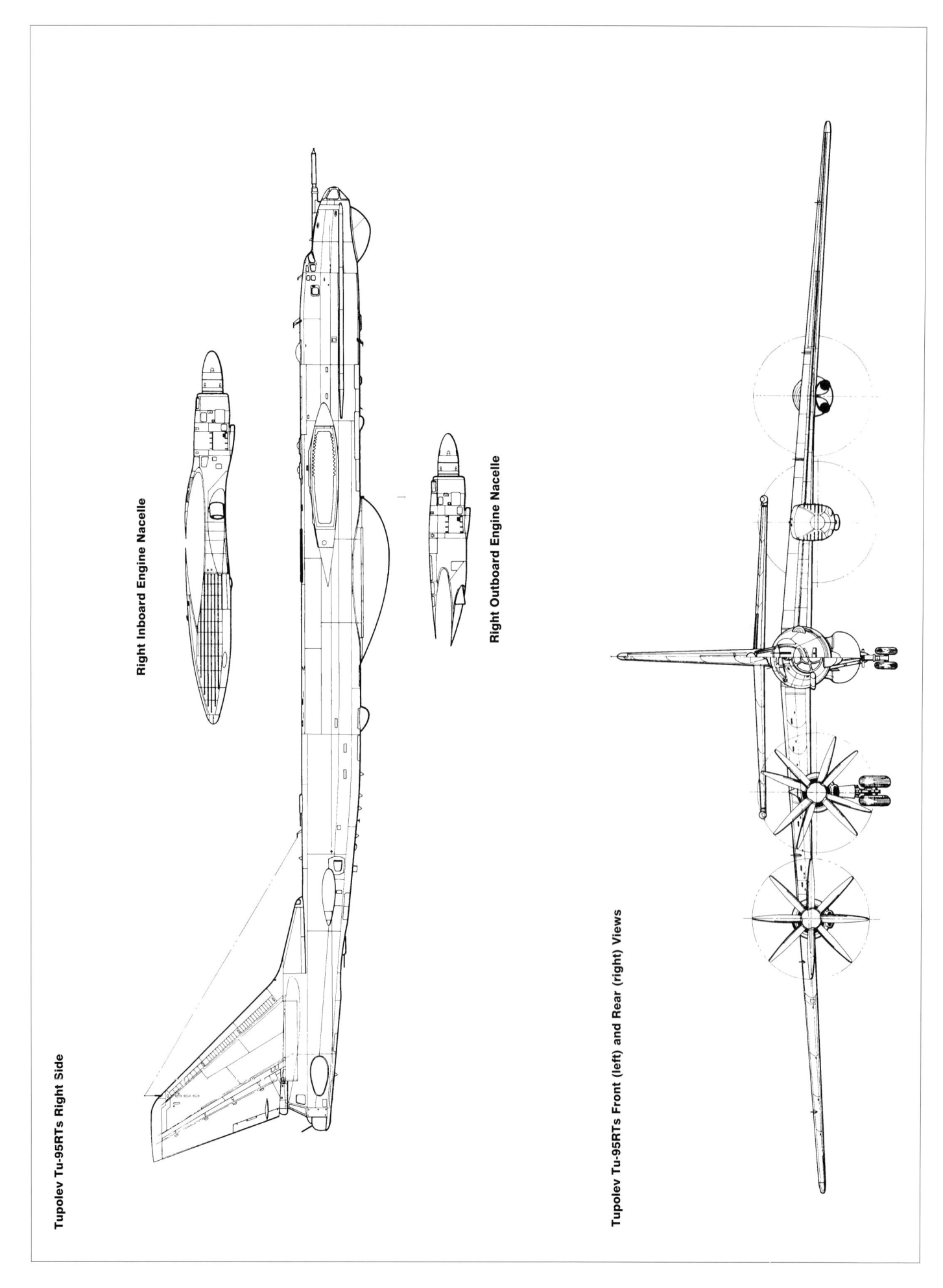

Right Inboard Engine Nacelle

Right Outboard Engine Nacelle

Tupolev Tu-95RTs Front (left) and Rear (right) Views

Tupolev Tu-95RTs Top View

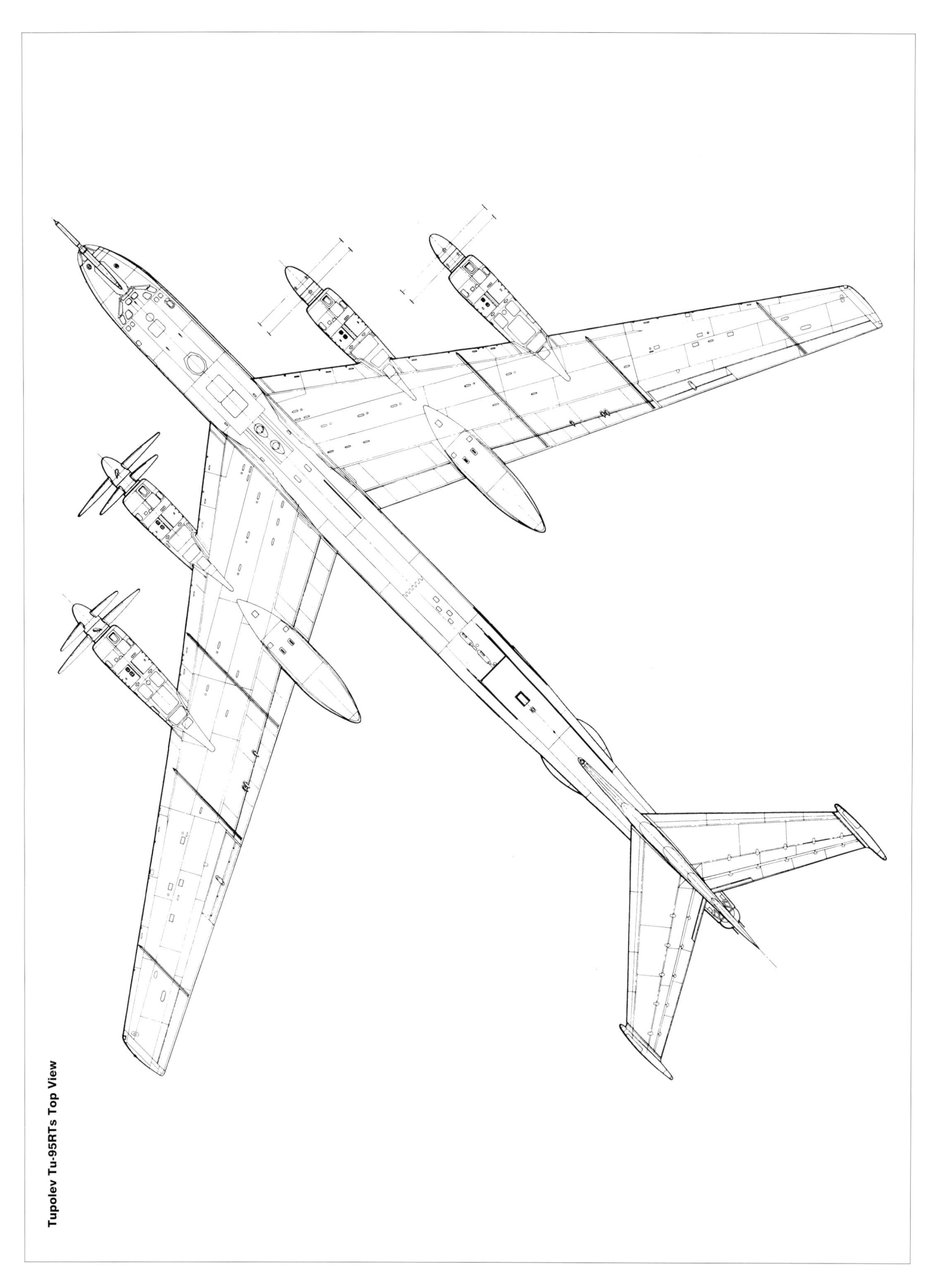

Tupolev Tu-95RTs Bottom View

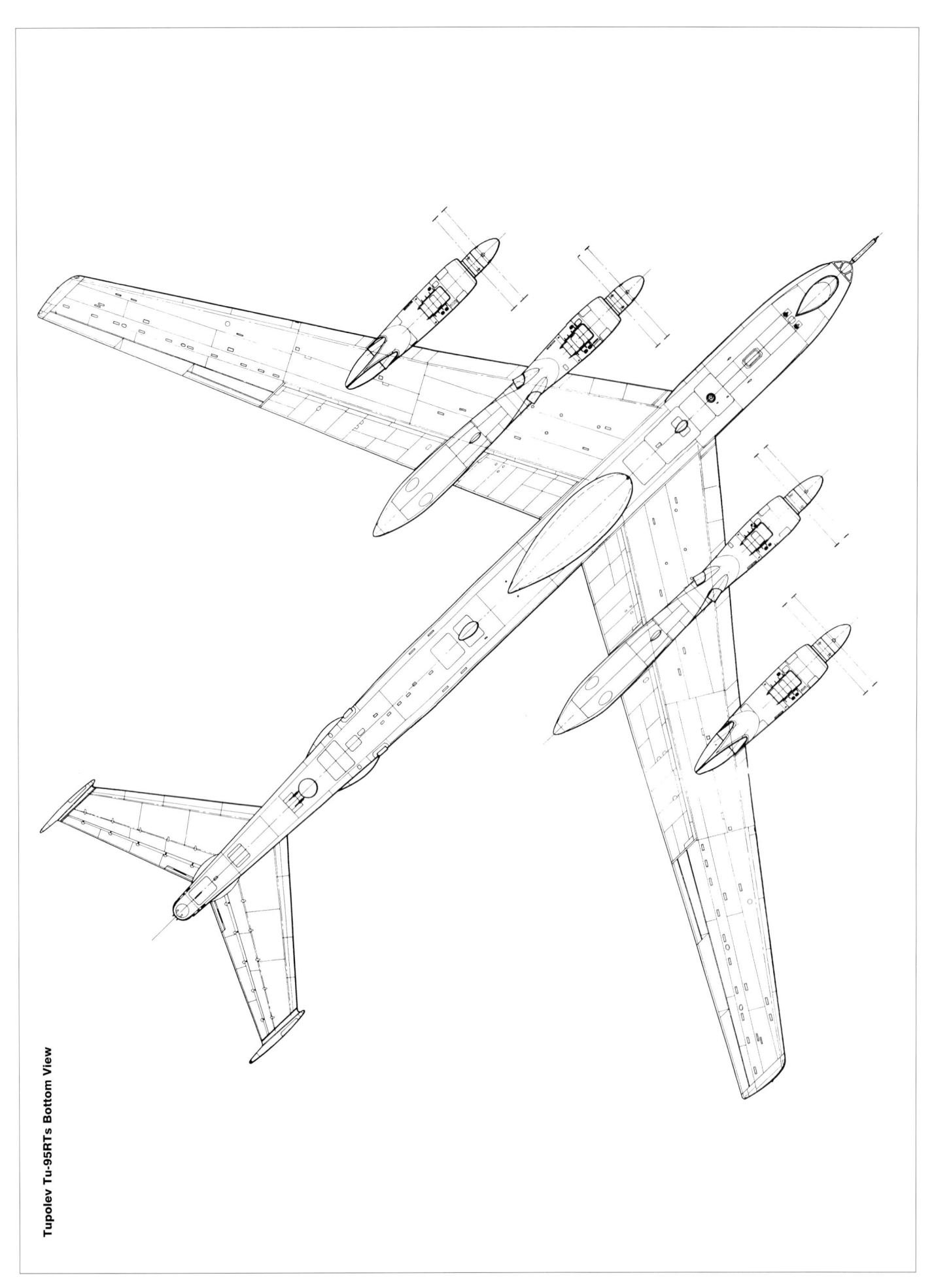

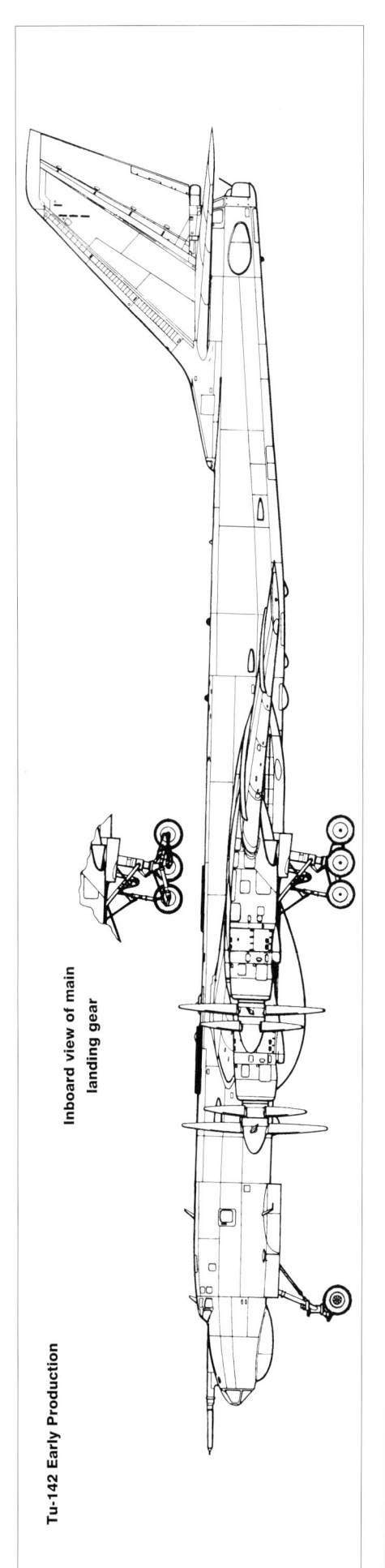

Tu-142 Early Production

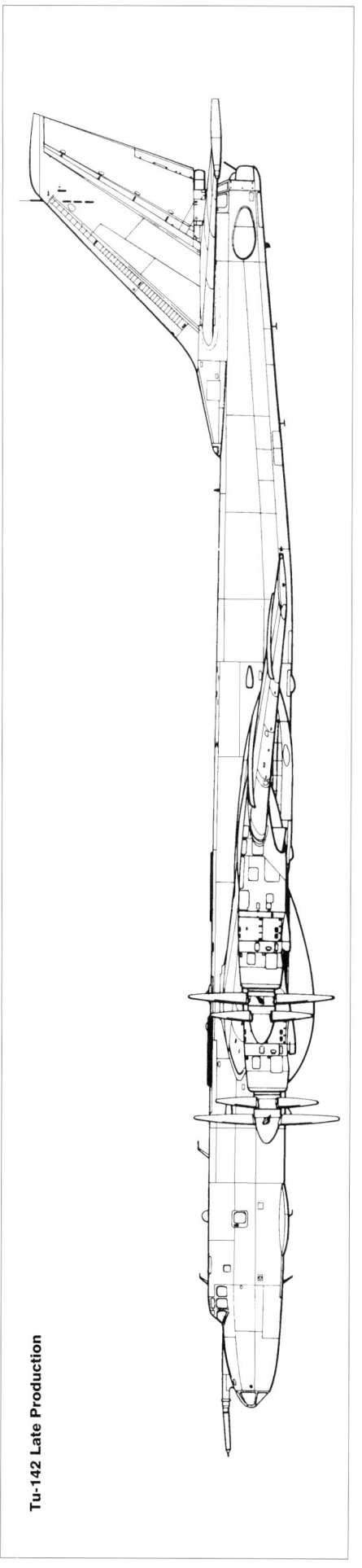

Inboard view of main landing gear

Tu-142 Late Production

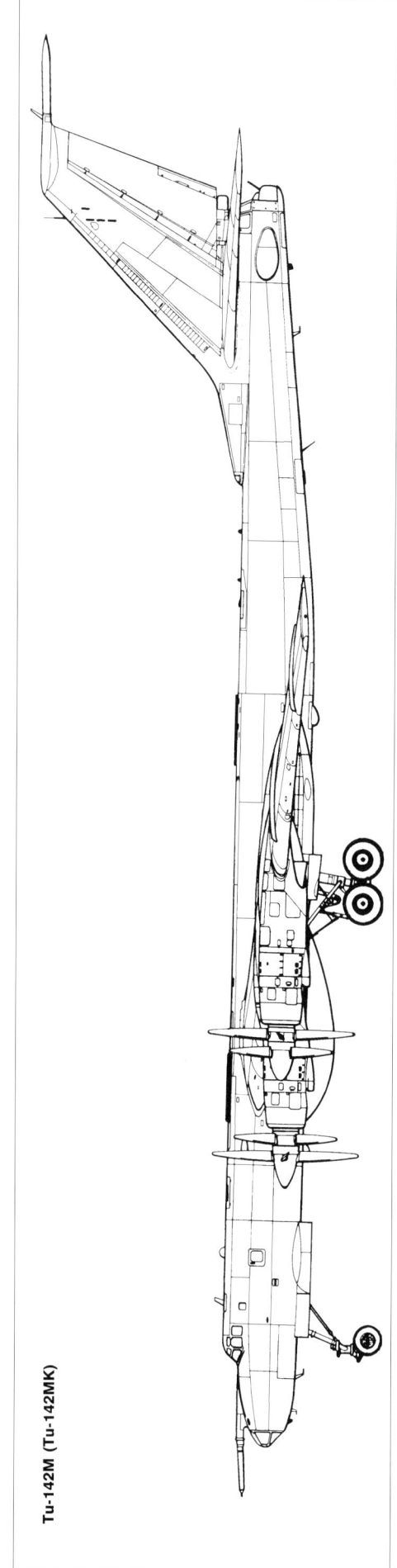

Tu-142M (Tu-142MK)

123

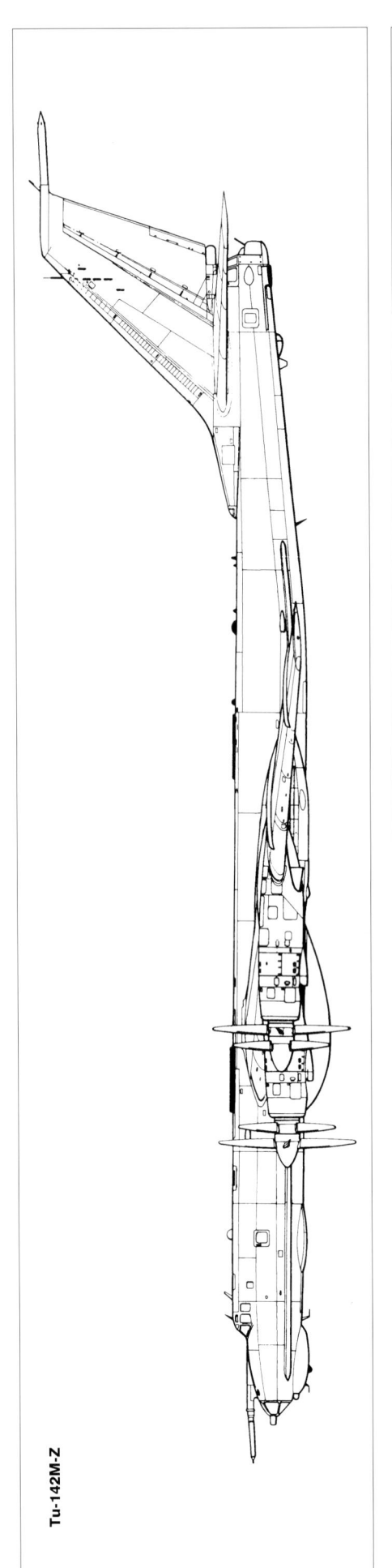

Tu-142M-Z

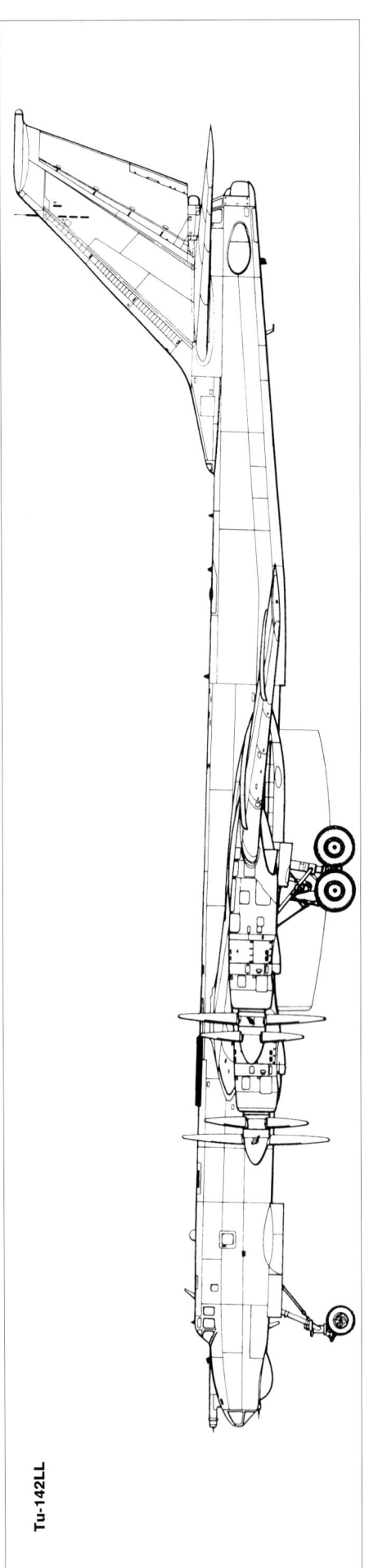

Tu-142LL

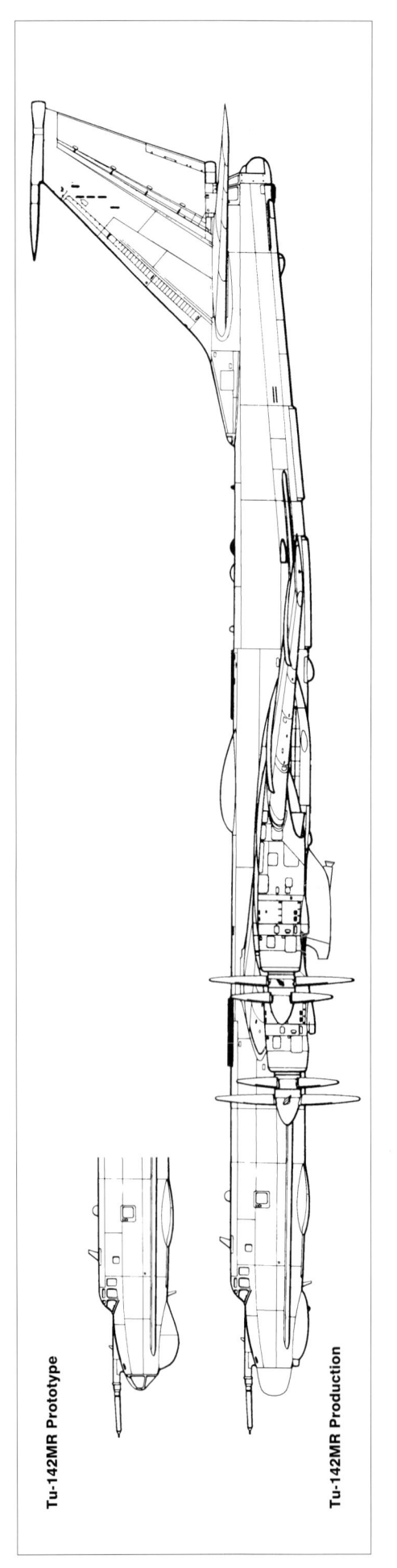

Tu-142MR Prototype

Tu-142MR Production

AeroFax

In 1982, American author Jay Miller published his first major book, the AeroGraph on the F-16, since when there has been a flow of widely acclaimed books from the Aerofax line.

After many years acting as the European distributors for Aerofax, Midland Publishing acquired the rights to this series, and many new titles are now in preparation, compiled by a talented team of internationally known authors.

Certain of these continue to be produced for Midland by Jay Miller in the USA, but are now augmented by others originated in the UK and USA.

These softback volumes are full of authoritative text, detailed photographs, plus line drawings. They also contain some colour and cockpits, control panels and other interior detail are well illustrated in most instances.

The previous categories of AeroGraph, DataGraph, MiniGraph, and Extra are now discontinued; all new titles are to be simply published as 'Aerofax' books.

The first two new-style 'Aerofax' titles were updated 'Extras', namely:

Lockheed-Martin F-117 (Jay Miller)
1 85780 038 9   **£7.95/ US $12.95**

Northrop B-2 Spirit (Jay Miller)
1 85780 039 7   **£7.95/ US $12.95**

Other new titles in the series are outlined alongside and below.

A listing of earlier titles still in print is available upon request.

Aerofax
CONVAIR B-58 HUSTLER
The World's First Supersonic Bomber

Jay Miller

Instantly recognisable with its delta wing and 'Coke bottle' area-ruled fuselage the B-58 was put into production for the US Air Force in the 1950s.

First published in 1985, this is a revised edition, which takes a retrospective in-depth look at this significant aircraft, from design studies, through its development and comparatively short service life, to and beyond retirement. It includes yet more amazing material, bringing the story up to date, and 80 new illustrations.

Softback, 280 x 216 mm, 152 pages
415 b/w, 14 colour, 100 line illusts.
1 85780 058 3 **£16.95/ US $27.95**

Aerofax
GRUMMAN F-14 TOMCAT
Leading US Navy Fleet Fighter

Dennis R Jenkins

Entering US Navy service in 1972, the Tomcat is one of the classic jet fighters of all time – and is inescapably linked with the film 'Top Gun'. It remains a formidable weapon system and is in widespread frontline use with America's carrier air wings. This work describes all variants, including the so-called 'Bombcat' attack version and the very capable F-14D. Colour schemes, aircraft production details, squadrons and markings, are all covered, also close-up details of cockpits and weaponry.

Softback, 280 x 216 mm, 88 pages
151 b/w, 39 colour, 22 line illustrations
1 85780 063 X **£12.95 / US $21.95**

Aerofax
BOEING KC-135
More Than Just a Tanker

Robert S Hopkins III

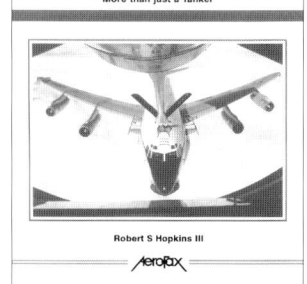

The highly readable text follows the development and service use of this globe-trotting aircraft and its many and varied tasks. Every variant, and sub-variant is charted, the histories of each and every aircraft are to be found within; details of the hundreds of units, past and present, that have flown the Stratotanker are given. This profusely illustrated work will interest those who have flown and serviced them and the historian and enthusiast community.
Due for publication 1997 (3rd qtr)

Softback, 280 x 216 mm, 224 pages
c185 b/w and 50 colour photos
1 85780 069 9   **£24.95/US $39.95**

Aerofax
YAKOVLEV'S V/STOL FIGHTERS

John Fricker and Piotr Butowski

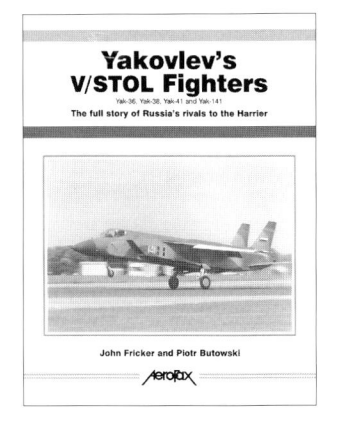

The story of Russia's programme to achieve a supersonic VTOL jet fighter can now be revealed, from the earliest Yak-36 'Freehand' experiments through the carrier-operated Yak-38 'Forger' and astonishing Yak-141 'Freehand', on to the agreement between Yakovlev and Lockheed Martin to help produce JAST, the USA's next generation fighter.

Using material never before seen in the West, this book tells the story of a programme that has to an extent, until recently, been shrouded in secrecy.

Softback, 280 x 216 mm, 44 pages
90 b/w photos, diagrams etc
1 85780 041 9   **£7.95/US $12.95**

Aerofax
MiG-21 'FISHBED'
Most widely used Supersonic Fighter

Yefim Gordon and Bill Gunston

The ubiquitous MiG-21 is unquestionably one of the greatest fighters of the post-Second World War era. It was Russia's first operational Mach 2-capable interceptor, and a stepping stone for many nations to enter the age of supersonic air combat. Access to the files of the MiG design bureau and other previously inaccessible sources reveal the secrets of the fighter that has flown and fought in more countries than any other supersonic jet.

Softback, 280 x 216 mm, 144 pages
335 b/w and 46 col illusts, plus colour artwork and scale plans.
1 85780 042 7   **£16.95/ $27.95**

Aerofax
MIG-25 'FOXBAT' and MIG-31 'FOXHOUND'

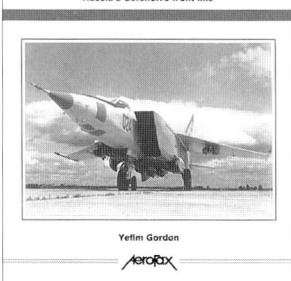

Yefim Gordon

This book takes a detailed, informed and dispassionate view of an awesome aeronautical achievement – the titanium and steel MiG-25, backbone of the USSR defensive structure. Its follow-on was the similar-looking MiG-31 'Foxhound', very much a new aircraft designed to counter US cruise missiles and in production from 1979. Includes a large amount of previously unpublished material plus lavish illustrations and extensive full colour artwork.

Softback, 280 x 216 mm, 96 pages
92 b/w and 27 colour photos plus 91 line and colour airbrush illustrations
1 85780 064 8   **£12.95 / US $21.95**

Aerofax
EUROFIGHTER 2000
Europe's Fighter for the New Millenium

Hugh Harkins

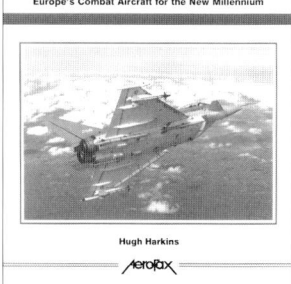

Eurofighter 2000 – of which five are flying with a scheduled entry into service date of 2002 – has been a subject of much debate. In Europe, coverage has centred on cost and timing. In the US, attitudes have been of cloaked awe – for the UK, Germany, Italy and Spain have developed a high-tech fighter with great export potential, in the face of existing US-built products.

The author had direct access to Eurofighter's files and has produced a detailed, yet readable, account.

Softback, 280 x 216 mm, 48 pages
60 col, 4 b/w photos, 2 3-view drwgs
1 85780 068 0   **£8.95 / US $14.95**

OKB SUKHOI
A history of the design bureau and its aircraft

Vladimir Antonov et al, with Jay Miller

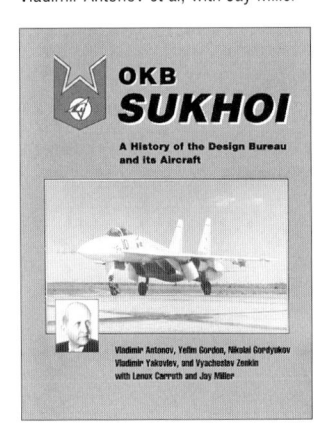

A team of authors have thoroughly documented the products of this famous Soviet aircraft design bureau, thanks to extensive access to the company records and photo files. A huge amount of unpublished information and illustrations are included. Each aircraft type is reviewed in detail, also prototypes, testbeds and projects, some of which never saw the light of day. Appendices detail test pilots and major personalities.

Hardback, 280 x 216 mm, 296pp
645 photos/illusts plus 23 in colour and 104 3-views and line drawings
1 85780 012 5   **£29.95/US $49.95**

OKB MiG
A history of the design bureau and its aircraft

Piotr Butowski, Jay Miller

Beginning with a comprehensive overview of Soviet military aviation, the text methodically moves from the births of Mikoyan and Gurevich through to the founding of the MiG design bureau during 1939, its war years, and the period of greatest importance, beginning with the advent of the MiG-15 and the Korean War and continuing via the MiG-17, -19, -21, -23, -25 and -27 to the MiG-29 and MiG-31 era. A highly acclaimed work.

Hardback, 280 x 216 mm, 248pp
800 photographs, over 100 drawings
0 904597 80 6   **£24.95/US $39.95**

LOCKHEED MARTIN'S SKUNK WORKS
The First Fifty Years (Revised Edition)

Jay Miller

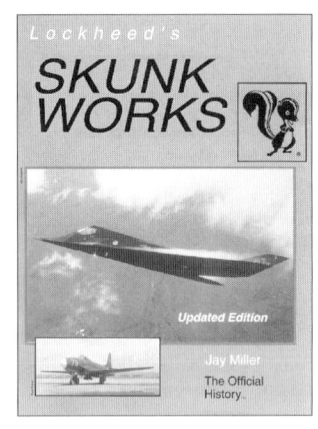

An updated edition of the original 1994 'Lockheed's Skunk Works' – written with the total co-operation of Lockheed Martin's Advanced Development Company. In a major 'pulling back' of the veil of secrecy, official histories of such products as the U-2, A-12, D-21, SR-71, and F-117 are finally brought to light.

This is the closest thing yet to a definitive history of this most enigmatic aircraft design and production facility.

Softback, 305 x 229 mm, 216 pages
479 b/w and 28 colour photos
1 85780 037 0   **£19.95/US $29.95**

LUFTWAFFE SECRET PROJECTS
Fighters 1939-1945

Walter Schick & Ingolf Meyer

Germany's incredible fighter projects of 1939-45 are revealed in-depth – shapes and concepts that do not look out of place in the 1990s. 95 pcs of colour artwork in contemporary markings plus data tables show what might have been achieved, and careful comparison with later Allied and Soviet aircraft show the legacy handed on, right up to today's stealth aircraft. This first English-language edition benefits from author revision plus approximately 20% additional information and illustrations.

Hardback, 282 x 213 mm, 176 pages
109 3-views, 63 drwgs, 52 photos.
1 85780 052 4   **£29.95 / US $44.95**

FOREIGN INVADERS
The Douglas Invader in Foreign Military and US Clandestine Service

Dan Hagedorn and Leif Hellström

The Douglas A-26 Invader is without doubt one of the most unsung of combat aircraft, serving worldwide in many roles until the 1970s, including the CIA's notorious 'Bay of Pigs' invasion of Cuba. This book focuses on its non-US military use, covering service in 20 countries including use by a host of paramilitary forces and clandestine users, in over a dozen wars, conflicts and coups. Deeply researched, with many rare photos, it refutes some long perpetuated 'facts'.

Hardback 282 x 213 mm, 200 pages
265 b/w photos + 8pp colour.
1 85780 013 3   **£22.95/US $34.95**

FIGHTING GRASSHOPPERS
US Liaison Aircraft Operations in Europe 1942-45

Ken Wakefield

Some 3,000 American liaison aircraft – mainly Piper L-4 Cubs and Stinson L-5 Sentinels – served with the USAAF in Europe on low level recce and front line courier duties with 9 liaison squadrons of the 9th Air Force. With Army ground forces, liaison aircraft served as Air Observation Posts with Field Artillery.

Official USAAF/USAF records, Army After Action Reports, diaries and log book extracts, were used to produce what has been widely acclaimed as 'the book' on the Grasshoppers.

Hardback 280 x 212 mm, 160 pages
185 photographs, 4 maps
0 904597 78 4   **£17.95 / US $29.95**

We hope you enjoyed this book . . .

Aerofax and Midland Publishing titles are edited and designed by an experienced and enthusiastic trans-Atlantic team of specialists.

Further titles are in preparation but we always welcome ideas from authors or readers for books they would like to see published.

In addition, our associate company, Midland Counties Publications, offers an exceptionally wide range of aviation, spaceflight, astronomy, military, naval and transport books and videos for sale by mail-order around the world. For a copy of the appropriate catalogue, or to order further copies of this book, and any of the titles mentioned on this or the previous page, please write, telephone, fax or e-mail to:

Midland Counties Publications
Unit 3 Maizefield,
Hinckley, Leics, LE10 1YF,
England

Tel: (+44) 01455 233 747
Fax: (+44) 01455 233 737
E-mail: midlandbooks@compuserve.com

Distribution in the USA by Specialty Press – see page 2.

Index

2TV-2F engine   12-14, 25, 28-29
'64' bomber studies   6, 13, 113
'94' bomber studies   12
76th Regiment   68
'95' aircraft   13, 14, 25-26, 29, 114
'95-2' aircraft   48
'99' aircraft   37
'105.11' aerospace aircraft   48
'130' aerospace aircraft   48
'202' bomber study   6
'302' bomber study   6
392nd ODRAP   35-36, 68
'471' bomber study   8
'473' bomber study   8
'474' bomber study   8
'485' bomber study   8

A
abbreviations   4
acronyms   4
Aeroflot   75-77
Agavelyan, S D   26-28
Alexandrov, A P   49
AM-23 cannon   69
AM-3 cannon   78
AM-3 engine   12
Amet-Khan, Sultan   41
Antonov An-22   78
Antonov, D A   15
Antonov Design Bureau   78
APR-1 missile   66
ASh-473 TK engine   8
ASh-73TK   11
ASh-73TKFN   10
AT-2 torpedo   67

B
Bay of Biscay   36
Bazenkov, N I   15, 28
'Bear' designation   30
'Bear' family tree   31
Belay air field   34
Beriev Design Bureau   82
Beriya, L P   5
Berkut   54-55, 57, 62, 67, 105
Bobriikov, V K   77
Boeing B-17   5
Boeing B-29   3, 7, 9
Boeing B-50   9
Bolshakov, A M   27
Borzenkov, L I   25, 27
Brezhnev, L   55, 58
Bulgakov, V N   66

C
Cerkov airfield   34
Chelomey, V N   34
Chernov, A F   27
Cheryomukhin, A M   14
Chrom   36
Consolidated B-24   5
Convair B-36   9, 11
Course   75
Cripton   79
cruise missile carriers   65
Cuba   69, 75
Cuban Missile Crises   71

D
Da Nang air base   68-69
Design Bureau 18   13
Design Bureau 19   30
Design Bureau 23   15
Design Bureau 120   12
Design Bureau 126   15
Design Bureau 156   13, 15
Design Bureau 276   28-29
Deyneka, V G   66, 69
Dimitrov, G   55
Dobrovolsky, V   75
Dobrynin VD-4K engine   10
'Doubler'   37
Douglas DC-3   5
Dubinskiy, V I   55, 65

E
Eastern Express   73
Eger, S M   13

F
factory no. 18   14, 33, 35, 74, 79
factory no. 156   14, 26
Falkland Islands   36
Fedotov, A S   36
Fuchs, Klaus   5

G
Gabalov, V N   66
Gelyi   77
Gigarev, P F   26
Gladkov, I F   36
Gordon, Yefim   3
Great Patriotic War   3-4
Gromov, A M   58
Groozin, V V   67-68
GSh-23 cannon   69

H
Haritonov, N N   70, 77

I
Ilyushin A-50   82
Ilyushin Il-14   76
Ilyushin Il-38   57, 105-106
Ilyushin Il-62   76
Ilyushin Il-78   73
Ivan   46
Ivanov, V   82

J
Junkers Jumo 022 engine   12

K
K-20 system   39
Kamchatka   30
Kantsendahl, V N   69
Karpinchik, A A   66
Kerber, L L   30
kerosene T-1/T-2   90
KGB   25, 27
Kh-20 missile (Mikoyan)   39, 43, 71, 100
Kh-55 missile   65, 71
Khabarovsk   30
Khramtsov, G A   69
Khrunichev, M V   27
Khrushchev, N S   30, 46, 75
Kibal'nik, V A   67
Kinasoshvili, R S   28
Kipelkin, V S   77
Kipelovo air base   35, 65, 68
Kirichenko, S S   25, 27
Kirsanov, N V   15
Komissarov, I E   25, 27
Kondorsky, N S   11, 74
Konus   42
Korean War   11
Korolyov, S P   48
Korshun   55, 57-58, 60-61, 67, 69
Kosygin, A   55
Krasnosel'skiy, A I   36
Krypton   60
KSR-5 missile   45
Kub   53
Kuibyshev factory   13, 29, 34-35, 37, 45, 54-55, 73-75, 79
Kulikov, S M   46
Kurchatov, I V   5, 46, 49
Kuznetsov Design Bureau   32, 36, 37, 51
Kuznetsov, N D   12-13, 29
Kvadrat   53

L
Ladoga MAD   58
Lashkevich, N V   27
Liana   79-80
'Lincoln" carrier   71
Lira   81
Lisunov Li-2   5
Lozino-Lozinsky, G E   48

M
MAD gear   60
Makarevsky, Dir.   29
Malhasyan, K I   75
Mayiorov, N F   25, 27
Meteric blind landing system   36
MGAB bombs   59
MiG-15   11
MiG-19   40
Mikoyan, A I   48
Mil Mi-6   68
Minker, K V   28
Mir   77
Monino (AF Museum)   47-48
Morozov, V N   65-66
Morunov, V P   25, 27
Moscow   3, 75
Moscow Factory No. 23   13
Myasischev Design Bureau   13, 38
Myasischev M-4 (3M)   11-13, 29, 31, 33, 35, 39, 42, 79
Myasischev, V M   6, 11-12, 15, 29

N
Nadashkevich, A V   46
Nashatyr'-Nefrit   61-62
NATO   30
Nerchinsk sonar   58, 60
Nezval', I F   47, 50
Nikel   36
'Nimitz' carrier   71
NK-6 afterburner   48
NK-8 engine   76
NK-12 engine   70, 88
NK-12M engine   31, 52, 78, 105
NK-14A engine   51, 78
NK-25 engine   64
NK-144 engine   48
North American B-25   5
Novaya Zemlya   47
nuclear weapon program   5, 7
Nyukhtikov, M A   30

O
Okean-75   66
Orbita computer   57
Ostapenko, N S   66

P
P-6 missile   34-35
P-8 engine   37
Pasportnikov, V S   77
Pavlov, V I   66
Perelyot, A D   25, 27
Petlyakov Pe-8   5-6
Phainshtin, A S   50
Popov, V S   77
Pritok   42, 48
Putilov, A I   79

R
R-4 air-to-air missile   81
R-7 rocket   48
Rastyapin, A G   36
Romb   35, 43
'RS'   47
Rubidiy   33-34, 36, 77
Rubin   33, 45
Ryazan air base   21

S
SALT agreements   21
Sayany defensive system   58
Semipalatinsk   50, 70, 73, 78
Shamanskiy, Lt. Col.   65
Sheremetyevo airport   75
Shmel   82
Shvetsov, A D   37
SM-20P testbed   40
Solovyov, A I   28
Solovyov, P A   30
sonobuoys   56, 58-60, 62, 68-69, 105-106
Spiral   48
Stalin, Joseph   3, 13, 28
'Star' aircraft   48
Strela   58
Suhomlinsky, I M   75
Sukhomlin, I M   30, 80

T		Tupolev Tu-95 inert gas		Tupolev Tu-115	78	*Vega*-M	82
Taganrog	55, 62, 69, 82	system	96	Tupolev Tu-116	76, 115	*Vishnya*	35
Tanya	46	Tupolev Tu-95 landing		Tupolev Tu-119	51	*Volga* system	45
Tat'yana	46	gear	87	Tupolev Tu-126	79	Vymyatin, V K	36
Ter-Akopyan, A M	27, 30a	Tupolev Tu-95 Missile		Tupolev Tu-128	81		
TIDS	58	Carrier	38	Tupolev Tu-142	49, 53, 55123	**W**	
Tomilino facility	50	Tupolev Tu-95 oxygen		Tupolev Tu-142 specification		*Way*	75
Tosky proving ground	7	system	96	table	67		
TRD engine	12	Tupolev Tu-95 pneumatic		Tupolev Tu-142 technical		**Y**	
TsAGI	26, 38	system	95	details	103	*Yad* radar	45
TsIAM	28	Tupolev Tu-95 powerplant	88	Tupolev Tu-142LL	64, 118, 124	Yakimov, A P	75
Tsibin, P V	47	Tupolev Tu-95 rescue		Tupolev Tu-142M	17-18, 22, 49,	Yefimov, I A	65-66
Tupolev, A N	6, 11, 15, 27-29, 54	system	97		55, 97, 123	Yeger, S M	28
		Tupolev Tu-95 specification		Tupolev Tu-142M-Z	61	*Yel'*	57
Tupolev Design Bureau	54	table	52	Tupolev Tu-142M2	20		
Tupolev Tu-LL	29	Tupolev Tu-95 technical		Tupolev Tu-142MK	55, 61	**Z**	
Tupolev Tu-4	7-10, 15-16	details	83	Tupolev Tu-142MK-E	61	Zacepa, N S	77
Tupolev Tu-4LL	13-14	Tupolev Tu-95 wing		Tupolev Tu-142MP	63	Zaikin, Gen.	28
Tupolev Tu-16	7	and empennage	84	Tupolev Tu-142MR	19, 63, 124	Zarechye	62
Tupolev Tu-22	48	Tupolev Tu-95A	32	Tupolev Tu-142MS	65	Zhdanov, K I	12, 36
Tupolev Tu-70	15-16	Tupolev Tu-95DT	34	Tupolev Tu-142M-Z	123	Zhukov, G K	30
Tupolev Tu-75	15	Tupolev Tu-95K	19, 39, 115	Tupolev Tu-142MZ-C	62	Zhukovsky flight test center	
Tupolev Tu-80	9-11, 113	Tupolev Tu-95K-10	41	Tupolev Tu-144	47, 64		25-27, 30, 34,
Tupolev Tu-85	11-12	Tupolev Tu-95K-22	44, 73, 116	Tupolev Tu-160	65, 73		38, 46-47, 53,
Tupolev Tu-95	25-26, 28, 31, 114	Tupolev Tu-95KD	42, 116	Tupolev 'Tu-200'	9		57, 73
		Tupolev Tu-95KM	43, 48, 100, 116	Tushino	3, 30	Zhygarev, P F	28
Tupolev Tu-95 with additional fuel tanks	32	Tupolev Tu-95KU	41	TV-2 engine	11, 13		
		Tupolev Tu-95LAL	49, 51, 119	TV-2F engine	12		
Tupolev Tu-95 armament	90	Tupolev Tu-95LL	48-49, 64	TV-4 engine	12		
Tupolev Tu-95 de-icing system	95	Tupolev Tu-95M	20, 26-27, 32, 83, 100, 114	TV-10 engine	12		
				TV-12 engine	14, 29-30, 37		
Tupolev Tu-95 ECM aircraft	33	Tupolev Tu-95M-5	115	TV-16 engine	36		
		Tupolev Tu-95M-55	65	TVD engine	12		
Tupolev Tu-95 electrical equipment	90	Tupolev Tu-95MA	32				
		Tupolev Tu-95MR	18-19, 21, 23, 33, 97, 117	**U**			
Tupolev Tu-95 equipment	91			*Udar*	57		
Tupolev Tu-95 fire-extinguishing system	97	Tupolev Tu-95MS	20-24, 69, 117	UR-200 carrier aircraft	48		
		Tupolev Tu-95N	47, 118	*Uspeh*	53		
Tupolev Tu-95 flight control system	90	Tupolev Tu-95PLO	53	Uznia air field	34		
		Tupolev Tu-95RT	22, 34				
Tupolev Tu-95 high-altitude equipment	96	Tupolev Tu-95RTs	119-122	**V**			
		Tupolev Tu-95V	45, '47	Vaiman, K I	27		
Tupolev Tu-95 hydraulic system	95	Tupolev Tu-96	36	*Vanya*	46		
		Tupolev Tu-114	73	VD-5 engine	37		
Tupolev Tu-95 Hypersonic Aircraft Carrier	47	Tupolev Tu-114PLO	78	Vedernikov, I K	34, 53, 57, 75, 77		
		Tupolev Tu-114T	78				

Below: **Posed aircrew shot in front of a 'Bear F'.** Yefim Gordon collection